SURVIVING QUEENS ANTHOLOGY

ANDREA MAYNARD-BRADE   CORNITA TAYLOR
MAE TERESA   JANETTE BARRETT   SARA MAYNARD
MAXINE PALMER-HUNTER   ANCHILA KAMALA
KIMOLA KAY   MAUREEN ELIZABETH WORRELL

Edited by
MAUREEN ELIZABETH WORRELL

SURVIVING QUEENS ANTHOLOGY

CONTENTS

ANTHOLOGY CONCEPT BY
ANDREA MAYNARD-BRADE

Surviving Queens

Surviving Queens Copyright © 2021 Analia Publishing Website: www.analiapublishing.com
Email: analiapublishing@hotmail.com Telephone: 07949 433 804
Published by Analia Publishing - September 2021 ISBN:9798497406535

Please be aware that some chapters contain references to sexual abuse, domestic violence and trauma

AFFIRMATION QUOTES

There is no greater agony than bearing an untold story that is hidden inside of the depth of you

Self-love, self-respect and self-worth

There is a reason that they all begin with 'self' You cannot find your-SELF in anyone else

Heavy is the crown and yet we wear it as if it were a mere feather upon our bent and burdened heads

There is strength in our hearts There is determination in our eyes

The will to overcome and to survive resides within our souls This is me and this is you

We are warriors, champions, fighters, survivors and Queens!

REVIEWS

There had already been quite a hype around this forthcoming book called 'Surviving Queens', amongst my peers and colleagues located near and far and that had instilled in me an eager excitement to get my hands on a copy.

Each individual chapter will resonate with readers, both male and female, and each chapter certainly stands out on its own merits with the additional bonus that the whole book from start to finish flows seamlessly and beautifully.

The chapters feel as if each writer is interacting personally with the reader and the clarity and honesty shared has an effectiveness in relating their life experiences and how they overcame such various and diverse challenges.

As a woman and as a professional, I must admit that I shed a few tears, not because I was sad, but I think because the overwhelming feeling I had in reading this book was one of gratitude and admiration for the courage and determination it must have taken for these inspirational women to open their hearts to share such detailed and personally hidden fears and secrets with us and the wider audience.

Each chapter illustrates an honest and genuine account of what it took to survive, and these women should be proud of their gifted achievements as I can only imagine it cannot have been an easy journey to decide, act upon and then complete such a beautifully written work of art.

I loved the additional positive affirmations at the back of the book and enjoyed reading the personal testimonies and dedications by the Surviving Queens writers. It gave me that extra time to get to know each of them a little better, which was very lovely.

I do not think there is anyone, man or woman, that I would not recommend this book to and who would not benefit from reading this unique and lovingly crafted book.

Dr Sabrina Collins - Psychologist - Bristol UK

The various insights into the lives of these women are not only enlightening, powerful and an honour to read, but they take you on a journey of complexities, resilience, heartaches, joy and celebrations, through a snapshot of their lives and their ups and downs.

Not only will you feel like you are there, but you will also sit back with gratitude and awe at what these ladies have been through.

The Surviving Queens Anthology book is a fantastic read and very inspiring indeed!

Vanessa Nosa-Oviasu ~ Head of Year ~ English Teacher ~ Secondary School UK

I was initially taken by surprise when I was asked to read a sample of the book that is called Surviving Queens, as I have never written a review before. Plus, I am a man and wondered if I could do justice to a review of a book written by women!

I read the few chapters I was sent, several times over. Mainly because I couldn't get my head around how eloquently and superbly these ladies had expressed themselves. I know some of the chapters are somewhat hard to read at first because they speak of atrocious and painful past experiences, but I felt privileged to be granted permission to peek into their world of how they survived and came out the other end so much stronger and wanting to help others to not go through what they themselves had experienced. We hear that phrase so often, breaking the silence, but these ladies are doing exactly that, and their courage must be applauded and recognized of their true intentions in sharing, which is to help to create a much safer world for all victims and survivors.

This is such a wonderful example of a book that can change lives and inspire so many other people, too. I can categorically state that I loved this book! I will be buying a copy and telling my family and friends about it too.

Keep up the good work ladies and thank you for showing us who and what our Queens are, do and represent.

Surviving Queens is a must read!

Mr. K A Adebayo - Clinical Manager - Manchester UK

Being on maternity leave I was more than happy to spend an hour or so to read some chapters taken from the Surviving Queens Anthology book for a written review, forwarded to me by a mutual friend of one of the inclusive authors of this book.

I settled down with the extracts and with an open mind, anticipating a quick and enjoyable read. By the time I had read the first page I had turned off the TV so I could better take in all that I was reading.

These chapters were magnificent! I love too how even though each chapter is different, they flowed nicely together, one after the other.

How brave are these women? Their courage and determination are astounding and so uplifting to see and witness through the words on the screen.

*I was so impressed with **how** they survived, and I really liked the added poems in the book. They enhance and compliment so well each of the chapters too. I am not a great fan of poetry, but I liked reading these poems a lot. Like the chapters, they touched something in me.*

Very well done to you all and I have no qualms about recommending this book to everyone for them to read and enjoy.

Mrs. C R Kumar - Child Psychologist

INTRODUCTION

This Surviving Queens Anthology Book is dedicated to all those who wish or need to have their voices heard after survival of their innermost and previously hidden lived experiences of challenges, trauma, devastation and courageous journeys towards inner healing and hope.

This book is dedicated to our Ancestors on whose shoulders we have the privilege of standing with our heads held high in appreciation and acknowledgement of their sacrifices made so that we can give thanks for life and honour their belief in us, the future generations, in knowing that we are enough.

This book is dedicated to those whose enforced silence of suffering and pain has yet to be acknowledged because it is important for you to know that your voice is worthy of being heard through your written words.

This book is dedicated to those who believed in the victims, stood by them and supported and loved them through the trauma of having the courage to reveal and seek help. We thank you all.

Surviving Queens Anthology book is dedicated to all the future Surviving Queens whose voices will be heard through their written words as this first and original Surviving Queens Anthology book is just the beginning of a beautiful and long-lasting healing journey for each of you.

It was the recognition of the passion of Andrea Maynard-Brade's desire to bring together a group of phenomenal women to share their stories of overcoming adversities and life challenges that made it possible to accept her offer to be a part of this awesome project and journey that is the Surviving Queens Anthology book. To be invited to be included has been a privilege and an honour. We were inspired by her intentional goal to not only give a voice to those who have suffered in silence but also in creating a unique coming together of like-minded individuals who have demonstrated such an empowering courage of determination to push through their revisiting of past hurts and pain in order to show others how they succeeded in coming through to the other side of having once been a victim and showing up as survivors. Survivors who have thrived through their personal healing journeys. Thank you with much love and sisterly affection.

We love to be inspired. Thank you to all the other Queens in this Anthology for the privilege of getting to know the authenticity of who we are as women and survivors. It is a blessing in having the opportunities to be still with your minds, hearts and souls as we all embrace and learn from your personal courage in sharing your truths of survival. Witnessing the dismantling of the fears that once controlled you has humbled us and leaves us grateful for the lessons learnt from each of your chapters. We continue to marvel at the greatness revealed through your survival of past traumas. We salute you all and thank you all.

ACKNOWLEDGMENTS

Acknowledgements and appreciations are extended to those who took the time to read the extracts from the Surviving Queens Anthology and then submitted their Readers Reviews to be included in this book. Your support and encouraging words have served to uplift the Writers of this wonderful book and to validate our sharing of our past pains and healing journeys. We thank you.

Thank you to Maxine Palmer-Hunter for assisting us with publishing our individual stories as our book. As individuals we come together united with a purpose borne out of compassion and understanding to assist each other through inner healing and in not being afraid to shine a light on our greatness as women, women of colour, as empowered females. Thank you for your part as a Publisher in helping to turn our desires for our voices to be heard into a printed and published reality.

Unconditional love and respect are extended to all the Queens who have participated in and contributed towards creating this superb Anthology book. Your chapters will undoubtedly inspire many others to know that they too can achieve all they wish for and to witness that their dreams can come true in positive ways, also. Thank you for your immense courage and determination in pushing through the difficult barriers to stand firm and tall in your truths. Thank you for being authentically inspiring and phenomenally awesome examples of empowered, confident women. We salute you and honour you by hearing your once silenced voices through your beautifully expressed narratives.

Thank you to Maureen Elizabeth Worrell, the Editor of the Surviving Queens Anthology, for your passion in wanting to help women who have lived and suffered in enforced silence for so long, in offering them a unique and compassionate bespoke service so that their voices can be heard through their written words. Your belief in other women whom you proudly proclaim as your siSTARs, no matter their creed, age, status or location in this world, is something that is appreciated and inspiring to behold.

INTRODUCTION TO SURVIVING QUEENS ANTHOLOGY VISIONARY AND LEADER

The Surviving Queens Anthology Project is the concept of Andrea Maynard-Brade, which she first thought of back in November 2018.

After working professionally in the field of domestic violence for more than twenty years and having been a victim of domestic violence herself, Andrea felt the need to do more, not only for herself but specifically for the wider community and even on a world-wide level.

Having successfully written her own book which chronicles her survival through having endured years of domestic violence and witnessing the ongoing cycle of familial abuse within her own family towards women, she shared her story in the hope of giving others the motivation to know that they too can heal and progress forwards in positive ways in their own lives.

Her book, '*Suffering In Silence*' was published in 2021 and has received several positive reviews and is considered as a useful tool in written narrative to assist others to learn how to re-empower themselves to emotional and mental wellness and illustrates to readers that they are worthy of so much more than their abusers had shown them thus far.

Her goal in conceptualizing this Surviving Queens Anthology book of inspirational chapters was borne out of her desire to honour those victims and survivors who had a wish to have their voices heard so that they could at last begin their healing journeys to mental, physical, emotional and spiritual wellness.

Her vision for Surviving Queens has always been to see that all Queens are uplifted and supported in their courage to fulfil their desires to have their voices heard after having suffered in silence whether that be through fear or abusive threats.

Surviving Queens is a platform from which all survivors from abuse, trauma, exploitation, violence and personal life challenges, will be embraced in love and respect without judgement or ridicule.

Its aim is to illustrate how to courageously and lovingly reveal and share their past experiences, good and bad, and how to trust the process of learning how to forgive themselves and others in letting go of past and painful memories attached to negative and abusive patterns of behaviour that no longer serves their higher purposes in life.

This first Surviving Queens Anthology book is hopefully the first of many that will be created and shared with the public. There are so many women and men out there who wish to have this opportunity of having others with similar experiences to share the gift of being supported, encouraged, guided and loved through the process of sharing their most intimate and hidden stories of overcoming and surviving.

Surviving Queens are:

Successful, unique, respected and valued. They are imaginative and do not need validation about standing courageously in their own truths. They seek inner peace and create positive new beginnings. They are Goddesses. They are quality Queens of this unique Universe. They are empathetic with a vibrant energy borne out of love for all. Queens are nurturers of mother earth, strong, spiritual survivors who are re-empowered and unstoppable.

FOREWORD

Surviving Queens Anthology – is the beautiful result of the commitment and determination of a group of beautiful and soul-filled Queens who have delved deep into their darkest recesses to relive and share a pain that often has literally bought them to their knees. Their overriding desire to help and inform others is an illustration of their intentional willingness to confront those internal turmoil of physical, mental, emotional and spiritual adversities so that others may know that they are not alone.

These Surviving Queens Anthology chapters are truly engaging and powerful and will inform and teach others the valuable lessons learnt from lived experiences and of overcoming a diversity of immeasurable challenges. The telling of their stories illustrates that in dismantling the fears that once controlled them and every aspect of their lives, they have opened themselves up to the possibility of being receptive to all that the Universe has waiting for them in positive abundance. They have shown us that by being authentically true to themselves that therein lies a powerful re-empowerment of self and worthiness. Sharing their stories gives them and us, permission to rise above all obstacles and to live confidently in our greatness, to treat ourselves and others with love, kindness and respect.

In unburdening ourselves of doubts and self-loathing, we reveal the magic of internal spaces that were once clogged and occupied with feelings of unworthiness. We are enough.

These phenomenal Queens are demonstrating to us that hidden courage can be reborn and unleashed as we shed the shackles of our concealed sorrows and insidious cycles of fearful silence.

Our gift to you is to embrace the knowledge that you have it within you to allow new chapters to unfold as you let go of negative energies and fears that are holding you back. When you take that leap of faith, everything else will align itself and fall into its rightful place.

As survivors we raise our voices, not so that we can shout, but so that those without a voice can be heard also. We cannot succeed when so many are still suffering in fearful silence and anxious trepidation.

It is not our job to try to figure out what other people want to hear from us, but rather that we figure out what we have to say.

Your voice matters. All our voices matter.

Speak up. Believe that you are worthy. Take that courageous risk. Permit yourself to evolve into living your authentic and beautiful life.

A woman with a voice, is, by definition, an empowered woman.

As a Surviving Queen, I come as one, but I stand as ten thousand individuals representing my siSTARs, brothers and all humanity from across the globe.

C. S. Lewis once said...

The world places so much emphasis on physical and external things.

But what REALLY matters and counts, is the ESSENCE of your Inner Self and Being.

Blessings with Love and Respects Maureen Elizabeth Worrell

Surviving Queens Anthology Non-Generic Editor

Author of Surviving Queens Anthology Chapter – 'The Definition of
I & I'

BIOS & CHAPTERS

CORNITA L. TAYLOR

My name is Cornita Louise Taylor, and I am the Founder of '*Cornita Taylor Health and Wellbeing*'. I live in Birmingham. I am a woman who, throughout my life, has experienced so many highs and lows, but I always find a way to get back up and begin anew. As a mother to a beautiful daughter who is the love of my life, my priority will always be to protect and nurture her to the best of my abilities. I am also one of seven siblings, a daughter, grand-daughter, niece and friend to many.

During my twenty-five years as a Massage Therapist, I have been fortunate enough to have been able to travel the world for nine years and during my global explorations, I have assisted in setting up two Spa facilities. Now, I have my own business, formerly known as Head 2 Toe Massage, but has now been rebranded as '*Cornita Taylor Health & Wellbeing*'.

In 2019, I was a finalist for 'The Most Influential Businessperson of the Year,' award, which was a great achievement for me and one which humbled me to realise that my peers and others considered me to be a positive influence on others.

My Surviving Queens Anthology chapter is about how, at the age of just nineteen years of age, I was systematically groomed by a man who was seven years older than I was. He verbally and physically abused me and during that period, I felt helplessly locked into this toxic relationship with him. After becoming pregnant with his child, he then proceeded to force me into having an abortion. Now, when I say that he *forced me*, I mean exactly that. He beat me with a curtain rod and then he pushed me into one of those walk-in clothes closets. In sharing my story of domestic abuse, I hope to help other ladies who have not yet found their voices and for the younger generation to know that they do not have to be fearfully silent or silenced and that they can use their voices or their written words for good and positive intentions. We, all of us, must take actions to break this cycle of being abused so that we can learn to do and be better. We can use our collective voices to let the abusers know how their abusive and aggressive actions damages their victims, sometimes for the rest of their lives. You can do anything that you put your mind to. Just believe in yourself and learn to value your self-worth. We all have a purpose in life so let us all learn to embrace it and tap into it in positive and uplifting ways.

My chapter is entitled, 'Aborted but not dead'.

CHAPTER 1

ABORTED BUT NOT DEAD

CORNITA L. TAYLOR

It was at the age of nineteen that my mum had kicked me out of the house, her reasoning being that two grown women cannot live in the same house.

With nowhere else to go, I ended up sleeping on the couches and floors at various friends' houses until I felt it necessary to ask my cousin if I could stay at her place until I could sort myself out and she had kindly agreed, and I had gratefully moved into her unoccupied flat.

After two weeks of aimlessly roaming from one place to another, my mother had asked me to come back home. I had felt the need to decline, due to my stubbornness, but more so because I was feeling hurt and rejected by her and I was too scared to return home to her only for her to repeat her behaviour, to leave me feeling abandoned all over again. In hindsight maybe I should have taken her up on her offer, but it had felt far too risky in an emotional and mental way, for me to do so.

At the time I had been attending college, studying for my BTEC Sports Therapy course and working part-time to support myself financially.

In due course, my cousin had decided to return to live at the flat with me. She had been dating a guy and naturally he had a friend that my cousin then introduced me to. His name was Phil. I had not been interested in him at all as my main priority had been to concentrate on my studies and to eventually find a place of my own. Phil had been very insistent and just would not take no for an answer. He refused to back off and eventually he had caught me off guard, which is how I came to find myself participating in one of his conversations with me. I had been surprised to realise that whilst in his presence and during our communications, I had found him to be quite humorous and he had made me laugh. Even though he was much older than me, I slowly began to think that maybe he was ok. He had this charming way about him, always knowing the right things to say, at the right time.

Almost without really realising what was happening, I swiftly found myself interlocked into a full-blown relationship with him, despite my intentions to take this apparently flourishing relationship at a slower pace. I had politely turned down his offer to move into his flat with him. I was still harbouring a desire to find a place of my own in which to live.

One night, he and I had accompanied my cousin and her partner to this club. Whilst there, I had recognised a guy whom I had known from my younger days and we had naturally greeted each other and engaged in a conversation, sharing a joke or two.

Although I had noticed Phil glancing over at us, I had not thought much of it at the time.

The four of us had returned to my cousin's flat after leaving the club and I had asked him why he was so quiet. His response was to question me about who the guy was and despite my explaining that he was just an old friend of mine, Phil had seemed reluctant to accept that explanation and seemed to be extremely upset with me for some reason.

Before I had a chance to comprehend what was happening, he had pinned me against the wall, hissing at me that I should never do that again!

I recall thinking to myself that he was only feeling jealous, and I had honestly not even given it much thought as to why he should feel it was acceptable to react in that way over nothing.

As our relationship continued, Phil was as charming and persistent as ever, trying to persuade me to move in with him. I had finally found a flat of my own and had moved into it, content in knowing that I had my own space and was happy for Phil to come over and spend the odd day or night with me. But he obviously had other ideas and almost immediately he started bringing over black bags filled with his personal belongings and in the blink of an incredulous eye, he was in possession of a key to my flat. So now I found myself co-habiting with a man whom I initially did not even want to be with.

As the weeks passed by, I then began to see another side to this man, one which I did not like at all. He started calling me nasty names, damaging goods in the flat and constantly telling me that I would never amount to anything. He would spit at me and hit me. Too late, I grew to understand what a nasty and horrible person he could be. I found myself living in fear for my life and felt on edge all the time. I wanted to escape from this relationship but could not see a way of how I could do that safely or permanently, without him hunting me down to either force me to return home to him or to further harm me. My heart kept telling me that nobody should live in fear inside their own home, but in my head, I could not seem to join the dots to figure out a way of how to get from under that highly toxic, abusive and volatile situation.

It was a few months into this relationship when I discovered that I was pregnant with his baby. I had been on the injected version of the contraception, but because of the massive stress I was living with, I had completely forgotten to arrange for a top-up injection at the clinic.

It is an understatement to say that I was nervous about informing him of my pregnancy, but I had still harboured a silent prayer that he would be pleased and excited about it and that it would prove to be the cata-lyst for him to cease his abusive behaviour towards me.

I had felt so sick and frightened to tell him that I kept putting it off, but eventually I had to share the news with him. I remember feeling all kinds of emotions when he had told me bluntly, that he did not want me to have the baby. I had felt hurt and rejected all over again and I had replied to him that, given a choice, I had not wanted a baby with him either, but it was what it was.

Over the following few weeks and months, I had informed my mother and my friends of my pregnancy. Despite the terrible but hidden circumstances I was living in and having to suffer, in my head, I had been determined to have the baby.

Would you believe that even one of his friends had approached me to advise me to terminate the baby! I had felt compelled to ask him if Phil had sent him to tell me that, but he had replied no, that he himself, had felt it necessary to warn me to not have a child with that man, as he, the friend, felt that I was too nice a girl to be having Phil's child, knowing that Phil would not treat me good once I had the baby. Deep down, I had already known this would probably be the case, anyway.

I still wanted this baby and the thought of terminating the pregnancy had not even entered my thoughts and was not an option for me, personally.

It must have been around the time when I was about ten or twelve weeks pregnant and was standing in our bedroom, in just my under-wear, when he had again forcefully expressed his demands for me not to have the baby and that I should get rid of it. I had told him that I had no intention of aborting our child.

Before I could even process what he was about to do, he had grabbed hold of a length of wired curtain rod, folded it in half and had proceeded to viciously beat me with it. He had then aggressively pushed me into the walk-in clothes closet and slammed the door shut on me.

I have no idea how long I sat on the floor in the closet, holding my stomach and quietly talking to my baby inside of me, telling the baby how sorry I was that I had to get rid of him or her. For as long as I live, I will never forget that experience. That terrible and frightening moment will remain painfully etched onto my brain for the rest of my life.

The very next day I had made my way to the clinic to make an appointment to have a termination. On my arrival, the nurse there had informed me that I was anaemic and that they had to prescribe me some medications to remedy the lack of iron in my blood. Ironically, they had to cure that ailment to make sure that I was healthy before they could abort my child.

My broken heart had felt that had been a sign that I should not have the termination, but I felt that I had no other choice but to go ahead with it.

After they had completed the procedure, I had called him to come collect me, but he had heartlessly told me that he was unavailable and that I should call someone else to bring me home.

There had been nobody else that I could ask to come for me, and the clinic would not allow me to leave on my own. I had felt so abandoned and had cried tears of frustration at being the last one there to be discharged. It had been such a horrible feeling to know that I had no-one to be there for me at that time. The lady at the clinic had suggested I could go home using a taxi, but she had been concerned also as I was feeling nauseous, having not eaten all day. The longer I was detained in the clinic, the more I kept reflecting on my then current situation and how I felt towards Phil. I knew that I had to somehow find a way to leave him. That life was not for me. I had already emotionally and physically detached myself from him and whenever he touched me, I had felt dirty and physically repulsed by him.

I had asked the taxi driver to stop so that I could pick up something for me to eat. I recall feeling so weak and ashamed, overwhelmed with trying to figure out how I had allowed myself to be so mistreated and abused.

In my angry thoughts towards him and myself, to be fair, all types of thoughts were spinning in my confused brain. I had mental visions of contemplating how I could kill him, but fortunately for me, those thoughts were fleeting. I believe the Almighty God saved me from taking that destructive path of acting on my vengeful delusions, stimulated by physical and emotional pain and the loss of my baby.

One evening my cousin and her partner were visiting us at our house. As they sat chilling in the front room, Phil and I had been in the kitchen when he had suddenly decided he would be horrible to me, saying some hurtful, nasty and demeaning things to me. I can remember picking up a knife with the intention of stabbing him with it. Fortunately, or unfortunately, depending on which perspective you are thinking on this, I was not quick enough, and he had grabbed my hand, bending it painfully backwards, causing the sharp edge of the blade to graze my thigh instead.

Another time and opportunity had arisen for me to cause him harm, when we had both been in bed, sleeping. I had leaned over him and started to strangle him as he slumbered peacefully. He had then suddenly woken up choking for air, so I had quickly leapt off him and pretended that I was sleeping. It was then that I had realised that my attempting to kill him was not the ideal way for me to escape from that toxic relationship.

I had felt desperately compelled into acting on my suicidal thoughts but that had not worked either.

I pleaded with God to tell me what I had done to deserve this punishment.

Eventually, I had reached the conclusion that I just had to accept that this was my life and there would be no light at the end of the long and dark tunnel for me.

There was one day when I had ignored him after he had asked me a question as we sat in the bedroom. He had then thrown a shoe at me, which had struck me painfully on the head. Surprisingly, my immediate reaction had been to pick up the shoe and throw it back at him. He had accused me and raged at me for thinking I was a '*bad gyal now*', meaning I thought I had the right to feel that I could now no longer accept his mistreatment of me. I had repeated that he should not throw a shoe at me. In the next moment, he had walked out of the bedroom and into the living room. I had followed closely behind him and had seen when he had picked up the telephone to make a call. I had told him to put my telephone down and his response had been that I could *never* tell him what to do. He had made it clear that he felt that I had no right to disagree or argue with him. He had refused to listen to me so in my anger, tinged with an undercurrent of fear, I had stooped down and pulled the telephone cable from the wall socket. It had been at that point that he must have realised that I was not playing with him. Things had quickly escalated, and we became embroiled in an aggressive and physical fight.

It was after that fight that he had come to accept that I had had enough, and he had reluctantly handed over the keys to the flat, to me.

I remember thinking that if that was all it had taken to get rid of him, to remove him from my life, then it was a pity that I had not stood up to him much sooner.

After he had packed his belongings and left my flat, it had taken me awhile to believe it was now a reality that he was finally gone for good. I could not fathom that I was now a free woman, free from being abused, violated and treated so disrespectfully.

It took some time before I could allow myself to accept that he would not and could not come back into my life and that he had finally seen that I was no longer prepared to put up with any more of his bullish and aggressive behaviours towards me.

Having gone through those experiences of domestic abuse, I came to understand that it is often a case of fright, flight or fight.

I may have felt extricated from his physical abuse of me, but in my mind, I still felt trapped. The fear that he would return was real for me. What if I were to accidentally bump into him on the street, what would I say or do? Would I still be frightened of him?

I still had not told any of my family members or friends of what I had been suffering behind closed doors, so everything still felt awkward and unsettled for me as I felt the need to keep it all a secret from them.

In the beginning when I had started dating my abuser, I had felt somewhat giddy with excitement about being with him and interested in everything that spewed from his lips. As time went on, I had been forced to acknowledge that he was a person who was happy to tell me lies and who knew how to manipulate people for his own selfish gains. He was extremely intelligent and should have been a lawyer as he was exceptionally good at talking and freely expressing his opinions. Apparently, it had been noticed that I had reduced myself to being deafeningly quiet when I was around him and other people, to the point where I was very withdrawn. I had somehow forgotten how to be the bubbly and talkative person I used to be when part of a social group of people or crowd.

It was not until I had watched the film 'Sleeping With The Enemy', that it had occurred to me that I myself was embroiled in an abusive relationship. I had been telling myself that I ought to be grateful that I was 'in love' with a man who had rescued me with his love and kindness. In fact, he had just been using me whilst playing Russian roulette with my already fragile and shattered emotions. I came to realise that it had been fear that had kept me shackled to him. To say that I was truly scared of him and his temper and aggressions, would be an understatement. My distaste and repulsion at having him touch me or having sex with me grew and I despised him for reducing me to a withering and cowering shell of my former self, to the point where I consistently feared for my life.

Despite my euphoria at him leaving, I am not going to lie and pretend that suddenly everything was so much better. There were days where it still felt difficult and upsetting to know that he would not be coming home. It had felt somewhat odd not hearing his key turning in the front door lock. In hindsight, I think I was more grieving for what could have been and not for what was my reality before he had finally left me.

Wanting to get back on track with being in control of my life, I threw myself into my studies for my last year at college and I made the effort to spend more time with my family and friends. Getting back into some form of a routine was going to help me to move on, I hoped.

It had felt exciting in a nervous kind of way to be told by my teacher, John, that I could be working on the cruise ships as a Massage Therapist. I could not quite get rid of that little voice of Phil's in my head that kept telling me that I was not good enough and that I would never achieve or reach my goals in life.

There was a huge sense of relief for me when I finally completed my training course and had graduated. My mental health and thoughts were all over the place at that time and it had taken me a little while to fully acknowledge that achievement, even to myself.

A friend of mine's, Tom, wanted to work on the cruise ships also so we had both completed the course and had both attended interviews. He had wanted it more than I did, I recall. The interview involved a trade test and an interview with one of the representatives from Steiner. During the interview, she had questioned me on where I envisioned myself within the Steiner company in five years. I had replied that I could see myself in the management position. I had been so happy when she had offered me the job and in knowing that John would be working on the same cruise ships with me. Whist I was walking out of the college, he had informed me that he had not secured the job. I had felt so bad for him as I could see that he was so disappointed in not getting the job he wanted.

A few short weeks later, I was involved in a terrible car accident. I was lucky to be alive and felt that God was trying to teach me a lesson as I had suppressed my doubts about working on the cruise ships. That car accident and the injuries I sustained, had proven to be like a wakeup call for me.

It had taken me several more months before I had decided to go for it and to begin working on the cruise ships. I had given up my flat, which had held both good and bad memories for me. More so bad than good, but I had somehow survived it all. It had proven to be a traumatic and strenuous journey back to full health after the terrible car accident. But now, I was feeling more ready to start living my life again, to begin a new chapter. Travelling to London for my training in preparation for my working on the cruise ships, had proven to be an experience, too, especially when I took the time to reflect on how I had progressed from being trapped in a toxic and destructive and abusively violent relationship with a man to sharing a bunk bed with a roommate from a foreign country. It had been such a lot to take in, but it also showed me that life can change so quickly, from one minute to the next. I had felt lucky that things were finally changing for the better. It had felt as if I was on this journey of self-discovery and learning how to love myself again.

My first contract had involved working with seventeen other girls from all around the world and for the first time in my life, I had been forced to face the ugly truth and the sad reality of the impact of racism. I cannot even pretend that I knew how to react to it. I felt afraid of being fired if I complained but I also did not want the racists to think that I was being 'soft' in just accepting their bigotry and racist remarks. I had eventually mentioned to my manager my having experienced racism. In response I had received an abrupt and brief message back that I should grow some balls and learn how to stick up for myself. I had been shocked by her callous and non-compassionate response and had spent hours on the telephone calling home, crying, telling my loved ones that I wanted to come home. I had felt further conflicted with my grandmother telling me to stay and my mother telling me to return home.

I felt God was not hearing my prayers for an answer as to what I should do, even as I fell to my knees and earnestly prayed every night.

I had felt more upset in thinking that I had escaped one violent bully only to be confronted with another form of bullying, born out of other people's ignorance and lack of acceptance, respect and understanding of different cultures and people.

In the stock room, one day, I had been harassed and disrespected by a racist individual, when from nowhere, I had felt a sudden urge to tell her to "fuck off!" I could not believe that I had been so rude to her, but it appeared to have worked as she never once bothered me again and neither did the other girls. I was so proud of myself for having the courage to stand up for myself. For me, it also meant that I could finally enjoy the rest of my time on the cruise without feeling like I was being targeted purely for the colour of my skin. It had taken time, but I had eventually earned their respect.

Being a black girl from England on that first cruise, had been interesting, to say the least. There were other people of colour on that cruise, like Kevin, who I had first sighted when I had come on board the ship. He was tall, dark and handsome and worked as the Assistant Manager Housekeeper. Before long, he was asking about me just as I was making enquiries about him. I found out that he was from Costa Rica and spoke Spanish. We were finally introduced to each other and sat up all night talking, even though I could hardly understand most of what he was saying as his Spanish accent was so pronounced. But in the end, it had not really mattered, and we started dating and soon became inseparable. Kevin was very loving and caring and very sexy, too. Soon, it was approaching the time where his contract would be coming to an end, and I was devastated to think that I would never see him again. He had then asked if I would follow him onto his next cruise ship and fortunately for us, we were able to continue our relationship. It is usually impossible to get onto the same cruise ship as your partner, but we were lucky in that regard.

As time passed, our relationship became more intense and our feelings for each other grew. He was constantly and verbally expressing his love for me, but my brokenness had prevented me from believing his declarations of love, most of the time. Three years into our relationship, I had discovered I was pregnant with our child and for the briefest of moments I had been convinced that it was a sign that we were meant to be together and that our baby would be born to parents who would love and cherish it. But again, it appeared that God had other plans for me and my life. It was whilst I was giving a massage to a client that I felt my baby detaching away from my womb and with silent tears streaming down my face, I had somehow maintained an air of professionalism as I completed the massage.

Losing the baby had happened so quickly it had left me feeling achingly numb. Telling Kevin that I had suffered a miscarriage was so painful for us both and he had tried to reassure and comfort me by saying that we could try again. I remember feeling hurt by his reaction as my body was still reacting to the pain and devastation that I was experiencing. I was increasingly concerned about that too as the physical pains were not decreasing at all. My friend Debbie suggested that I go to see the doctor which resulted in them having to admit me into the Miami hospital to perform an operation on my uterus.

Everything kept happening so swiftly, but I just could not bear the level of pains I was in for another minute.

The day after the operation, I was lying in my hotel bed, recovering and resting from the surgery when the Housekeeper, who spoke no English, began pointing to me and shouting 'Dead! Dead! Dead!'. As I woke fully from my medicated sleep, I looked down to see that the bed was saturated crimson with the red of my blood pouring out of me.

I had not sensed that I was bleeding at all and wondered where all that blood was coming from. It was a good thing that the Housekeeper had come in at that time, otherwise I may have bled to death. After being rushed back into the hospital, the doctor told me that I was haemorrhaging profusely.

My unexpected stay in the hospital for an additional week had meant that I was unable to return home as planned and then to return to the cruise ship after that.

During this time of being so ill and recuperating, I had lost so much weight that the girls on the ship had not recognised me. Things between Kevin and I seemed to have changed too. He was so distant towards me. It was shortly after my return that I had learnt that he was in fact cheating on me. In my devastation, I could not believe that the man I had loved could do that to me, even as I was still recovering from losing our baby and the operation that had saved my life. Now I had lost the man I loved and that relationship, too. I felt that I had no other choice than to say goodbye to all of that and him. I had experienced being hurt once before and I was not prepared to put myself through that again, to suffer through being hurt and disregarded like that and having everyone knowing and laughing at me behind my back. The hurt and humiliation was just too much to bear.

As time went on, I worked on other cruise ships in my role as a Massage Therapist. I even managed to take a well-deserved break for a little while. When I then returned to working on the ships, I was promoted to Senior Therapist Assistant Manager and then to the Manager post. I had laughed to myself because to be honest, even though I had stated in my initial interview that I had wanted to be a Manager, that had not really been the case or something I had been serious about working towards achieving. But those promotions were certainly a huge step for me in my professional career. In my new role I was responsible for a large team of younger and older staff members, and they had all been relying on me in my role as Manager to show up and be what I needed to be in that managerial role. It had been a lot of responsibility to shoulder and at the same time, it had also lifted my spirits and increased my self-esteem and self- confidence. I felt I had a purpose and that my staff respected me. At times it had proved challenging, and it was hard work, but also it was a rewarding job, especially when people had managed to reach their set targets. Although at times, I had missed being a Massage Therapist, I quickly grew to love my new job.

With my promotion, I was introduced to a man named Stewart, who was the Head Broadcast Manager. He had assisted me with learning the details of management and he ensured that I attended all the relevant meetings. In time, we started to casually hang out together in our spare time. We would talk and laugh together, a lot. One day I was in his cabin when he had offered to cut my hair. I had short hair at that time, and it had needed shaping up and trimming. As he begun to cut my hair, I could feel his warm breath on my neck, and I started to notice a certain feeling come over me. It was in that moment that I realised how much I liked him. He must have sensed how my feelings were getting stronger and stronger because in no time at all, we had found ourselves locked into a sensuous embrace and we were kissing each other passionately.

It had felt almost magical, and I recall feeling happy that we had built up a solid friendship first before finding ourselves entwined in this next phase of our relationship. It had felt right.

From that day, every time I saw him, I felt butterflies in my stomach. Even the sound of his voice left me weak at the knees. We had spent more and more time together, going to parties, hanging out at the beach and going to different restaurants.

When he was transferred to another cruise ship, I had been convinced that would be the end of the relationship. I had consoled myself that it had been short but sweet. I had therefore been shocked to hear Stewart say that he wanted us to continue our relationship. I knew it would not be easy to maintain a long-distance relationship but every day, several times a day, he would call me. My roommate used to laugh that he certainly had it bad for me. Stewart and I had continued like that until my contract had ended and I had returned home. He still carried on calling me every day.

That Easter, I had travelled to his hometown, to spend time with him and his family. We had rented an apartment for the two weeks holiday. I had been slightly anxious that the holiday would be like a test run for our relationship in meeting his family and friends. So far, we had spent more time apart than with each other, but it appeared to be working for us. He had even come over to England to meet my family and friends and to spend more time with me. It had been lovely to see him in my home surroundings as I had seen him in his. I had returned to his hometown for the Christmas celebrations.

Before too long, I found myself yearning for more from this relationship. I wanted to become his wife. His response was to tell me to be patient and that it would happen. I had made the decision to quit working on the cruise ships and I looked for a job that would enable me to be home so that I could start a family. That had been in 2009, but I was still just his girlfriend.

Stewart continued working on the cruise ships. In 2010, I severed my relationship with Stewart as he was not giving me what I wanted or needed. He had begged me to not finish with him as he stated he loved me and that we would get married. But I had been determined to stick with my decision. He had asked that I come out onto the cruise for my birthday as he had a surprise for me. I had declined his proposal as I had been feeling tired of the whole situation. My friends and family had kept on at me too, advising me to go as I did not know what he had in mind to propose or offer me. In the end I had taken their advice and had gone out to see him. Upon my arrival, there had been an obvious tension between us. I recall how I called a friend back home, crying that I should not have gone to see him. He had met someone and although it had been recent, he had liked her. We had then had a massive argument. All I had wanted to do was to go home. It had been a good thing that I had known several of the people on the ship so I could hang out with them instead. On the last night of my trip, he told me how he still had feelings for me and that we could still make it work between us. I had disembarked the cruise ship, knowing that it would be the last time that we would see each other.

Stewart would still call me to check if I were doing ok. He had somehow convinced himself that I was pregnant, even down to thinking he knew when the baby was due. I had laughed and ignored him. I knew that he had already moved on with his life.

I had gone away overnight for a training course, aware that my periods were due. I must have gone to the toilet at least three times, each time noticing that there were no signs of my menstrual cycle coming.

Sat at my desk one day, it had occurred to me that maybe he had been right and what if I was pregnant. I had gone to a walk-in clinic to ask for a pregnancy test. The lady there had informed me that I needed to go and pee in a bottle. I had already been to the toilet before reaching the clinic as I could not hold it in any longer, so only a dribble came out as I was trying to wee into the sterile bottle. But the lady in the clinic had said even that tiny amount would be fine. In a few minutes, she had then turned to tell me that I was pregnant. She told me that I was due on the 11th of March and Stewart himself had predicted that I would be due in March. I had felt excited but scared. We were no longer together as a couple, and I did not want us to get back together just because I was pregnant with his child. His response after I had called to tell him the news was to tell me 'I told you so'. He said that he just knew that I was expectant with our child. I thought it was crazy that he had known before I had because after all, it was my body and not his.

From the start of my pregnancy, it had not been easy. There were complications where I had nearly lost the baby.

Even though I was a mature woman at age thirty-one, I had been living with my grandma then and I had felt apprehensive about telling my grandmother my news. I knew she would be disappointed with me as she would have preferred that I be married and settled down before having a child. But life does not always go according to our plans or wishes. With the ongoing complications the pregnancy resulted in, I had to go to the hospital, not knowing whether I had lost the baby or not. My sister had been rather insistent that grandma had to be told but I had felt reluctant to say anything before having confirmation as to whether everything was ok or not. Despite my pleas, my sister could not wait and had informed our grandma. Big mouth! On returning home, my grandma had asked me why I had not told her, and I had been honest in expressing my fears that she would be so disappointed in me. She had gently chastised me, telling me that I was a grown woman and not a teenager. I think if I had not been living with her, in her house, I may not have felt so bad about my predicament. But grandma was one of my biggest supporters and was there for me and the baby.

Others were happy for me as they had thought that I would never be able have a baby. I had also been anxious to inform my boss at work as I had not long started that job, but she had turned out to be pleased for me and was supportive throughout my pregnancy.

I was aware that the level of emotional tears I was shedding on a regular basis was down to more than just hormones. I was almost in a state of grieving for my lost dreams of having my first baby as a married woman, happily living with a partner, a soul mate, who would be by my side and supporting me through all the necessary pre- natal and doctor appointments. It felt to me as if I were mourning for a socially acceptable union between two people who were deeply in love and who were planning to have a family.

For the sake of my sanity, I had to learn to quickly let go of that idealist dream that had been cemented inside of my brain for so long. It was time for me to move on and face things head on.

In time I soon learnt to embrace the excitement I was feeling about buying tiny clothes and outfits for the baby, unisex colours as I still had not known the sex of the baby I was carrying. I had been hoping for a girl and knew that Stewart did too. He had been there for part of my pregnancy, but in a mental way, not physically.

I was around five months into my pregnancy when I had taken some time off work with having hospital appointments to attend, hoping to finally discover the sex of my baby during one of the scheduled routine scans at the hospital.

It was the first day of my time off from work and I was in the Housing Office. Having succumbed to the urge to use the toilet, it was there that I had discovered that I was bleeding heavily. I had been immediately overwhelmed with confusion and anxiety. I called my friend, Diane, who was desperately trying to calm me down and instructed me to drive to the hospital if I were able to and that she would meet me there. I had driven through the busy streets, not caring that I was being so visibly hysterical behind the wheel.

Arriving at the hospital I could barely speak with the amount of crying I was doing, and the receptionist had called for the doctor immediately. They had then quickly whisked me off to a room and all I could do was to keep repeating that I had lost my baby! Every time I begged for them to tell me if my baby were alive or dead inside me, all they would say was that in the morning they would let me know. That had caused me to become even more hysterical and eventually they had agreed to place the monitor on my stomach, the one that picks up and monitors the baby's heartbeat. They had been insistent that they could not tell me the reason why I was bleeding so heavily, at least not until the morning.

In my head and heart, I was sure that God was punishing me because I had terminated my first pregnancy.

My family and friends soon arrived to offer me support but it was just a matter of waiting and hoping.

Once I had been connected to the monitor, I had been too frightened to look at the screen, but my friend had pointed out to me that it was ok to look, and so eventually I had peeked at the blurry images on the screen. The relief I felt in seeing and hearing the baby's heartbeat was huge. My sweet, tiny baby was still alive.

Early the next day, the midwife and doctor had arrived to escort me to another room where they would be carrying out tests to try to determine what had caused the heavy bleeding. I was feeling so nervous and scared that the baby would arrive there and then. It was far too early for that, and I squeezed my eyes shut as I tried to calm myself down.

The midwife was kind and tried her best to engage me in neutral conversation, asking me what I wanted to have, telling me that if the baby was healthy, that would be the main thing. After a few minutes, she had confirmed that it was a baby girl that I was having.

Further tests and painful internal examinations had revealed that the cause of my bleeding was because the placenta was blocking my cervix. They told me that if the placenta did not shift of its own accord, that I would need to have a c-section performed to deliver my baby safely. I had not been overjoyed about that prospect, but I figured long as my baby was delivered and born safe and sound, that was all that mattered the most to me.

I had eventually been discharged after the medical experts were satisfied that I was well enough to go home.

I had been outside my grandmother's house. It was the 4th of February. Suddenly and without warning, my waters had broken. Arriving at the hospital, they had said that I needed to stay in so that they could monitor and observe me closely.

Two days later, on the 6th of February, they had taken me down to the operating theatre to induce me as they were concerned that I might contract a water infection which would ultimately be harmful to the baby.

On the 6th of February at 9.25pm, my daughter was born. She had arrived five weeks early. She was so beautiful with her eyes wide open, looking as if she had been here on earth, before. I had been instantly engulfed with the wonderful feeling that comes from being a mother.

After giving birth to my daughter, it had been a weird feeling in many ways as I had never once thought that I would be a single parent. It is hard for me to say 'single mother' as my family is superbly supportive and very present in my daughter's life and nurturing.

The job I held at the time of her entering this world, had been demanding with long hours. I did not really have a life as such. I wanted to dedicate my time to my daughter, but I had also possessed a desire to have a career. For many, it is so difficult to achieve the two simultaneously.

With her father and his side of the family residing in another country, I only had my family to rely on for help and much needed support. My daughter was in nursery from the age of ten months. She was so tiny having been born prematurely so everyone thought she was younger than she was. I had felt constantly guilty in having to work such long hours and my daughter had spent so much time at her grandparents' house. I had missed so many precious moments with my child like eating meals with her, getting her ready for bed and reading to her at bedtimes. It had proven difficult when she had started school and I then had to make changes to my life in order to achieve a better home and work balance that suited us both. She is my world and the very reason why I arise each morning and go to work to achieve my goals. I know that one day it will all prove to be worth all the sacrifices I have made.

In May of 2017 I was able to walk away from my job to start my own business. From that moment onwards, I would say that my life became more balanced, and I would not change it for the world.

After having cruised around the world for nine years, working as a Recruitment Consultant, becoming a mother and being baptised, I had decided it was the perfect time to be starting my own business.

Prior to having made that life-changing decision, I had been on a programme called Ester's Academy, a workshop where a lady had been speaking about worth of self. It had felt as if she had been speaking directly to me. I recall leaning across to my friend and telling her that I was going to leave my job. She had thought me crazy, but to me, it had felt right and the right time. The following week I planned to hand in my notice on the Friday. On the Monday morning, during a team meeting, the Manager had stated that there would be one-to-one meetings coming up and I had requested that if it were possible, I would like to be the last one scheduled, as I had a lot of work to complete. He had stated that he had no problem with my request, and I had returned to my desk to write out my resignation letter. It had been something I had wanted to do for the past four years but had always avoided doing through fear and a lack of courage of my belief in myself, really.

During the meeting with my manager, he had been shocked when I had presented my resignation letter to him. With his head in his hands, he had wanted to know my why. I had replied that the big man above had told me to do this, now. My manager had made a concerted effort in trying to persuade me to stay but I had known this was the right time to be moving onwards and forwards.

I was literally stepping out in faith. I had no savings or concrete plans. All I had was my passion and love for what I do plus a few loyal clients.

For me, it had been a long and challenging journey, but I would not change that journey for the world.

When my mum had kicked me out of her house when I was just nineteen years of age, it had proven to be a difficult time for me and my anger with her had simmered and grown as I had not been a bad daughter to her. Throughout all those following years when I had suffered the abuse and for many years after I had escaped from living with it, I had still felt such bitterness and anger at the life I had felt forced into living and I had partially blamed my mother for it.

With time and wisdom, I had eventually prayed to God to allow me to forgive her as I knew that I could not forever blame her for all the misfortunes that had occurred in my life. I love my mum now more than ever before. She was the one who had given me life and I know for certain that if I needed her that she would be there in a heartbeat.

It is only with hindsight and in learning to put everything into perspective that I have come to realise that despite my past sufferings and experiences with domestic violence and abuse, in stark comparison with many others who were around me at the time, I was still fortunate in having lived a relatively good life. Thank you mum and I love you very much.

I now have my self-esteem restored, and my self-confidence and self-respect are intact. I am respected by my peers.

I no longer shy away from recalling those hurtful words spat at me during the duration of the abusive relationship that I was once trapped in, when I was told repeatedly that I would never amount to anything. Instead, I choose to remember those words as they serve as a reminder that I am more than he or I ever believed that I was, could and will be.

Being fearfully trapped within an abusive relationship at a young age, had been horrifically difficult and had stripped away my personality. It has been a slow but steady progress in rebuilding my self-esteem and self-confidence and if I am honest, it is still a work in progress for me. I have learnt that the more I share my story, the lighter I feel inside, and I can sense the old but new Cornita returning! Hip-hip- hooray!

My personal life journey has been one of lessons experienced from which I have learnt that life can be straight forward, chaotic and can suddenly veer off to the left or the right, forwards or backwards. But there is always a light at the end of that dark tunnel, no matter how hopeless or alone we may feel at the time.

I now also know that I am here to give hope to those ladies who have gone through domestic abuse and who have yet to find their voices, whether that be verbally or in written form. Until they do, I will be their voice and reasoning beacon of light, motivation and inspiration.

I am no longer accepting of being brutally forced to be cowering fearfully in the dark corner. I am stood tall and proud front and centre and rearing to go. There is no stopping or hindering me now.

My final advice to those suffering in silence is to learn how to look after and protect your temple and crown, as it is the only human and spiritual vessel that we have.

My life journey has served to remind me that I am indeed a Surviving Queen.

MAE TERESA

Psalm 23:1 The Lord is my Shepherd, I will never want, for He maketh me to lie down in green pastures. He restoreth my soul'.

God, our Father, had laid it upon my heart to write a book, my book, my life story, some time back, but I had consistently procrastinated for a long time, until one Sunday morning in church, the Pastor, a humble man of God, had suddenly paused in his ministrations of preaching his sermon, and he had proclaimed: "Sister Mae Teresa. When are you going to write your book or books? The Almighty has blessed me with the divine message that you have three books to write".

This book that I am now in the process of writing and sharing, is the Lord's divine blessing to me, so that I may help myself to heal, to remove all the old feelings that I have hidden so well, deep inside of me. This is to be my way of revealing and acknowledging my life's journey, inclusive of the breast cancer experiences that I endured and went through to survive and to emerge triumphantly at the end of that and many other personal and life changing traumas.

My written words will also help to give me emotional and mental closure regarding the profound sadness I have felt, the disbelief, the fear and ultimately will no doubt serve as a testing of my deep faith in God. I do believe that God has cleansed me spiritually.

My prayer is that my story helps those who read it to feel empowered, supported and encouraged. I know that God can and does keep His promises to us, to help us through our darkest moments. He will come through for you, in Jesus Christ's mighty name of Nazareth.

Psalm 121:1-2 I will lift up mine eye unto the hills, from whence cometh my help. My help cometh from the Lord, which made heaven and earth.

Life itself has been a phenomenal challenge from the very beginning of my life to the very last chapter of my book journey. I include one of my chapters from my forthcoming book here, which is my written gratitude of hope, love, and faith.

My Anthology Chapter is called: 'My Path To Divine Empowerment'.

CHAPTER 2

MY PATH TO DIVINE EMPOWERMENT

MAE TERESA

I had a decent life growing up with my brothers and I had been blessed with not feeling deprived or of longing for more.

My mum was a hard worker and had been employed on a part-time basis, doing cleaning jobs, with her working hours being fitted around being at home for us at the appropriate times when it was time for her to be present whilst we hurried in the mornings to get ready for school and for when she wanted to be home in time to prepare our evening meals.

Even though my parents were married, my mum had been the proactive parent who had made the concerted efforts to be fully involved in helping us with school and homework projects. My dad had not finished his early years education and he had therefore not gained any academic qualifications, but when it came to the skills of carpentry and design, my dad had possessed a great and skilful mind and capability for precise measurements and in visualising what his products and ideas would eventually look like. He had produced some fantastic works, which had been admired not only by us, his family, but by many others as well. To this day, we still are in possession of two beds that he had crafted for us as children and those same beds are now lovingly utilised in our family home that was built in the Caribbean.

I had once asked my mum how and why she had become a cleaner, and she had explained to me how when she had first arrived in the UK, and after giving birth to me, she had secured employment cleaning offices during the very early hours of the morning and had also been fortunate in getting an office job that she had trained for, during the day.

In those days, there had been limited access to qualified or governmentally inspected child minders, but rather it had been a case of relying on friends of friends. One day, my mum had collected me

from the child minder to find that I was tearful. It had only been once she had arrived home with me in tow, that having fed and then changed me, she had realised that the same nappy she had put me in that morning had not been changed! She had double checked and confirmed her suspicions by recounting the number of nappies she had carefully packed into my bag, that morning. She had never taken me back to that child minder and had instead, embarked on taking on her office cleaning job on a full-time basis.

Mum had eventually trained as a nurse and had applied herself to that role diligently, after the birth of my third brother. After my mum had become pregnant with my last and youngest brother, she had given up nursing all together.

Growing up, I can remember my dad having issues with my mum's undertaking of professional training courses and her desire to better herself and her various attempts to elevate her professional status and self-worth, had caused many heated arguments between them.

Witnessing this had taught me, later in life, with a fuller understanding, that men who had no formal education or academic qualifications, usually felt too much egotistical male pride to pursue remedying their lack of educational qualifications and so therefore they had resented the women they were married to who had chosen to do and pursue what they were pridefully fearful of doing for themselves. There had been times when my dad, who had worked for the Ford Motors company, had refused to go into work because he had a headache or a cold and this had meant the absence of his wages had put a great strain on my mum, as she was the one who had been burdened with solely having to pay the bills. This, also, had been a source of contention between them and had resulted in further heated words being exchanged between them, sometimes in our presence.

When I had turned thirteen years of age, my parents had planned a holiday to the island of their birth. They had not owned a house of their own back then, but arrangements had been made for us to stay in a town house owned by relatives as they spent a lot of their time in their other home, situated in the rural localities of the island.

I had felt excited as it had been my first holiday abroad and the first time that my brothers and I would be travelling by aeroplane. When my parents had arrived in the UK, they had travelled by boat, the *Windrush*, so it had also been a first for them, too, to be flying in an aeroplane.

The morning had eventually dawned, and we were all ready to go, and I had been dressed up in a similar two-piece, flared trouser suit and blouse, just like my mum. We had reached the airport and after all the finalities of checking in, we finally boarded the huge aeroplane. My brothers and I had been so excited, we could barely contain our joy. It had been a long seven-hour flight to Antigua where we had disembarked to make our connecting flight to our destination. It had been here that we had experienced what it felt like to be bitten by mosquitos. We had finally arrived onto the island of our parents' birthplace.

My younger brothers and I were overwhelmed with awe and excitement. My youngest brother, he had been but a toddler, so he had naturally just gone with the flow of our combined joy and laughter and so forth.

During our stay there, after about a week or maybe two, there had been a knock at the door and I had gone downstairs to open the front door, to find one of my cousins stood there. That had been the moment that he had seized the opportunity to squeeze my nipples so hard that it had frightened and shocked me and from then on, I had made every effort to avoid him like the dreaded plague. Every time I had thought of what he did or even just having the images of his face flash through my mind, I could feel my temper rising and recognised it was because I had felt violated by him. He had not stopped trying to get me to be on my own with him but each time, I had quickly moved away from him.

One Saturday, my Grand Aunt had visited. She had literally lived just down the road from us. She and my mum would sit and converse in their language, not realising that I could understand their every word. During their conversation, my Grand Aunt had asked my mum if she was not going to introduce me to my dad. My mum had stammered and looked flustered. I had stared at them both in shock. Eventually, my mum had managed to respond that *"No-one else is her dad, other than the man who has raised her"*.

I could see that my mum had been clearly upset and had most likely buried the thought of her having to reveal this secret to me, way back somewhere in her once fractured mind.

The next day, my mum had mentioned the context of this family secret to me, and I had eventually gone on to meet the man who was supposed to be my birth father. I am going to call him IL.

To be truthful, during our first meeting, I could not bring myself to react positively towards him as I had felt stone cold and confused. He, on the other hand, had been over the moon to see me and my mum. I could not bring myself to even pretend to share his enthusiasm though, as I had felt hurt, angry, and resentful.

Our holiday of six weeks had been generally very enjoyable, and we had loved experiencing the local juices, foods and delicacies of the island. The time had soon come for us to return home to the UK.

I had made the decision that I needed to question my mum about my biological father.

I am now a woman in her fifties, but I had grown up feeling such intense anger towards men in general. I had little or no respect for them, and I would argue with them whenever they tried to correct me on anything to do with my wellbeing or even if they attempted to encourage me to find another way that would serve to help me on a personal level. I used to wake up aware of this suppressed rage within me which dictated that I would be in a foul mood all day and I truly had no significant understanding of the reasons why.

It was sometime last year as I was laying on top of my bed, having a quiet moment with God, when He had shown me the reasons behind my constant feelings of internal suppressed rage, and it had become clear to me just where that anger had originated from.

I have always heard that when a woman is pregnant with child, that the baby can sense and absorb all the emotions from within the cocoon of the mother's womb. God had shown me that my unhealed anger had stemmed from my mother. I had inherited her own anger and pain as a result of her feeling hurt and betrayed from being assaulted and raped. As a born-again Christian, I now finally understood that my previous behavioural patterns were not directly from me but rather from what my mother had unfortunately experienced in her life. Her rape had led to my birth. Essentially, I had been born as the result of a violent act being perpetrated against another human being.

After receiving those messages of hope and clarity from God, I have had to learn how to alter my thoughts to evolve from being dark and toxic ones to more happier and positive thoughts. I do still get upset sometimes when my mind wanders to the way how IL had brutally violated my mum, causing her so much pain and distress, not only to her but also for myself as I had been the direct result of that forced violation on her body, mind and soul.

It saddens me that such a dark and heavy cloud has followed me for most of my life. I give thanks that I was able to eventually find my faith and my God because my path in life has changed so much since then, for which I will be eternally grateful.

Mum had explained to me that this man had been hungering after her for ages, even though she had shown no interest in him.

My mum and her brother had been raised by their grandmother, as their own mother, my grandmother, had shown no interest in raising

her children. Their mother had never wanted my mum and had blatantly told my mum that she had tried to get rid of her during her pregnancy, by drinking all sorts of concoctions, but to no avail, and my mum had remained cocooned inside her mother's womb, despite the attempts to forcefully flush her out. I can only imagine how my mum must have felt in hearing that from her own birth mother.

My mum had told me that the only way her mother had shown any emotions towards them was in the form of severely beating and scolding them. Their mother had, without question, willingly believed every complaint that had been delivered to her ears about her children, usually uttered by the neighbours.

My great grandmother had ensured that my mum and her brother had attended school and I believe that my maternal grandfather had helped in this accomplishment, also.

My mum had eventually progressed to working as an accountant. She had attracted several admirers but only had eyes for one specific gentleman. He had taken her out for ice-cream and whatever else social ventures they had had going on during those times, back in the 1940's. IL, my biological father, used to bring food and various goods for my great grandmother, a tradition that I believe was and still is embraced and implemented by my mother's culture and many other cultures, too.

As I have mentioned before, my mum had felt no desire for or had any interest in this man, IL. In listening to my mum, she appeared to have been quite a serious lady, born and raised in the town and slightly snobbish or 'stuck up', as people might label it. If you were not employed in a certain type of job, for example, my mum had no interest in you. I have heard friends of my mum's, who knew her from her younger days, describe her as a hard nut to crack. According to her friends, she had also been beautiful, with big pretty eyes, a head full of healthy hair and very deep dimples which were evident whenever she smiled. She could certainly hold her own, as they say.

It had been a Saturday afternoon and my mum had been home on her own, happily reading a book. Apparently, she had been an avid reader of the Mills & Boons books publications.

Mum related how IL had knocked on the external door and pushed his way in and had then forcibly raped her. She had described it in graphical details, how he had pushed her underwear to the side and had aggressively taken her in that way. She had felt shocked and humiliated.

At that time, my grandmother had travelled to the UK and met her husband, who I had grown up calling my grandad. After a month or so after my mum's shocking experience, mum had come to realise that she was pregnant with me. There had been a doctor who had offered my mum the option of having an abortion, but my mum had refused. She had instead turned her thoughts into wondering how she could possibly find a way to leave the island quietly. She had felt embarrassed, hurt, and angry at her situation and enforced circumstances. She had even written to her mother in the UK, asking for her to send her some money with the promise of paying it back. Apparently, my grandmother had given her a hard time, stating that she was getting married to my grandfather and had needed all her money for that forthcoming expense. However, I do believe that my grandad had given her the money and my mum had travelled to England by boat. Despite her constantly feeling ill on the boat, she had still managed to meet and interact with some lovely people, she said.

When mum had landed at Tilbury Docks, her mother had been shocked and immensely disappointed as she had been unaware that her daughter, my mother, was expectant with child. Fortunately, for my mum, my grandfather was a loving and understanding man and he had embraced my mum with a warm welcome. Her mother, on the other hand, had not been at all happy but there had been nothing that she could really do about it.

Her mother had allocated her a room that was situated in the corridor and that is where I was born and where my mum and I resided. Mum's labour had started on the Saturday, and I was born on the Tuesday. It had been a painful breech birth and the medics had to turn me several times, which must have been excruciatingly painful for my mum to bear. Mum had lost all the birth fluids during her prolonged labour and the result had been a very dry and extra painful birth of delivery. The doctors had struggled to pull me out by using medical forceps in the end. Mum remembers me being born and looking really pale with matted black hair stuck to my head.

Mum said also that IL had told her that when he had found out that he had gotten her pregnant, that she never wanted him near her or wanted anything to do with him. However, mum would always remember the difficulty she had in birthing me and had this following reminder of how I came into this world.

Proverbs 18:21 Death and life are in the power of the tongue and those who love it will eat its fruit.

Mum never forgot how she and I had to reside in the draughty corridor, where people came in and out frequently, as my grandmother was always entertaining her friends. In the fifties and sixties, this was considered normal for the Caribbean communities as they went about their daily work lives and then determinedly enjoyed themselves on the weekends.

My mum eventually met a nice man. I will call him JB. Whenever he took my mum out, I was left with his Aunt, who had loved me like one of her own grandchildren. I remember her well. My mum and JB had dated for a while and had been happy together. I had often been told, what with having similar complexions, that I had looked like him and he had, in fact, loved me and treated me as his own, even though he had no biological children of his own. People had always assumed that I was his biological child.

My grandfather had a cousin who had been one of those people always visiting my grandparents' home. He had apparently loved or lusted after my mum from afar back home in their homeland and had been overjoyed when he realised that he had found her here, in the UK. My mum had felt no interest in wanting to know him back home as she had considered him to be a country man as opposed to her being a town girl. I shall refer to this man as BS.

Mum had been enjoying her flourishing relationship with JB and had been immune to the proffered and unrequited attention from BS. He would visit my grandparents often, bringing foods, alcohol, cigarettes and so forth, always alerting my grandparents to how he felt about my mum and boldly declaring his interest in wanting to marry her.

My grandmother had consequently begun to give my mum a hard time about JB as he was not, as I would put it, one of those men who would try to buy his way into a family. His interest in and his love for my mum and myself were pure and uncomplicated. But my grandmother had pushed and cajoled and basically harassed my mum until such time as my mum had agreed to marry BS. My grandmother had apparently been more impressed with being flattered with material things more than with appreciating true love when she saw it. My mum had not been at all happy with the idea of this arranged marriage but had felt distressingly powerless as she had not wanted to cause further upset to her mother, so she had eventually agreed to marry BS. Her decision to agree to this arranged marriage had been reached out of not wanting to further disappoint her mother and out of feeling she had little choice in the matter.

During their engagement party, my mum had been dancing to the pulsating rhythms of the Jamaican ska music, calypso and so on, as BS had just remained sat morosely on the stool at the bar, drinking vast amounts of alcohol and getting increasingly upset with my mum as he watched her enjoying herself and socialising with those invited guests that were present. Mum stated how he had hit her during that party and how she had then grabbed a flask and broken it over his head. It would have been normal to have considered that that would have signalled the end of their relationship, but my mum had so wanted to please her mother that she had allowed the marriage plans to still go ahead.

BS had agreed to adopt me and to give me his name. But, in hindsight and from the memories I have, I had never really felt any love from him towards me. I do not recall ever being physically or emotionally embraced by him.

I was five years old when my brother was born. I had felt so happy. I finally had sibling company. Unfortunately, for my mum, she had again experienced a difficult time in giving birth to my younger brother. The medical staff had deemed it necessary to keep my mum in the hospital for further observations and care and my brother had come home with BS, who was now my dad, too.

I can remember the time, as a teenager, where I had been visiting my godmother and she had informed me how when my baby brother had been discharged from the hospital, that BS had refused to look after me and had brought me to my godmother's house instead, telling her that *"I will look after my own and I am leaving her with you and her godfather as she is yours"*. On hearing that, I had felt deeply hurt.

By the time I was six, mum had realised that I was having difficulty with my eyesight and as a result I was finding it hard to read properly. I can remember going into work with my mum during the school holidays and it had been her manager who had pointed out that there was an issue with my sight, and she had suggested to my mum that she take me to see the opticians. They then had discovered that I could barely see out of my right eye and had slight vision in my left eye. Part of the treatment was to provide me with prescribed glasses, which I had hated as they had solid thick lenses with a wired pink frame that hooked around my ears, causing me some discomfort.

When I think back to my birth, I sometimes believe that the way in which I was pulled out of the womb may have caused some damage to my eyes. Maybe they had used too much force when clamping the forceps onto my head. This is only my personal and reflective thoughts and not a medical diagnosis.

Growing up as a teenager, I was teased mercilessly and called names, like four eyes and ugly. In the area where I lived, I was walking past two Caribbean women one day and overheard them talking and saying how because I was so ugly, that men would just use me and impregnate me with endless numbers of children. Hearing those words had affected me in so many ways. It had taken me some time to realise that I found it hard to accept a compliment. When I looked in the mirror, all I could see was this ugly and unworthy person, someone who had no hope or dreams of her own.

It is so important to speak positivity into children's lives because what you say can have a negative impact on them, one which they will most likely retain and carry around with them for a long time, if not for the rest of their lives. This is one of the important lessons I am learning as I continue onwards with this evolving, spiritual journey of rediscovering who I am.

At age fourteen, my mum had signed me up with a modelling agency in Bond Street. Despite my horrible thick glasses, I had been accepted onto their books. During my training to be a model, I had learnt how to walk down the catwalk and I still remember the instructions of 'hip, toe, hip, toe' being drummed into my ears. Applying make-up was not as easy as it had appeared to be, but in time and with practice, my self-confidence had accelerated from zero to believing that I could do this. Unfortunately, I had not pursued a modelling career as many family members were constantly feeding negativity into my mum's mind about the industry. But training to be a model had served to stimulate me into wanting to find myself, because as a teenager I had previously felt so lost and unsure of who I was.

When mum had another child, my fourth brother, the fights between her and our dad had continued. Her pregnancy was a miserable one. Friends used to encourage her to take it easy.

I recall during some type of altercation between them, how I had picked up a piece of wood with the intention of using it to lash out at dad, wanting to hit him with it on the back of his head. But mum had screamed out my name and I had been abruptly stopped in my tracks.

There had come a day when the teachers had called my mum into the school, wanting to speak to her about my younger brother, the one who was born after me. Mum had left the school building that day heartbroken and having made the decision during her journey home, that she would be divorcing my dad, BS. The constant fighting was beginning to affect my brother's schooling and education and he was consistently being found crying by one or more of his teachers. When he had been questioned as to why he was so upset, he had explained that he was afraid of my dad who kept on beating our mother.

Around the time their divorce had been finalised, my youngest brother must have been around eighteen months old, and he had no clue who our dad was. Even now, he does not feel entirely comfortable in joining in conversations about the experiences the rest of us shared as children as he does not remember any of that.

Just prior to my leaving school, I had finally been fitted with contact lenses and it was like a fog had been removed from the ogling eyes of the opposite sex. I began noticing that I was getting admiring glances and interest from boys and men. There had been a boy in the school, called MR, whom I had fancied for ages. He, however, had always considered me unattractive, due to my thick glasses, I presumed. As soon as I had stopped wearing them, it had been like, hey presto, interest galore! My belief remains intact that some men are truly just visual and cannot see beneath the surface.

At age sixteen, I had taken my mock exams and then I had left school.

Everything I learnt from then on was through my jobs and the courses I took at college during the evenings. One of the main reasons I had left school so early was that my mum had been struggling with paying the bills, so I had gone out to work and found a really good job at the post office. Despite helping my mum with grocery shopping and buying clothes for my brothers, I had still been able to afford to live a fun-filled life, partying and even travelling abroad on my own and consequently loving the experiences of discovering other countries and cultures.

It was around that same time that I had met and fallen in love with my daughter's dad. I had been naïve in not knowing how to behave in an intimate relationship but had trusted my limited judgement in believing that being faithful, intimately giving and in love, would be enough to sustain and maintain a healthy and intimate relationship. He had shown me love also, but he also had an eye for the ladies and had loved to gamble. Even though his actions and behaviours had caused me hurt and stress, I had remained completely faithful and loyal to him.

I was twenty-three when I fell pregnant with my beautiful daughter.

Unfortunately, he and I had been unaware that we were both carriers of sickle cell. We had both had the sickle cell trait which meant that our daughter was born with having full-blown sickle cell anaemia.

In due time we had eventually bought our home and moved in together. Our co-habitation and life together had not been the easiest, but we had built a life together, as a family of three.

During her younger years, our daughter had suffered many instances of sickle cell crises and as her mum, it had almost broken me to see her suffering in that way. I had cried often. I had no clue how I could take her pain away for her and make her feel better. She had been on medications for years, like penicillin and folic acid, to name a few, but she had still persevered to grow into a beautiful woman, with an inner strength that is to be admired and inspired by. I had taught her from early on that she was in charge and in control of sickle cell and that sickle cell was not in charge or in control of her.

Aged seven, she had travelled abroad with my family and had apparently caught some type of infection and had become seriously ill to the point of almost dying. The Consultant in charge of her case in the Caribbean hospital had told me that she did not think that my daughter would make it, despite the emergency blood transfusions they had given her. Several hours after the Consultant's shift had ended, she was still there by my daughter's bedside, offering us comfort and words of care and positivity. I just had no words of how to thank her for her dedication and care.

That near-fatal situation had really frightened us as her parents and the whole family, too. When I had arrived there, I saw how my mum's hair had turned silver almost overnight. She had left the UK with a head full of black hair, but the emotional intensity and anxious grief in seeing her granddaughter at death's door, had shocked and affected her badly.

Some of the residents who lived in the area had started to tell my mum that her granddaughter would not live past the age of nine! I had told my mum, that with all due respect, those people were not God and that my child would not die until the good Lord was ready to take her. The scripture that immediately came to my spirit was: *Psalms 118:17, I shall not die but live to declare the works of the Lord.*

In giving God the glory, I am thankful that my daughter is now a grown woman, a graduate, in employment and a partner in her own business. As I type this, a song comes to me: '*I shall have what God has promised me, what He said in his WORD, is mine'.*

Sadly, her father and I had parted company when she was seven. I had woken up one morning realising that I had endured enough. I could no longer suffer his infidelities and constant cheating and extensive gambling. I had once had confidence in myself but that had been broken down by his insensitive behaviours and relentless disregard for my feelings or happiness. I could no longer trust the opposite sex. I grew to feel more and more angry with him and with men in general.

I had walked out of our marital home with our daughter and had moved back into the family home. My family and friends had not really understood what was going on with us, within our marital relationship, as I had shared so very little information of what I was suffering.

I had harboured a lot of resentment in my closed heart. It had then taken me another two years before I had started to date again, but I had possessed the attitude that I cared little if these liaisons lasted or ended. I had taken no prisoners. I had been comfortable in carrying around a baggage load of unforgiveness, grudges and hate. At that time, I had no clue of the emotional and mental damage that I was inflicting on myself. I had been seeking love from the wrong men. In truth, I had not loved myself enough, either.

Not so long ago, we, as a family, had reached out and made connections with our brother on the BS side of the family. It had been so overwhelming to see him, his children and so many grandchildren. I could see and feel my brother's excitement upon meeting us. It had felt good to be called Aunty by grown children and their own children. Still, on the other hand, I had also felt a certain distancing within myself, a wary and anxious cautiousness that stuck painfully to the lining of my soul and heart. What would they say when they found out that I was not actually a 'blood' relative and was in fact adopted by their grandfather? Would they still receive me with open arms and continue to love me? On the IL side of the family, would they be willing to accept that the man they called their father had raped and violated my mother?

My question to God is, *"Where do I belong?"* I have never felt the unconditional and special love of a dad, only the unique and appreciated love from my mum and my loving brothers. I still feel like a small vulnerable fish in a big sea. Living with this yearning, this longing, for the love of a father, is one of the hardest things to endure as an adult. But the Heavenly Father has shown me that this life journey of mine is not just about my inner healing and deliverance, it is far greater and more meaningful than that. It is about reaching out courageously and with faith in wanting to help someone else who may have gone through or is going through a similar journey as I have, in trying to find, understand and appreciate Self.

During my many years of asking God, *"Who am I?"*, and beseeching him to expose any hidden secrets, I began to feel more positive about myself and the journey I am taking, divinely guided by God. There were times during my praying when the tears would pour profusely down my face and I would feel an internal shift, which in turn allowed me to form a better sense of positivity and release.

I sincerely believe that I was going through a spiritual cleansing.

I thank God for the Pastors to whom I am spiritually accountable to. Being in a mentorship programme has not only assisted in helping me to pray strategically but it has also helped me to find that inner courage with which to dig deeper into my thoughts and soul to deal with the hurts and emotional and mental pains of being the product of rape.

I grew not knowing or experiencing the love of a father in the way that my daughter has memories of the times spent with her dad.

I became an expert in hiding my true emotions, burying them so deep and sweeping them under the carpet where they could not be seen or heard. Being a mentee under the guidance of my Pastor has served to help me to delve further into my sub-consciousness to uproot the roots of my hurts, to find answers to the questions that had for so long burnt and etched their way into my soul.

The harder I prayed, the more those hidden secrets were revealed to me. Bringing those unspoken secrets to the surface helps me to pray in earnest and to free myself from the tentacled demons that were always lurking in the deep dark corners of my mind.

In life, those secrets and unspoken hurts have a way of coming out and being passed onto the wrong people, especially during times of upset, distress or stress. My spiritual mentorship involvement helps me to learn how to handle and cope with healing from those painful emotional traumas.

I would recommend that if you are a believer and have faith, that you find a spiritual mentorship programme to help you to heal from within. Mentorship under the guidance of the right person for you, will help you to navigate the process, to restore in you trust of humankind and will help you to forgive those who caused you previous harm.

God promises us freedom from the trauma and hurt and He is the same yesterday, today and tomorrow. God not only heals the physical body, but also the mind, soul and spirit. He is the deliverer that delivers us from brokenness so that we can remain whole in Christ Jesus.

It had been a busy day in the office and I and my colleagues were all working, laughing and enjoying our usual banter between us all. Suddenly I had felt an intense heat directly over my left breast. I had ignored it and continued typing away on my keyboard. I recall when a clinical member of staff had come into the Administration office to speak to us, and I had then felt a strong urge to scratch away this itching on my breast. It was then I had felt a hard lump. I kept discreetly touching it and eventually it had filtered into my spirit that I may have just discovered what every woman is fearful of, which is cancer.

Sweat had settled profusely on my forehead as I experienced a hot flush from within my body. I had tried to digest what I was truly feeling and questioned silently how this could be happening to me.

I had walked out of the office in complete shock, making an excuse to those I had been talking to. I had called my GP and fortunately there had been an appointment available for the following morning.

The rest of that day had gone by in a blur. My mind wandered left, right and centre, even though I had said nothing to anyone, not even my daughter.

I had felt horrified in thinking that I may be afflicted with a disease that for many had proved fatal. My mind refused to stop whirring and went into overdrive imagining the worst scenarios possible. My anxiety levels went through the roof. And this was all before even having seen a medical professional.

As I sat waiting to be called in to see my GP, I found myself studying the faces of the other patients and wondering what their diagnosis would be and if whoever they were with would be supportive of their needs. My mind had drifted as I aimlessly watched the television screen that was attached to the wall. I tried to imagine how my daughter and my family would react if it were bad news and then my mind drifted unfocused to thoughts of what I would cook for dinner that evening.

I could not help but think of all those times I had spent in the hospital with my daughter when she had suffered through one crisis to another, due to her having a serious blood disorder. I thought of all those nights spent in the A&E department, watching her curled up in excruciating pain and how my heart felt heavy, and my hands symbolically tied, in not being able to physically help her to ease her pains. The only comfort I could give her was to wrap her in my arms until her pain medications kicked in to ease her hurting. There were moments when I could see the fear etched on her little face and there I was, trying to suppress my own fears of the unknown.

Eventually it was my turn, and I was called in to see the doctor.

During the examination, the look on the doctor's face had confirmed my worst nightmare. She had tried her best to compose herself. She had taken my blood pressure and then she had explained to me that she was referring me directly to the walk-in breast clinic at Northwick Park and that they would be contacting me shortly. Later that same day, I had received a call from the breast clinic. They were offering me an appointment to come in to see them on the Monday of the following week.

Psalm 91:1 – He that dwelleth in the secret of the Most High, shall abide under the shadow of the Almighty.

Monday morning had finally arrived, and I had felt a massive increase in my anxiety levels. My daughter had driven me to the clinic appointment, but I refused to allow her to come inside with me. I had wanted to face this part of my journey alone. I was a mother trying to protect her child from absorbing the tremendous fear I was feeling. Having made my way to the outpatients' department, I had given them my name and was asked to take a seat.

My name was duly called out and the doctor had introduced herself to me. We had spoken at length and then she had proceeded to examine me. She had busied herself in making some notes and then she had called in the Macmillan Nurse, telling me that the nurse would be my contact nurse for the next few years. The nurse had informed me in detail about everything to do with breast cancer and what the next steps would be. An appointment was then made for me to have a scan and biopsy.

My mind had swayed equally between thinking negatively and positively but thoughts of not surviving this trial and tribulation of having cancer was uppermost in my thoughts. Would I live to see my grandchildren? Would I enjoy seeing my nieces and nephews grow into adults? Would I be fortunate enough to survive to see their children and be a part of their joy and special moments? Would I live to experience spending time with my family at Christmas and for their birthdays yet to come? Would my breast need to be removed and even though I was single at that time, would I be considered as unattractive to the opposite sex?

I had no life partner with whom to share my worries or the experiences of having cancer, with. Nobody to tell me that I was still attractive and desirable. Nobody to tell me that they loved me as a woman ought to be loved and desired. To say that I was worried, was a massive understatement.

Once again it had been my daughter who had driven me back to the hospital to have my biopsy procedure done. On the way there, the reality of having cancer and what that meant, had begun to really sink in and I could feel a tsunami of emotions threatening to overwhelm me. We had made our way to the X-ray department where the Radiologist had patiently explained the procedure to me, in detail, inclusive of the injection that would numb the area they would be taking the biopsy from. To this day I remember the noise the piercing of my skin had made in my ears. It had sounded like a gun and even though the area had been numbed, I had still felt everything. Afterwards, I was sent back to the breast clinic where they had explained that once the results were in, I would be contacted and asked to return.

My daughter and I had hardly spoken as she then drove me to work. We had both been lost in our own thoughts. My journey of being diagnosed as a breast cancer victim had truly commenced.

They say that God does not give you more than you can bear. He might let you bend but he will not let you break. Amen.

The dreaded day had come when I had to go back for the results. I had been aware of what the Holy Spirit had already told me but in my mind, I was still telling myself that I would be fine and that there would be no trace of any cancer.

My daughter was with me as they had confirmed that I had breast cancer. It had turned out to be the kind of cancer that kills most women as it grew slowly, and many women had no idea that they had it.

As the Consultant had been speaking, the tears I had been withholding, had finally spilled out and rolled down my face. I was given a date for surgery to be performed in the November. I recall questioning why I had to wait so long as I had wanted that cancerous and intrusive lump removed and gone.

Over the following weeks, my sister-in-law and her son visited me in my home to say prayers for me and with me. It had been during that time that God had revealed to me that the cancer I had was spiritual. That revelation had broken me as I could not believe that someone could be so intentionally wicked to wish me such devastating harm. It had been shown to me that that same person would be in touch with me to check how I was doing. That person had contacted me literally days after I had experienced that revelation. I received a telephone call asking me how I was keeping. My response had been to go further into prayers and fasting, trusting in God that His words would come to pass and that I would be delivered well and healed at the end of this trying journey back to wellness.

Would I survive or would I die?

I had no hesitation in placing my faith in God throughout the whole ordeal of being diagnosed and operated on. My relationship with God grew and I started to reach out to Him more and more and in understanding further the path that lay ahead of me. I chose to not share my illness with the church hospitality team, but I had confided in my Church Lead and in the Bishop of my church.

If I survived, what part would I then play in the Kingdom of God and within the world? What could I do to help other women? What method could I use to encourage and empower others who were diagnosed with cancer, knowing the tumultuous and uncertain journey that they would have to face?

My thoughts had turned to the strong women depicted in the Bible. Hannah, who had prayed ceaselessly until God had blessed her womb as she had so desperately wanted a child and had prayed for a son. She had promised God that she would dedicate her life to Him. It was written in the Bible that Hannah's faithfulness had never faltered. Could I be anything like Hannah?

Psalms 91: 4-6 – He shall cover you with feathers and under His wings you shall take refuge. His truth shall be your shield and buckler. You shall not be afraid of the terror by night nor of the arrow that flies by day. Nor of the pestilence that walks in darkness, nor of the destruction that lays waste at noonday. Amen.

I give Thanks in the Almighty's name for being a child of God and in remembering that I am a Surviving Queen!

JANNETTE BARRETT AKA MS LYRICIST B

I am a wife, mother and grandmother.

I work as a freelance Mental Health Awareness Community Practitioner, and I too have endured traumas in my life. This has been my chosen career as I am aware of the consequences of experiencing triggers and yet I still felt exposed in thinking about writing a book about me, knowing I would be standing alone in revealing and sharing, and I was unprepared to take that step. So, it was with some measure of relief and gratitude when I spotted a social media post that was looking to embrace several Queens into a space of love and support and who had journeyed through their personal paths of past or present abuse which had been perpetrated against them.

I felt hungry to be a part of that community, one which I knew would hold me with linked chains of love and compassion, and not with the previous chains of rusty captivity that had held me down for so long, forcibly connected to my untold secrets. To be a part of this anthology is akin to hearing our voices crying out in jubilant triumph, filling the air with harmony and unity so that we can all finally breathe a little easier. I had been craving that feminine support that would uplift me and I have found it here, surrounded by women, queens, whose reputations and genuine love for each other preceded them as each one of us bathes in the encouragement received to be strong in our vulnerabilities as we collectively and openly share our stories and lived experiences of overcoming challenges and adversities in life. My smile is now genuine as I feel whole despite everything that I endured. My husband, children and grandchildren can now have the authentic me that they so deserve as my writings have helped to heal and free me from any inner turmoil I may have suppressed.

I am a published author and my trilogy of books, *The Transition Series*, is available on both the Amazon and Waterstones websites and the sharing of my journey, the disrobing of my innermost thoughts and secrets, is dedicated to those I know and do not know. My wish is that you come to know that you are not alone as through my written words I wish to embrace you all into this inner circle of friendship and sisterhood.

I have also written and acted on stage in a play based on my books. I sang the songs that I had written that helped to expand my soul as I harmoniously released the shackles of the chains that were keeping me locked into not being who I wanted to be.

My Anthology chapter is called 'The Secret Lining of my Hidden Suitcase'.

CHAPTER 3

THE SECRET LINING OF MY HIDDEN SUITCASE

JANNETTE BARRETT

I was born in the era known as the 'swinging sixties', in a small town called Handsworth in the city of Birmingham UK. The sixties were labelled as a time of free love and free expressions but both of those statements, as wonderful and liberating as they sound, were not something that everybody could display and certainly that had not been the case in the lives of my parents or anyone else with even a hint of colour in their skin. For those with white skin, this was not a problem originating from the colour of their skin.

Simple and daily activities like playing and listening to the types of music they loved or cooking the foods they enjoyed eating, were met with hostile opposition. As for people of colour daring to have an opinion – that was certainly not encouraged.

The reality is that my parents may well have been subjected to racial remarks due to the differences in their skin tones.

The following is my interpretations of those times lived, based purely on a desire to ascertain whether racism with all its connective barbarism had played a pivotal part in the decisions my parents made when raising my siblings and me. It has made me more than curious because their decisions, especially those decisions that lacked a way of communicating to us and educating us as to what to expect in this world, would prove to have a catastrophic effect on how I saw myself. Were those same decisions to omit teaching us certain aspects of the reality of life, one of the reasons why I had ended up being a woman subjected to years of abuse and domestic violence?

Racial segregation had been rife in the areas in which we lived and yet we came from a seemingly tight-knit community. I can only assume that my mother and father had experienced their fair share of verbal and possibly physical abuse for some time before we came along. Why do I say, assume? I use that term because my parents have never disclosed anything of that nature to us. Like so many others, they lived in a vacuumed vortex of cultural silence. Most of the racial incidents were met with compliance to show conformity to what was already expected of them. Keeping quiet after being abused was just one of the things they were expected to endure. Their apparent willingness to remain silent was born out of shame, embarrassment and a need to keep up an almost invisible appearance to the external world of whiteness personified.

The fear of revealing any situation that would stigmatise them or their families was real and never spoken about, and the fact the devastating happening may even have been a rape, had no significant influence over them remaining locked into their conspiracies of fearful and shame-filled silence. It appeared that the lesser of the two evils was to allow a poor woman who had been assaulted to be viewed as a loose woman having a child out of wedlock rather than to admit or acknowledge the possible presence of abuse or violence. Worse still, a secretive abortion would have been sorted and preferred, rather than a family handling their affairs in a moral and humanely orderly fashion. They would rather keep it hidden than to admit they needed to seek help from any other than their immediate families. It would have been a damn sight better for us if our parents had spoken about the effects of racism or the consequences of being Black.

It would have been far easier to have heard it from them instead of having to have experienced finding out about all that consequential racial trauma in the way we had.

Some of the abusive remarks we were subjected to were so ugly to hear. Even when there had been witnesses to what we had encountered, nobody had defended us. People would turn a blind eye and happily walk the other way, determined not to get involved. We were left alone to defend ourselves and to create and live by a 'dog eat dog' mentality, which is part of the reason why we felt compelled into forming gangs. It had felt as if we were left with only that choice of doing so as a way for us to get by, living in a world motivated and dominated by racism, prejudice and unjustified hatred. There were times where the racial abuse had been subtle and at those times it had been more an aware-ness to be quick witted, but at other times, we had been blatantly harassed, with racist people crowding into our personal spaces and up close to our faces. There were times we had to resort to using bricks, bottles and fists to fight our way out of a dangerous and potentially fatal situation. It had proven to be a far cry from the innocence of our younger childhood days where the freedom to play and express ourselves amongst our peers of all races, had never really forced us to see any of our skin tones as an issue that would cause hostility and mistrust between us.

From the time we had begun secondary school, during the 1970's, those issues had manifested into an unexpected thunderstorm that seemed to come at us thick and fast and without pause or reprieve. Those carefree days when our smiling faces were met with their smiling faces was replaced with unbridled expressions of uncertainty and unspoken distrust. The simplicity of running in and out of each other's houses had seriously started to disappear. The atmosphere within the school I attended, which had once been my sanctuary, even with its disciplinarian ways, suddenly felt like a whole different experi-ence. Bullies were no longer people whom I could handle easily with my quick wit. Instead, now their racist remarks felt seriously threat-ening and intimidating.

Another thing that had become apparent and rather profound, was the 'Watch with Mother' children's television shows and the wrestling followed by the numerous spaghetti western films, which were amongst the very few shows that we were permitted to watch. 'Watch with Mother' was a cycle of children's programmes broadcasted by the BBC and aimed specifically at pre-school children and their mothers. The intentional title was meant to deflect fears that television might become a nursemaid to children and therefore encourage bad mothering habits.

Mum and dad had started to watch these television shows during the week. Shows that were cleverly scripted to highlight how people of colour were integrated into the community and the community's reactions to their arrival and presence. Initially it had been with the influx of those now referred to as the 'Windrush Generation', then the Asians migration that followed. The racist undertones and nuances were blended into those television comedies to assist with society's reluctant and conditional acceptance and/or tolerance of us as people of colour. The television shows used banter as a way of diluting our cultures and traditions and along with everybody else watching, we, as Black people, had laughed, especially if it was a visualisation of our own race that was being mocked and ridiculed or when they answered back the white folks and got away with it. All I can say is, thank goodness for shows like 'Top of the Pops' which seemed to counterbalance those other shows. 'Top of the Pops' came along as a non-threatening alternative with its shiny and happy environment depicted on the screens. Occasionally, I felt happy that at least some of our music was getting through onto the show. There were times when we sat and viewed how we were both depicted and thought of as a race of people and we would laugh. We even snickered at the way all men, black and white, appeared to treat women, giving them an uninvited slap on the bottom or ogling at their chests.

Mum and dad had laughed, so we did too. We had absorbed all the wrong that is now viewed as chauvinistic, egotistical and unacceptable patterns of thoughts and behaviours.

We have probably all encountered where something that is concentrated was needing to be watered down, yes? In some incidences, it is common sense to do so, after all.

What if it was told to you that your skin colour was deemed to be too dark and that you should dilute it to a lighter colour, somehow? Being 'too black' was a common utterance said to many and they were also informed that the darkness of their skin made them unattractive, also. I myself was not considered dark-skinned but I was called 'red-skinned'. Being considered as red-skinned, meant that you were not light enough to get by without problems, according to my mum. Imagine hearing as a child from your own mother and your aunts, also, that the 'darkies' would bring trouble to you so you must heed the warnings and steer clear of them. Is that not shocking to hear or to be told that? I think now I get it and understand more why they said it, but I most definitely do not agree with it. This is a prime example of how the fear of experienced racism manifests itself and affects people.

My mother and her siblings were all light-skinned to the point of looking white with a suntan and not only that, but their facial features were more European than say African or Caribbean. I have honestly seen much darker shades of white people on holidays.

My dad, on the other hand, who was born in 1909, was a rich shade of coca brown. He had spent time serving in the American Naval forces. That was one of the reasons I had assumed that he must have suffered serious incidents of racism before he had settled in the United Kingdom, where he most likely experienced racism in a more subtle manner. I would not have been surprised had he and my mother experienced racism as a couple if they had been spotted walking down the street arm in arm, and she had been mistaken to be a white woman stepping out with a black man. Had that been the reason why she and her siblings had felt the need to warn us of the 'darkies bringing trouble with them'?

Such prejudice had certainly not dissipated completely amongst us, unfortunately, and neither in many other cultures that are visibly non-white. Racism has affected so many people that millions have resorted to trying to bleach their skins in order to appear lighter or white and to be accepted into the stereotype of what is considered normal or preferable. Bleaching of the skin is a sad and tragic form of self-abuse, a form of self-harming and it saddens me deeply. The word abuse, in this instance, feels almost too small to cover the myriad of layers of self-loathing that must be felt to consider bleaching to make yourself beautiful in the eyes of those who dislike you because of the colour of your skin. I am guilty of both, I am afraid, and it was not an easy thing for me to admit openly, but for me to deal with the ugliness of it I must first be prepared and courageous enough to own my personal issues and actions, in being honest about what I had inflicted upon myself, and others. That is the only way that I can move forwards and in so doing, learn to eventually forgive myself. I need to do that before I can ever ask forgiveness from others. One of the most difficult things for me, as I discovered through my healing journey, was to forgive my abusers for what they had done to me.

In school I had been the victim of bullying and had been called names like, 'coconut' and 'red'. In the minds and through the eyes of some, I had not been black enough nor had I been white enough. There were those who had been extremely envious of my luscious mane of hair. I was often told how my hair made me favour a 'coolie'. 'Coolie' is an awful and derogatory term used to describe an Indian person. The older generation would simply say 'You got that good hair' so I had grown up confused in wondering if my hair was good, then why all the hurtful and vicious teasing about it?

My experiences of being bullied at school was also because my sister had a stammer and because I had a flat chest. It had felt like all through school, I had to constantly fight to defend myself and my sister. What confused me even more was being told that I was pretty, too.

Looking back on those years, I would not necessarily describe them as being overwhelming, but it had been constant, and for me, that is where the dangers lay. I felt as if I was becoming institutionalised by the constant and insistent bombardment of it all. In having to cope with the bullying and teasing outside of the home, I then had to come home to more of the same. I was the sixth child of the seven children my parents brought into this world, and I had to literally fight for my place in the home, to be heard, to speak, to be me. I used to have to tolerate being called 'hooter' because it just so happens that I was born with a broader nose than my siblings had been. The teasing about my nose had been relentless but nothing heavy handed or anything like that, just the usual, everyday sibling rivalry most families go through, but those squabbles did have their consequences.

I have already given you a brief insight into who my parents were. My father, a dark-skinned man, born in 1909 and who had married my mother, a very light-skinned woman, and I have also expressed my suspicions of the possibility that they had experienced racism.

It is an unfortunate factor that people often actively repeat what they know or what they learnt from their own childhood.

With that in mind, I can only surmise that my father must have experienced some serious beatings whilst living in America, because when he disciplined us children, all girls apart from one brother who was the eldest of us all, father was truly harsh even when there was only a slight disagreement between us siblings over nothing that was important or significant. But still, father had seen fit to punish us mercilessly, regardless.

I am not speaking of a relatively simple smack, either. The word beating is fitting because that is exactly what we got. Beatings that were delivered with force and painful precision and with the handle of a broom, a thick leather belt, a saucepan, a slipper, a piece of curtain wire or indeed anything that had been within his reach. It had been the way of how our parents and others disciplined their children back then and it had been so regular that we had readily accepted and expected that kind of physical punishment. We used to compare our bruises and scars with other children from other families. For us all, it had been accepted as the normality and not the exception.

Dad was just about retired by the time I came along and then of course my sister came after me. He was always a good provider, doing everything that he could to help make ends meet and to keep himself fully occupied. He had always been the predominant homemaker too, doing the cooking, tidying, cleaning, shopping and ironing. Oh, my days! Dad ironed our clothes until they were shiny, and the material had thinned and felt like fragile paper, not to mention how he pressed those seams until they were as sharp as a knife's blade edge. He was meticulous with all things, my dad. The pride he took when polishing our school shoes was certainly a learnt and ingrained chore of duty from his years in the American Navy, I suspect. As for mom, gosh, I had so wished that I could be like her. She was always so elegant, beautiful and sharp-witted, but she had not been around much. My busy, strong and active parents, who had so loved to dress up and go ballroom dancing, had eventually become ill and had then divorced.

How things and our previous family life which had been so structured and disciplined had turned to chaos, still affects me if I allow myself to think too deeply of those times and those severe beatings we endured.

The schools had their own disciplinary processes in place, which usually involved six vicious whacks with a piece of bamboo, referred to as the cane. Just hearing the swooshing noises that it made as it was lifted high into the air in preparation for connecting with our bare flesh, was enough punishment for some, especially the boys as for the girls, there had been the ruler. The ruler was made of wood and was used to strike us across the bare knuckles of the back of our hands if we had been very naughty or on the palms of our hands if what we had done was considered as a minor display of disobedience. I was always a fighter in school, so I got punished by both chosen weaponised instruments: the cane and the ruler. In those days it had been referred to as corporal punishment or discipline, but now, it is correctly seen as abuse!

From all aspects of my life, I was subjected to visions of abuse, from watching men on the television treat women like sex objects to seeing how women could be sexually harassed, to hearing how grown adults spoke to each other with the usage of such negative and corrosive language and belittling tones of voices. It was no surprise then that I had felt immune to it all. It was also no surprise that all of that plus racism had affected how they showed up in their own lives which in turn impacted on me in the way they treated or spoke to me.

Whichever form we choose to share our personal stories of abuse is an act of courage and not to be dismissed lightly. There are those who consider writing it down instead of verbalising it is cowardly. I would vehemently disagree. To admit to yourself that you were a victim of abuse in any shape or form, my goodness, that takes a lot of soul searching and having to dig deep to acknowledge that hurt you once endured. It also takes courage to speak to someone about that kind of pain that you have never dealt with before and then to write it and to share it with the world, opening yourself up to being vulnerable, like I am doing now along with my fellow writers in this anthology book, now that is courage personified on a whole other level. I feel honoured to share this space with each of these ladies and I honour their life experiences and this healing journey that they and I are now travelling. I applaud every one of you brave women, Queens, who have boldly stepped out into owning their truths.

My personal story and the other stories contained in this anthology is shared with the hope that those out there who are living with a depth of secret fearfulness from having suffered abuse of any kind, will heed the messages of hope from reading about our transformations from victim to survivor and be inspired to begin unravelling and under-standing their own past or current situations as being unacceptable. I pray that you will read and hear our words of uplifting armour against abuse and tragedies suffered and use it as your metaphoric shield and sword to cut down any enforced barriers that have been preventing you from liberating your mind, heart and physical body towards personal freedom and spiritual growth.

This chapter is my truth which I had originally written down onto pieces of maths paper, folded them up tightly and had then concealed them, placing them safely but secretively into the lining of my hidden suitcase.

My suitcase was secured within the depths of my ottoman, hidden under my shoe boxes which I had covered with the old winter blankets my mother had once used and which I no longer wished to keep, but I could not fathom up the will to part with them just yet. This old ottoman has travelled everywhere with me, from one home to another, safeguarding my closest held, suppressed and unuttered secrets.

My theory had originally been that if I kept those awful truths, the dreaded details of my abuse folded up real tight, then none of that truth would ever be revealed or be likely to leak out, somehow. Part of my reasoning for this was because I had wanted to protect my family and to avoid the possibility that my husband might look at me with different eyes, with an altered expression on his face. But most of all it had been because I had known that I was not in possession of any answers to potential questions I may have been asked. Not knowing the answers had not been a case of my lack of trying to seek them out, either. Would you believe that I had even been into prisons looking for answers? In that regard I had learnt a lot about myself, like how tolerant, forgiving and patient I had become.

Regardless of my feeling comparatively whole now, I am always mindful of the possible reactions of my family and even the readers of my stories plus of how I may handle those reactions and any possible triggering moments I may suffer as a direct result of revealing that which I had for so long kept hidden within me. Walking the path of releasing past hurts is never an easy one to trod, and I had known that I was capable of disrobing in solitude but not yet strong enough to consistently and continuously walk alone. With exposure comes the need to have a safety net beneath your feet, a direct impact of having been abused. It is wanting that supportive harness around us that allows us to stand tall in our personal truths, no matter how ugly it may be. I was fearful of feeling stranded and alone, so I am grateful for the support I have from my husband.

Being inclusive in this powerful anthology, I know that these Queens are my metaphorical ambulance, paramedic and hospital bed, all rolled into one. It feels right to be here.

I was never your average three-year old toddler, not by a long shot. I was a young carer to a sister who was eleven months younger than me. Being responsible for her had given me a mature mindset, one that was aware of things that may have seemed a bit off-key, to me. We had an uncle who used to live with us and who had remained a bachelor for all his life until he had passed away, all alone. Maybe karma had a hand in that, who is to know for sure. He had been dearly loved by his siblings, my mother and aunts, but never by his nieces. I myself had certainly been very wary of him as he had been over six feet tall with a huge personality and an aura of intimidating presence, but he had smelt strange to me. His hands were as large as garden spades and once they were clasped firmly around my waist, there had been no escaping from him, leaving me feeling like I was trapped inside one of those straight-jacket contraptions. I had wriggled furiously, trying to escape his clutches, feeling repulsed by his tobacco-stained fingers as he held me aloft so that he could look directly at my bottom. He had a devious way of holding me so that his heavy hands were either clamped around my waist or my chest area. He would swing me between his legs, making sure that I was facing him so that the front of my head and my face would deliberately brush against his groin area. He would do this several times and the foul smell of him left me feeling sick to my tiny stomach.

In my flashback type recollections, I can see him in those dirty beige trousers he seemed to always be wearing, with stains scattered all around the zip area of his pants, which were so tight you could easily see the protruding bulge through the material of his pants. Of course, at the time, I had no idea what that bulge was, although every time he forced me to sit on his lap, I could feel it turning from spongy and warm to firm, more so with every bounce he initiated whilst he had me trapped there, sitting on his knees. I shall call it what it is because my mother knew that her brother was a paedophile. There was no mistaking that fact. Why else would she warn us that we should go in twos when we visited his flat once he had eventually moved out of our house and into his bachelor flat? She had known, just as they all had known, but it had been considered too shameful a thing to speak openly about. I always felt that what he did and how he behaved was wrong, and I could always remember the details, unlike some victims who gradually forget the intimate details as they grow older. The images, the rank odour of him, the taste, the doubts. It had remained with me throughout the whole of my life and had even intruded into my marriage at times. I can only speak of my own experiences, but I am aware that there were other family members who had been subjected to and traumatised by his perversions and fetishes.

After the birth of my elder brother, us sisters had come along at a rate of one every year and a half, except for my younger sister and I who are only eleven months apart. Once my sister, who came before me, had started school, leaving just me and my younger sister at home, the deviously sneaky patterns of perverted behaviours by my uncle had started. Our house was so huge that uncle had use of one of the front rooms as his private accommodation area and other lodgers lived upstairs. As far as my parents were concerned uncle was more than a lodger, he was family.

Mother was always working so she had employed a home help to tend to us, but she could not come first thing in the mornings so for a couple of hours at least, my sister and I were left alone in the house with uncle and the other lodgers, who were basically strangers to us. Dad had been around somewhere, usually pottering around in his garden or doing some odd jobs around the neighbourhood. He had been retired by that time.

Those unsupervised couple of hours had been the perfect opportunity for uncle to come into our living quarters, him being family and all, it had been permitted. I do not think that my dad knew what my uncle was or was doing. No, in fact, I refuse to think or believe that he did know, otherwise I could not take that being a reality, not for a second.

Uncle had loved cooking liver, bacon and onions at any time of the day and my dad had loved eating the portions dished out for him. Uncle had seen this as his chance to come into our living space, always using the excuse that he was preparing some food for my dad. In truth, he was acting out his nasty little fetishes on my sister and me. I was however my sister's keeper, so I would position myself in front of her to protect her, but I was unable to do that all the time. There were occasions where I was missing as I had needed to use the loo and had not seen him coming. The high pitch sound of her laughing out loud had served as an alert to me to go running back into the room where she and my uncle were.

One of his 'games' had involved a series of tickles where he would tickle us so much that we often peed ourselves. It had always felt wrong and uncomfortable, but I had not known why even though I dreaded it happening, even whilst enjoying the reward that followed. One day I had returned from using the loo and had witnessed what he had been doing to my sister and it had been in that moment that I had been struck with the sudden realisation that his behaviour towards us was indeed so wrong. As far as I was concerned, it would never happen to her again, not if I could stop it from happening.

Before that, I had always been happy for him to help me to change into clean and dry underwear, because if my dad had found me like that, he would have punished me. The fear of my father striking me was too much and I would not be rewarded with any sweets, that was for sure.

Once uncle had removed my tights and pants, that overwhelming feeling of something being wrong would engulf me. He would get out his handkerchief and begin to gently wipe me down there, but then he would say, *'It's a bit too dry. Let me just lick you here and here',* as he proceeded to draw over the grooves of my vagina with his finger, *'And then I can wipe you again',* he had continued. His tongue licking me down there was very thorough and had caused me to wriggle and squirm and the need to pee again would cause me to giggle nervously so he would lick me even more as I tried my best not to laugh. Licking a handkerchief had not seemed such an odd thing to do as mum had done the same with me and my sister whenever we had any smudges on our faces which she would then wipe away. Surely that was the same thing as what uncle was doing to me? Well, that had been my thinking until I had seen him doing it to my sister. He had appeared so large as he stood stooped over her. I could barely see her body as his huge head moved over her body and she had been laughing, too. As children, it is such a tragic shame that we are taught to laugh at the wrong things because we absorb all that teaching without knowing right from wrong.

I had sprung into protective big sister mode, knowing that if anything happened to her, I would be blamed and punished for it. Even as I approached him this feeling of nameless dread had overwhelmed me. I knew what was coming next. I had forced myself to skip towards uncle, chanting, *'My turn now, is it my turn now?'*. He had raised his head with a look of surprise on his face, or maybe it had been a look of shock. He had then swiftly pulled up her underwear, despite her knickers being obviously wet and he had called me over to him. My sister had sat there watching, innocently sucking her thumb.

There had then been that extremely uncomfortable feeling, like having a poo from the outside in, with his warm thing pressing against my bottom, trying to get that thing inside of me. It had hurt so much.

That had been the first of several times I had volunteered myself to take her place so that I could protect her from his sexual abuse. It was I who would remove my own underwear before laying down and parting my legs. Uncle had been overly eager with this first sudden invite and had picked me up, his massive hands holding my entire body to his face. Cupping my bottom and my back he had used his thumbs to pull my legs apart. He had then plunged his face down in between my legs and licked hard. I had squirmed and wriggled intensely. That time it had felt different. His tongue must have been forcing its way into my vagina but had failed to penetrate it. Then he had laid me down and drew his finger over my private parts as usual, following its shape and flicking my undeveloped button. Nothing but pee had escaped. What else he was expecting I had no idea. His zealousness at my naïve and fear-filled invite must have distorted his mind. I was still a toddler and was not about to orgasm to give him free reign to enter me. He had been rougher than before, as he had turned me over, rubbing his hard, warm organ between the crease of my buttocks until he appeared satisfied with the creamy stuff that had spurted from his hardened thing. He did not have another handkerchief with which to clean me up so he had done the best he could, helping me to put my underwear back on, even as he handed me some pear drops as my reward. He knew that I had loved pear drops.

I had then taken my sister to the bathroom where I had washed the both of us with some carbolic soap after removing our underwear. I knew then he had not cleaned me properly because my panties had stuck to my skin and felt sticky when I had taken them off. I had hidden our underwear at the bottom of the wardrobe, hoping they would dry out on top of a blanket. I had been scared at not being able to find another pair of tights for my sister to change into, but fortunately, my dad had not noticed that she was now wearing an old pair of socks that belonged to another sister, with the heel part sticking out halfway up her calf.

Uncle had remained in our living quarters, sat there chatting with dad and eating liver and bacon sandwiches and drinking tea, as if everything was normal. All I had wanted was for our dad to tell him to get lost.

If it had not been my witnessing him abusing my sister, I would not have known that all of what he did was sexually abusive and wrong. I have felt that I owe my little sister so much, because I wished that I had seen it sooner. I wished it hadn't been her or anybody to be fair, but I just wished that I had known because there were more 'games' he had that were not right.

Uncle had in his possession magazines and books, which I know now were of the pornographic variety. Knowing the timetable of the home help, he would make sure to get his perverted 'fix' before she arrived. He appeared to have an early morning erection that he needed to release, and he sought that release through his magazines, books and me. When he was ready to relieve himself, he would put it into a little lid and call me over to watch as the sachet of sherbet he added to it made it fizz.

What he did next with that vile concoction has affected me all my life and still induces in me a devastating reaction that I cannot tolerate. He force-fed that fizzy concoction to me until I had froth coming out from my mouth and nose and he would caressingly rub it all over my face and clap loudly before stating, *'You look like a Christmas cake, good enough to eat'*. He had his stupid little one- liners which he thought were hilarious.

Poor little me had thought I was being clever at stretching out my tongue to lick as much of it off from around my mouth and face as I could. The sherbet bubbling inside my mouth had felt fantastic and after getting cleaned up again, I had received my expected reward of pear drops. They had tasted better than the strange tasting frothy fizz. The childhood sexual abuse he had inflicted on me could so easily have been rape, had he been successful in penetrating me. Maybe it had been a good thing that he had loved licking, because the alternative was too horrendous to contemplate fully.

I cannot begin to know or understand how his or the minds of other abusers' minds are wired to think that their behaviour was acceptable. Somehow, I do believe they know it is wrong though.

With that type of start to my life, did I even stand a chance of normality? Was it inevitable that I would fall into an abusive relationship when I was older? What visual or learnt point of comparison did I have to notice that he was mistreating me so badly?

I was only aged fifteen when the abusive intimate relationship stage of my life started. Things at home were terrible. There were illnesses with both mum and dad ill and on the verge of divorce. My older sisters were trying to find their own way in the world so they could not really be there to help me, and my brother was now a father himself. We had all been so confused and scared.

I had been living part time between where one of my older sister's lived, and with this boy. I had fallen pregnant, which was unfortunate as I had not even liked him. I had liked another boy from school, but he would just ignore me and diss me after a juvenile dare from his friends to kiss me. I recall how devastated and insulted I had felt by his rejection and that is how I had come to blindly allow myself to become involved with this other boy. The relationship had been dysfunctional with catastrophic results. He had grown into the most narcissistic man ever, gaslighting me beyond any recognition of who I was. I had only agreed to date him because he could dance. Of all the things to be impressed by to the point of basing that on starting a relationship with someone. I had been such an idiot. Back then music and dancing had been my happy place and the musically harmonious cement that had held our family together in times of uncertainty.

He had paraded a string of girlfriends in front of my face, showing no remorse whatsoever and his utmost contempt for me had been amplified by his mother because she had simply applauded and indulged his demeaning behaviours. For some unknown reason, she must have hated me deeply as she seemed to resent the very air that I breathed.

All through our relationship we had fought like bitter gladiators. He had raped and humiliated me constantly whilst intoxicated with drugs. It had not started out that way because we had created a child together before all that toxic chaos had developed and escalated, but the under-current of our tenuous foundations as a unit had turned into a whirlpool that had sucked the energies out of any connections that we had between us. His father had abused him and would chop off his dreadlocks every time they grew and then he would slap him in the face with them, humiliating him, not caring who he did it in front of.

For me, it had been a time when I had been searching for answers in my own life and I had turned to the Rastafarian ways of living, trying to find a semblance of peace of mind for myself. I am not sure if it was because of his father being black and his mother being white that I had perhaps harboured thoughts of seeing them as a replacement family for my own, as mine were splitting up. It may have been that which had lulled me into tolerating his abuse of me. I still do not have the answer to that question, except to admit that it was a catalogue of disasters with which I had no comparison to have known better.

My ex-partner was a man trying desperately to find his way, I believe. He had been in and out of prison for stealing. He hustled and imitated his gambling father's behavioural patterns of infidelity, having numerous affairs. My former partner had only behaved how he had seen it done and at the same time I had fallen into what I had known. We had physically fought because we knew no other way to be. We were each other's kryptonite and self-destruction and destruction of each other had bred easily from our toxic and abusive union.

His methods and manifestations of abuse towards me had been so degrading and public, just like how his own father had treated him. He had been a master manipulator, making me feel useless, ugly and weak. All the caring and nurturing skills I had gained in looking after and protecting my sister and which had strengthened me seemed to disintegrate in his presence and when I was in their household. Even after we had our first child, he had thought nothing of bringing other girls into our personal and intimate space, into our bed, fornicating on the very sheets he and I had slept on, whilst I had stayed downstairs. All of this had happened under his parents' own roof, and they had allowed things to run as he had wanted them to run. Those women were just as bad as he was and there had been one woman, who had deliberately gotten herself pregnant as if she had been in competition with me to snare this egotistical man. She had obviously been desperate in wanting to take on the empress role she imagined existed in the first place. She had only shown herself to be lacking in self-respect, ignorant, with no pride in herself and with no morals or sense of personal purpose. Still, he had made it clear that he preferred her to me, so I had just given up on myself. I had not known any better. I had no role models to show me the way or how a good relationship should feel and look like. No male role models to look up to, not even my father or brother.

It had taken a future pregnancy for me to finally wake up to what was happening to me and for me to want to change directions and swim against the current tide of upheaval and madness that had become my life. I had to find a way to climb out of the tsunami that had been pulling me down and draining me of all my energy. With my second pregnancy I had been expecting twins, but we had still fought like a pair of combative prize-fighters.

It had been after a particularly serious fight where I had fallen down the stairs and he had then viciously kicked me in the back, that I had fled that home, ending up in London. In my panic, I had left our daughter at the school. After seeking help so that I could go back for her, I had again fled, this time ending up in a refuge. I had lost one of the twins at birth due to that final vicious fight, but eventually I had returned to Birmingham, because I had thought it the right thing to do for my daughter as she had been constantly asking for him. She had never witnessed any physical harm that he had caused me, and I had refused to burden her with that or to use what had happened between her father and me as a bargaining tool to have full custody of her. It had taken me eight long years to get her back after he had her.

Of course, in hindsight, it had been stupid of me to date someone just because they could dance well. Back then music and dance had been my medicine to soothe all things that had gone wrong at home but now it had proven to be the non-harmonious poison that had turned what elements of myself I had left, to nothing. My ex-partner had treated me as if I were a painful and unwanted boil on his face, squeezing the life out of me and suffocating me with a symbolic heavy sheet of plaster so that I could not breathe. When we had first started dating, he had appeared to worship me, parading me in front of his friends, with apparent pride, advising me on what to wear, what to say and where to stand, like I was some type of innate ornament to be admired. Talk about red flags! They had been waving furiously in front of my eyes, but I had been blinded by naivety and a longing to belong. Yes, I see it all clearly now. At home I had fought my corner to have my say on things, but this was something else, this was manipulative control dressed up as what I mistook for caring and love. This was him exerting his masculine power over me in an abusive and destructive manner. He was the second son, and his brother was the taller and better looking one and he had two sisters that followed him. He had been familiarly overlooked, just as I had been. I thought I had understood him. I had believed that we had a unique connection, a bond, but he had proven to be the devil in disguise. He stole from me to the point where I had to resort to hiding my money behind the wallpaper that had come unstuck behind the dressing table due to the heat from the radiator. Imagine having to stick your money, your five- and ten-pound notes, with blue tack to the walls and then having to cover them up with the crumpled and dry wallpaper and praying that he never found them hidden there. Imagine too having to lay down with him on top of you, smelling of another woman's nauseating sex, staring up at the remnants of the drug coke, embedded into his nostrils, desperately willing for those three minutes to pass as quickly as three seconds as you hold your breath against his stench of betrayal and infidelity. He and I had been like oil and water.

Seeing ourselves as unworthy is a burdensome weight for us to carry around.

There is no-one on this earth who can remove us from the thoughts we repeat in our heads unless we are ready to face those negativities, hear them out and then deal with them and all the repercussions that may or may not follow. It can look and feel ugly when our dignity and pride is stripped bare, and our self-esteem is so low that it feels like it is buried below the earth's core.

It can be annoying when people keep telling us that things will be ok. We must be ready to hear that and sometimes we need time to be able to visualise it, believe it and then feel motivated to act on it. And ultimately, we need to have reached that place where we feel able to maintain the pursuit of our own happiness and peace of mind, so that we can feel whole again. Even once we feel we are well into our journeys of healing it still takes effort to keep working on staying there or moving forwards. Only then can we appreciate that it is time to remain mindful of being grateful for our struggles and achievements, and not be afraid to celebrate our journeys, all aspects of it.

It is our humane right to want to feel joy, love, admiration for our efforts and respect for ourselves and others. There is nothing wrong with wanting to embrace an influx of compliments to feel validated of the belief we now have in ourselves. Remaining humble is important too. We no longer need to suffer in wondering if others see us differently once we have spoken about our deepest secrets and fears. It is how and what we feel about ourselves that matters. Our secrets were only ever heavy anchors that had kept us trapped in the story we allowed others to define and narrate for us.

Labels that I had previously held on to internally, I have now turned them around. My victim is now my victorious as I have shed my past and risen above it. My abused became my ambition as I rediscovered my motivation to succeed. My traumas turned into triumph as I now use my experiences to help others.

I have learnt that it is not about how my life began or even how my life has been. It is about how my life is, right now. I am joyful and feel fulfilled, excited and happy to be spontaneous. These are words that I very much doubted that I would ever express or believe, until I was shown how to believe in myself by my current husband, Paul. I had no comprehension of how to begin to adjust my thought processes and feelings of what or how love should be or feel like. With an intense purpose and patience borne out of caring, loving and sharing, he has demonstrated how a supportive and intimate relationship should be, despite my repeated patterns of behaviour in being suspicious of his kindness and love for me. In the past I was consumed with negative and intrusive thoughts of asking myself what was it that he really wanted from me? With my self-confidence and self-esteem at its lowest point, I had convinced myself that once he had gained my trust and love, he would then cruelly discard me like an unwanted left-over meal, having succeeded in fulfilling his needs. Over the years, I had steadily constructed an emotionally protective wall so high that scaffolding was required to dismantle it.

Paul had more than risen to the challenge, painstakingly removing that wall, brick by emotionally damaged brick, taking his time whilst giving me time, to reveal our true selves to each other. Then, with an admirable higher level of patience, he had stood by my side as he showed me how to build another wall. That wall had represented and had been built from an inner strength of character driven by positivity, willingness, determination, courage and self-respect. Paul had lovingly nurtured, re-empowered and encouraged me to remember how to learn to love and to give love wholeheartedly.

I have delved back into that closet and have dug out and exorcised my skeletons and demons and now the energy-draining spirits of my past are dormant in the grave created by my learning how to let it all go. Now when I look in the mirror, I see a confident and capable Queen who is adaptable and fearless, staring back at me. I no longer feel like an imposter in my own body and soul. I have managed to cross that bridge that was once built out of shame, pain, confusion and of not knowing who I was. Having reached the nurturing border of another chapter in my life, I have now stepped into the land of my future, and it looks beautifully green and plentiful.

I have already begun planting new seeds of hope and self-love and am visualising their harvest of abundance and blessings.

I have only been able to achieve this through the mutual belief and trust that exists between myself and my life-partner, Paul. If I should fall, he is strong enough to catch me without faltering. He is strong enough to embrace and rejoice in my continued personal and spiritual growth. More importantly than his protective cradling of me however, there exists within me an inbuilt capability to confidently break through and rise powerfully and empowered above any of life's challenges and obstacles. I now know that I was born with this inner power of self and now I can walk with pride, with my head held high, because I know that I am worthy of doing so. The praise for that self-empowerment and love of self therefore goes to the Almighty.

There are still moments when I find myself seeking out that lost and confused woman that I once was, especially when I recognise that depth of empathy that I feel for one of my struggling Queens and all I want to do is to hug her tightly. But with every passing year the visual and mental memories of her fade more and more. I sometimes feel a sense of loss when thinking of her past ignorance, naivety and inability to comprehend where and what she had been blindly walking into. My sadness is felt for her loss of innocence.

Would I have felt as victorious as I do now, had I not lived through those tumultuous years of feeling like I had been navigating my way through a dense field of exploding grenades and situational bombs?

Victory is the result of battles won. And now, hopefully, my wins will be the inspirational and motivational gains for many others.

ANDREA MAYNARD-BRADE

 My name is Andrea Maynard-Brade. I am a published Author, Businesswoman, Master Health Coach, Reiki Master and Holistic Therapist. I was born in Birmingham. I am a mother to three wonderful children and the proud grandmother of six boys and two girls.

I work with vulnerable women and assist them in rebuilding their self- confidence and self-esteem towards regaining their health and wellbeing. I work with the ethics of providing positive influences and purposefulness to other women. I spend a great deal of my time contributing to my community, raising awareness regarding general and mental health issues. I teach self-empowerment, self-care and self-love to those who are striving to overcome life challenges. As part of the community work that I do, I have facilitated retreats in Wales for vulnerable women to enable them to raise their emotional, mental and spiritual vibrations.

I worked in social services for several years as a Social Worker Assistant, Occupational and Physiotherapist and became the Founder of *Positive Mouves Holistic Therapies and Training*. I am also the Founder of *Kamjersara,* an organisation that helps with decluttering your homes and in decorating event halls for all occasions. I held the position as a Senior Manager in *Rain International* and the CEO of *Embrace Health and Wellbeing.*

I have received awards for Woman of Power and Influence (2015), Health and Wellbeing and the Ambassador Award for my contributions to The Universal Peace Federation (2017). In 2016 I was awarded the Bex Live Health and Wellbeing Award. I have recently been nominated for the MBCC for a Shero In The Community Awards, due to take place in November 2021. I have previous work published in the *'Pain To Purpose'* and *'The Book of Inspirations For Women by Women'* publications. My first published book *'Suffering In Silence'* was published in March 2021 and describes my survival of domestic violence and breaking the cycle of abuse. I am the inspiration behind this *'Surviving Queens Anthology'* book and this project was created through the courageous sharing of personal stories of overcoming adversities by a group of phenomenal women. I have risen like the phoenix from the tyranny of domestic violence, and I stand firm in representing as a woman of exceptional resilience in overcoming life's adversities. *'Never let anyone steal your joy. We all have a purpose in life so find that joy and follow your dreams.'*

My chapter is called 'Knowing When To Draw A Line In The Sand'.

CHAPTER 4

KNOWING WHEN TO DRAW A LINE IN THE SAND

ANDREA MAYNARD-BRADE

Drawing a line in the sand – to set a limit beyond which a person cannot go without suffering serious consequences. Recognising there is a point, physically or decisional, beyond which a person will proceed no further.

Another word that is related to 'sand' is *'backbone'*. Had I chosen a man with no backbone?

It was June 2012 and a beautiful hot summer's day in Barbados when the love of my life had gotten down on one knee to ask me for my hand in marriage. We had officially met back in 2007 in a pub in Spring Hill where his brothers were playing that evening.

We had been walking along the boardwalk which stretches approximately 1.6km between Camelot and the famous Accra Beach on the south coast of the island. It had felt like the perfect setting to be with the one I loved, with our bare feet sinking gloriously deep into the soft white sand with the sounds of the waves of the sea gently lashing against the jagged rocks and the smooth pebbles. My friend had been present with us at the time, so she had started to film the memorable moment. At the precise moment that he had bent down to propose to me, the batteries in her mobile phone had died. I remember thinking to myself, *'Oh my Lord! Is that a sign that this was not meant to be?'* In hindsight, should that have been a pivotal moment when I should have drawn a line in the sand? We had all felt disappointed that the moment had not been captured on film.

He had previously had the opportunity to visit Barbados with me before then, but we had split up for a short time, due to my reluctance to put up with his moods, so I had cancelled his cruise as I am all about peace and love, not hostility, uneasiness and annoyance. Upon reflection, had that been another sign that I should have been more cautious in pursuing that relationship?

I do believe that a woman's intuition is a result of our closer connection to the Creator, as we are considered creators ourselves. I also believe that our intuition is developed as a natural defence as we, as women, do not typically have the physical strength in terms of protecting ourselves from a predator or potential harm that some men may cause us. Men generally have muscles. We women have gut instincts.

He and I had been seeing each other since the November of 2007. That year had been a heart-breaking time for both of us as we had both lost family members in September that same year.

My beloved brother Mark had passed away on the third of September and he had lost his niece. Our union had commenced whilst we were both still grieving, looking for love, comfort, clarity and validation for being alive and needing to be loved and cared for. We had fallen for each other after admiring one another from afar, for several years. We had both come together whilst grieving but I had never really looked at it in that way before. We used to bump into each other at social events where we would greet each other with a friendly hug. At the time we were both in relationships with other people, so we had kept things amicable and respectable.

We had known of each other's families for several years because one of my brother's was in a relationship with his youngest sister some years before, which had ended abruptly. None of us quite knew why and nothing was said and quite frankly, it wasn't anyone else's business and that is the way it had stayed. During their relationship though, I had visited the house regularly and had gotten to know the family quite well. My brother used to stay at their house sometimes and whenever he had one of his seizures the sister used to call me, and I would drive over there to collect them both so they could stay at my house. My relationship with my brother Mark, was special in every way, I can't recall us ever having an argument and if we did, we never carried any bad feelings about it. Mark was six years younger than me; he was always humble, loving and caring. He was a fitness freak, he played basketball, he loved swimming and walked everywhere. He always carried himself neat and smart, especially when he was going to work in his tracksuits and trainers or going to church in his suits.

Mark loved God with all his heart and served him until the day he passed away in 2007 at the age of forty. He was always respectful of people, loving, kind and loved his food. I couldn't falter him as a brother.

He and I had finally exchanged telephone numbers on the seventh of November 2007. I clearly recall the date because a friend of mine had just received her divorce papers and she was eager to go out to cele-brate. I had thought why not, and so we had headed out to the place where he had been playing music as a DJ. I had seen him as soon as I had walked through the door, and we had greeted one another with a hello. We had stayed there for a while and on my way out, he had called me over and had given me his number.

I had called him the next day and we had continued to have several conversations and then it had not been too long before he had started to visit my house. We had then soon after, began an intimate relation-ship with each other.

There is an incredible strain that accompanies grief and sometimes this can have an impact on a personal and intimate relationship and our grief had brought us together.

Another time that I maybe should have taken note of was when he had asked my dad for my hand in marriage and my dad had agreed. We had booked to stay in a beautiful hotel in St Lawrence Gap in Barbados for three glorious days as we were not permitted to share a room at my father's house as we were not yet married. Plus, it had been our first holiday away together and it had been lovely to have three days to ourselves and we had thoroughly enjoyed the three S's— sand, sea and sex.

On arriving at my father's house after our staycation at the hotel, we had made plans to go out that evening with friends. We had eaten dinner with my parents and then decided to have a quick power nap to feel rested for that evening. He and I had departed to our separate rooms, which my father had given us. A few hours later I had been awoken by a ringing sound, to discover that it was his mobile ringing.

I had eventually located it inside the suitcase we had our clothes in. As I had retrieved the mobile phone, I had seen a woman's name flash up on the screen. My first instinct had been to answer it but then I had quickly hung up as I realised that it would show up on his bill. I had automatically began scrolling down his mobile, taking notes of the times she had either called or messaged him. I had read some of those messages too. There had been too many to go through so I had instead logged the number into my own mobile phone so that I could call her on my return home. I had swiftly replaced his phone back into the suitcase as I could hear footsteps approaching my room.

My friend had picked us up from my parents' house and we had enjoyed a lovely meal, eaten on the beach under a luminous moonlight. Afterwards we had strolled along the beach, taking the opportunity to have a conversation about our past lives and how important it was for us to be open and honest with each other. Well, I had thought that we were for no matter how much I spoke about honesty and being transparent within an intimate relationship, he had not once mentioned anything about this woman whose name and numerous private messages I had seen on his phone. I had eventually tired of playing mind games, so I had asked him outright who she was. He had initially denied knowing the woman in question. In response to my enquiries as to why she was messaging him so frequently, he had told me that she was one of his male friends' woman, who happened to speak to him sometimes when she and her partner were not getting on so well. I wondered if he thought me so naïve even as I further grilled him about the contents of the messages that I had read from her to him. In the end I had informed him that he shouldn't mind then when I spoke to her myself upon my return home to the UK. It was my intention to have a three-way conversation with her and to meet her, I told him. My gut instincts were telling me that he was being untruthful. Alarm bells were ringing loud and clear.

He had just asked for my hand in marriage and despite my inner convictions that he was seeing her behind my back, I felt powerless to pause, stand firm and draw that line in the sand, there and then.

Once we had arrived home, I had seized the first opportunity to call her, once he was out and away from the house. In asking her directly why she was ringing my fiancé, she had sounded perplexed and then she had panicked. She told me that she had no idea that he was engaged to be married, that he was even seeing anyone else. We had agreed to meet.

I had taken the opportunity to meet the young lady whom he had been seeing behind my back and it became clear during our conversation that she herself had been of the belief that she was his woman and that he had no-one else that he was seeing. She had spoken in detail of how they had met and how she had helped him to furnish and fix up his flat, doing the cosmetic decorations and soft furnishings as the house was going to be theirs, to live in together. She had then gone on to inform me of how she had then helped him to find the house he lived in then, not knowing that he and I were together by that time.

That weekend I had to plaster a false smile on my face with the engagement ring on my finger and pretend to be happy as we made our way to a party we had been invited to. He had regaled to everyone how we were now engaged but inside I was hurting, and my heart was slowly and silently breaking. I had to be patient a little longer until I confronted him with the truth the next day. We had been intimately loving with each other that night and the next day we had gone out to eat as I needed to have that conversation with him, to get to the truth.

We had split up in July of that same year, not long after becoming engaged, due to his lies about not having a relationship with the lady whose number and texts had shown up on his mobile phone. We had split up for about six months and had then got back together and had commenced with planning our wedding. Yes, I had done it again. I had not followed my intuition to draw a line in the sand but had instead, followed my heart.

During the initial planning of our wedding, I had still been living in my property and he was living in his. He had visited me most weekends and after some time, I had visited him at his place. There were moments when his moods would upset my spirit and cause me to feel off balance. Being so busy with planning arrangements and work, I think I had ignored a lot of the signs that not everything was fine. When the time came for me to move out of my house, an inner voice kept telling me not to leave my home and to not go to his place to live with him.

Not listening to your inner voice can eventually be proven to be detrimental but I still foolishly kept packing my stuff in readiness to move out, despite the cautionary tears streaming down my face. It was September 2012 when I had left my house. Moving into his home had left me feeling claustrophobic as his house was smaller than the property I had left, but he hadn't wanted to leave the area in which he lived at that time. Feeling so confined in his home, I had felt restless.

Just before Christmas of that year, we had been embroiled in an argument and he had pushed me hard enough to cause me to hit my head on the kitchen cupboard. My head was bleeding, so I had to go to the hospital to have my wound attended to.

He had seemed scared when I was sat in the hospital speaking to the doctor, as if he was worried that I was going to tell them that he had pushed me. It had been Christmas Eve and his son, and my children were due to come over to ours for dinner and I had to then lie to them all that I had fallen and hit my head on the ground.

The uneasiness I felt around him from that point onwards had me questioning myself as to what I had let myself in for. Why had I moved out of my own home to go live with that man?

After that incident, he had been very apologetic and I had forgiven him, because I had loved him.

Okay, let us fast forward to 2013 and it had been two days before we were due to be married. My friends, family and I had gone down to the beach late that evening. It being a full moon we had gone to state our intentions and the date was the 1st of August 2013. We had strolled along the beach before sitting down to eat. We had laughed and we had prayed. My friend had no idea that deep down in my heart, I had wanted to cancel the wedding. It had felt as if I was organising a wedding celebration that I wasn't quite ready for. I had felt stressed and overwhelmed by it all, not sure if I was plagued with nerves or doubts. I don't recall having cried so much before that as everything was left on my shoulders to plan and organise.

I had felt so overwhelmed with all aspects of planning and organising the wedding and with the additional excitement that goes with paying attention to all the details required, I had convinced myself that it was far too late to halt or cancel anything. I therefore chose to ignore all the negative stuff I had been learning about him even though it had made me wonder if I was making the right decision. My intuition kept telling me No! My gut instincts kept screaming at me to stop everything, but it was over-ridden with the thoughts and knowledge that had I said something then, that I would be disappointing so many people who had travelled all the way from the UK to attend my wedding. Not to mention how disappointed my parents would feel and what would my husband-to-be think of me if I were to voice my doubts? I had experienced a wave of the possible shame and embarrassment I would feel and what of all the money that had already been spent towards this wedding? I felt I had little choice but to ignore my misgivings and to face the music and go ahead with it.

He had made sure to have his stag night out a few days earlier as he had wanted to be sober and rested on our special day and yet he had turned up for our wedding with a blood-shot eye after he overindulged in drinking alcohol the night before we were to become man and wife. After the Reverend had said *'And now you can kiss the bride'* and he had turned to face me and when I first saw the state of his eye, I could have shot him myself (not literally).

Grieving for a loved one or even for dreams unrealised, can cause many emotions to be trapped or stored within the body which causes even more complexities as a result.

I learnt to keep my pain quiet, deep within me. As time went on, I found myself feeling invisible, lonely and angry at myself. I felt tormented with not being able to talk about my feelings. I built walls to protect my mental and emotional being and I hid my pain from those around me. I even found it difficult to acknowledge the depth of my pain to myself much less to anyone else. I wore my masks well and silently and constantly fought an inner battle with myself.

In January 2016 I had commenced planning a trip to Barbados for the fiftieth year of independence celebrations. We had booked the holiday and he had promised to confirm those dates with his place of employment. As far as I was aware, he had done that, and everything was set to go ahead. Our plan had been that I would be spending five weeks there whilst he was staying for three because I would be finishing off working on a book project for which I was doing some writing for. I had noticed, whilst we were there on holiday, that he kept getting telephone calls from his work, but he never once said why. We had enjoyed a lovely holiday but on his having to return, there had been little communication between us, partly because he had been upset that I was staying on for another two weeks. I had not taken much notice of his behaviour because in the past he had often been sullen like that when upset about something.

Things had come to a head when I began noticing that bills that were paid by direct debit started to bounce and he wasn't answering his telephone whenever I called him. During the week before I returned to the UK, all communications between us had ceased as every time we spoke, we had ended up arguing or hanging up the phone on each other. The way things were, my mindset had been that on returning home, all I had wanted to do was to leave him.

He had finally admitted to me that he had no work and was in fact on disciplinary leave. I felt, as his wife, that I should support him through that crisis. I had contacted a solicitor friend of mine, who had helped him through the process of the disciplinary action, but he had still ended up losing his job. He had been there for fifteen years and was coming up to retirement age. He could have retired at age sixty and maybe even carried on working there until he was sixty-five.

He had attempted to explain it all to me by telling me that his work-place had not paid him any money and that is why he couldn't pay money into the bank to cover our bills. Yet, he could have and should have just communicated that to me. In truth, he had never liked taking responsibilities for what he needed to pay for to keep a roof over our heads, ever since we had moved into our new home.

He had insisted that he wasn't receiving any pay but then I had come across one of his bank statements, and there in black and white, it had shown that he was still in receipt of full pay from work. He had been receiving full pay and then a little after I had returned home from Barbados, his pay had been reduced up until the point where he had lost his job.

Again, I should have drawn a line in the sand, there and then. The lies, the deceit, all the signs were there, but still I stayed with him.

After that quite distressing episode, my cousin and I had actively assisted him in looking for a new job so that he could get back on his feet and to be fair, he had always previously been a man who had appeared to love to work, which had been one of the things that I had admired about him. Having to be in the house all the time, with no work, began to take its toll on him and he became depressed. We had continued to support him by filling out application forms and updating his CV. Our consistent support appeared to help him somewhat and he started to feel better until he eventually got himself a new job.

The signs towards warning me about drawing a line in the sand showed itself again when he was renting out his property and the lady stopped paying the rent. He had wanted to take control of the finances and then some months later, he had informed me that he had received a letter from the courts stating that they were applying for eviction. We had to attend court to ask the Judge to grant us three months in which to sell the house. With my hard work, we had sold the house and with those proceeds plus part of the pension, we had agreed to buy another property at auction, but those agreed plans had failed to manifest. I heard alarm bells ringing again as he now didn't want to go ahead with those plans to buy another house so that we could start our property portfolio and only God knows why or where his head was at the time.

The cause of enlargement of the prostrate is unknown, but it is thought to be linked to hormonal changes as a man grows older. The consequential raw energy is stored in our organs, tissues and muscles, which leads to health problems and undermines our general wellbeing. I believe this was the cause of his prostrate becoming enlarged. All the previous experiences and incidences of him having lived a rollercoaster life, was now taking its toll on his body and physical health. It must be so hard to keep lying to yourself and others and it cannot be easy hating and not loving yourself or those around you. Such darkness refuses to let the light or goodness to shine from within.

We had visited a new Testament Church of God at Spring Hill, for a talk about cancer of the prostrate. Soon after he had gone to his GP for his yearly check-up and when he had been diagnosed with the enlarged prostrate problem that required further investigations, I had known then how much I loved him because I hadn't wanted my husband to die. I could not imagine life without him. My love for him meant that I overlooked his faults and realised just how meaningful my marriage vows were to me. I had loved him unconditionally.

My concerns for his health made me even more radical than before. I made further changes to his diet to help him to eat even more healthier than before. I boiled herbs, cut out sweet and sugary foods from his diet and prepared more greens. We walked and exercised more and went swimming and to saunas. We enjoyed ourselves socialising, going to church, praying and going on holidays. We did everything we could to achieve a balance in our diet and lifestyle. We were on a mission to work, rest, play and pray.

That year had proven to be a much calmer year for us. I had been determined to love him back to full health and wished for him to be cured. I will never forget the day when we had been told by the Surgeon that he had been cured and that his prostrate had been reduced to 0.0, we had held each other and cried. I had sent up so many prayers of thanks and gratitude to the Almighty, that I was sure he was fed up having to listen to my prayers, now. It had been such an emotional time for the both of us.

The doctor had commented to us that he could not understand how my husband had recovered so quickly but a lot of his healing and recovery to wellness had been down to my hard work and to the protective blessings from God. Gratitude is a must.

During his healing process, he had still felt inadequate and for a while, we had been sleeping separately. It had taken him some time to regain his confidence after having his prostrate operation. We were slowly drifting apart. It had felt as if he was becoming like a stranger to me and the closeness we had once shared, had become non- existent.

I always felt a sense of feeling on edge when living in my own home. There was this constant feeling of unease. Even within the four walls of our house, there had been a vast distance between us. He stayed mostly in the living room whilst I was upstairs in the bedroom.

After living like that for more than a year, I felt as if I was losing my direction in life, just existing from day to day, month to month, with no focus or sense of where our relationship was heading. Our marriage was in crisis and yet we had no-one we could turn to, to speak to. We had no counselling and no access to our church as we were all in the middle of lockdown. We were disagreeing about everything. We had both continued praying and speaking to God, but separately, not together.

I had reached the point where it had become imperative that he vacate my space as all I could feel from him was bad energies. I no longer desired or wanted him or the marriage. It was time for me to draw a line in the sand.

During the whole of that lockdown period, he had been on furlough, and I was still working. Things had not been improving at all. I found myself willingly taking on overtime as I hated coming home and returning to the house knowing he was there. I had felt happier working outside the home than having to be around him. I had known my marriage was coming to an end and I wanted things sorted, dusted and over with before the end of the year. I just couldn't bear to be stepping into a new year with the same mask plastered on my face as if I was happy and as if everything between us was fine. I was so unhappy and needed to make a change.

During the days I was off from work and at home, I could feel the tension and the stress between us whenever he was around. There was such a negative vibe within the home that I kept myself to myself, mostly staying in my bedroom.

It felt like he had almost turned the living room and the downstairs of the house into his abode, and he spent all his time down there watching television, moving only to get something to eat or to use the bathroom. He appeared a bit defensive at times, when sitting there in the chair with the remote control in his hands.

It was the 1st of April – April Fool's Day – and I recall it clearly as if it were yesterday. The car had been booked in for its MOT service, so I knew I had to get up and get ready to take the car in. To be truthful

neither of us had been feeling well that day, but I had somehow managed to make my way into the bathroom to take a shower. Suddenly there had been a loud banging on the bathroom door. I had been shocked to hear him proclaiming that he felt unwell and that he was about to call an ambulance. To my dismay, realising I too was feeling ill, I had told him to hang on a minute as we needed to call 111 and not 999.

Before I could finish and leave the bathroom to check what was wrong with him, he had already dialled 999. He was on the telephone speaking to tb+he emergency telephone operator. He had been so impatient that he couldn't wait a few minutes and was already in conversation with the person on the other end of the line. She had informed him that because he was breathing, could speak and hold a conversation, that it did not warrant the emergency services coming out to him. She had then advised him to call 111 instead, something I had originally told him to do.

If he had been that ill, I would have cancelled the car MOT and taken him to the hospital myself, which was only five minutes from where we lived. No matter the issues we had between us, his health was a priority, no matter what. Once we had dialled 111, we had been advised to collect some antibiotics from the pharmacy, prescribed by his GP.

I had ignored how ill I was feeling and had driven from Walsall to Aston to make sure the car was serviced and then I had collected his prescribed medications on the way back. As I was driving, I was almost convinced we had both caught the Covid-19 virus, the way I was feeling so ill, dizzy and dripping with sweat. I wasn't sure if I could make the journey back home.

The roads were deserted due to lockdown, and it had felt like driving through a ghost town. I recall that journey clearly as I was fearful that with nobody in sight, no-one would notice if I was forced to abandon driving due to illness. It felt like I was driving into the wilderness, the unknown. I had been fearful of losing consciousness or of crashing the car. With the roads so empty, there would be nobody around to come and rescue me. If only he had made that journey with me, we could have looked out for each other and eased the burden of my solely worrying about whether I would make it back safely or not. But by the grace of God, I made it.

A friend of mine had been worried that I had driven so far and had not gone straight to the hospital, but I had explained to her how so many of my friends were dying in the hospital and that was the last place that I wanted to be. She had become very emotional, crying down the telephone as she was convinced that I needed to go to the hospital. My mind had already been in turmoil, and I couldn't handle that level of emotion then and there and had ended the call, promising to speak to her later.

All I could do was to pray for courage and strength to guide me home.

On the way home I had stopped at a friend's house. They had blended me some herbs for me to take once I reached home. Once home, I had literally taken a shower, collapsed in the bed and had remained there for four days.

I had felt so drained and weak and could not taste anything at all. My son had brought me some natural garlic to eat, and my daughter brought me some fruits and water, but I had little to no appetite.

A few days later I had attempted to eat a little but had swiftly thrown it back up. I felt delirious and was convinced I was about to die from this virus. I could barely walk up the stairs and felt so out of breath. I had known I was in a bad way as usually I could easily run up and down those stairs and now, I was fighting for breath. It was a couple more days before I could even sip water without feeling nauseous. I had tried eating a little but still I was throwing it all up, darting to the toilet so often. I had felt dehydrated. The most I could manage to do was to apply some herbs to my body to try to detox and heal. It had been difficult to drink the blended herbs, but I had to and did so, making sure he drank some too. I had been off work for two weeks, healing and self-isolating.

I could not believe what I was going through. After three or four days I started to regain some strength and to feel a little better. My appetite returned and I was able to sip a little Guinness and drink some water.

Considering we both suffered through the same illness, he and I still preserved our distance and gave each other space in which to physically heal in our own way and time.

As I returned to work, feeling much better, he continued to lounge around all day, playing with the remote control and watching television, eating and chatting with anyone who would talk to him.

One evening, I sat down in the living room, wanting to talk to him about what had happened on April Fool's day. I asked him why, when he had not been feeling well, he hadn't said anything to either myself or my grandson, who lived with us. I questioned him about whether it was because he hadn't really cared about us, knowing that he may have been suffering from the symptoms associated with the virus. Not to mention that he should have been self-isolating.

I had to make it known to him that my sole aim was to try to keep our family safe but what had really concerned me was how when I was not feeling well myself, I still had to find the strength and willpower to drive that long journey to get the MOT done for the car whilst he was apparently happy to sit at home. I had expressed my concerns that if something had happened or we had to deal with a crisis of some sort, I had no confidence in him that he would be there to help or support me.

It had seriously annoyed me that he was the man of the house, yet he was looking to me, a woman, to save him. I was tired of him and everyone else looking to me to sort things out and to make things better. He was supposed to be the strong one, the backbone of our family. He was supposed to make me feel safe and secure and to take some responsibility for his actions. Yet, he hadn't done so, not in the slightest.

I was always having to be the strong one, the brave one, the one who had to think about everything and make all the decisions. I was tired of taking on the burden of what he should have been doing and taking care of things within our household and for our family. I hadn't gotten married to elevate my stress. I had married for love and as a single woman I had needed a solid man to share the daily and financial responsibilities of maintaining a home so that we could be happy and remain and grow older together and in love. I had believed that as one, as a partnership, that we would be enhancing our lives, sharing the burdens and responsibilities, as we loved each other through thick and thin, ups and downs.

That certainly was not happening in our relationship or marriage.

I had unhappily but realistically reached the conclusion that the man had no backbone and that I should have drawn that line in the sand seven years ago. The arguments between us were becoming more frequent and during the last few years, they had been far worse.

After surviving the virus, I could only give God thanks for each day, moving forwards and for saving our lives, as so many of our friends had died or were dying.

I had ended that conversation with him, by sharing with him my thoughts, that now we had survived that scare, we should be praying and giving praises to The Almighty. I also made it clear to him that if there was any additional fussing and fighting over trivial and foolish things, then our marriage would be over.

I refused to continue living with a man who had no gratitude for life or for God and who obviously had no respect for me, as a woman or as his wife. I was so tired of his lies and half-hearted apologies and unworthiness.

It was time for me to let him and our marriage go.

All that had happened in April. Then, in May, his brother had died.

I had purposefully and willingly humbled myself so that I could support him in the best way I could. He had continued to behave badly with an ungrateful attitude. The almost tangible bad vibes, energy and toxic negativity hadn't changed at all around the home. I would rather have been alone than to have continued being disrespected by that man, but my heart kept telling me that it would not be fair or humane to kick a man whilst he was feeling down and grieving.

Once it had seemed like an appropriate amount of time had passed for his grieving, it was clear more than ever before, that he had to leave. So, in the July of that same year, I had packed his things, wished him all the best in his future endeavours and said goodbye.

His narcissistic traits and behaviours had become far too much to cope with or to endure. His characteristics had obviously stemmed from his personal life experiences, and I felt that the more I did for him and loved him, the more he appeared ungrateful and dismissive of me. I was living in a toxic cycle created by him and enabled by me, where we would constantly be taking ten huge steps backwards and never moving forwards. There was never going to be any meaningful or significant changes in his misbehaviours. Our relationship had become stuck and rooted in passivity. It was no environment in which any plans for our future could be made, even though I had desperately clung to my visions and dreams for our future together.

Several years into our marriage it had become unbearable as it was becoming increasingly difficult to communicate with him as he would inevitably turn what I considered a normal conversation into a full-blown argument.

His ego insisted that he should demand respect as he felt that he did everything so well! He was suffocatingly insistent on wanting my attention and affection all the time and exhibited signs of being jealous and resentful of my friendships with other people, especially when we were out socially, and especially if a man even said a simple hello to me. He would become territorial and would verbally abuse me by putting me down behind my back and sometimes in front of my family and friends, telling me that I was nasty, and he was forever accusing me of having an affair.

I had soon come to realise that the high degree of insecurity was with himself and not me, so I started to take little notice of his name- calling. I had to be constantly on alert to be mindful to retain my emotional and mental strength as his attitude and behaviour were eroding my self-confidence and self-esteem. Sometimes I would look at him and silently berate him as an asshole. I needed a man who was emotionally intelligent and mature, one who was loving, kind and caring. A man who would happily protect me and provide for me and my needs as his partner.

He had promised me so many things when we had first met but he had failed to see any of those promises through to fruition. He had made me promises to build a home for us in Barbados, to take me to America. In time, I grew to understand that I had been living with this man on false pretences as his lack of empathy made him to be so cold and unloving. Yet at the same time, he would insist on telling me that I did not show him love, that I never hugged or kissed him, when in fact, he was the one who refused to show me his apparent love for me in those ways. His hypocrisy was astounding as he would show me off to people as his wife, telling them how much in love we were! He was unbelievably cruel and had no conscience.

As the years passed, I trusted him less and less. I had lost faith in him and myself and could find no solutions on how to rectify that disheartening feeling of not believing that he could ever be the husband he had originally told me he would and wanted to be. The more I withdrew from initiating any kind of communication with him the more he reverted to having conversations on the telephone with all and sundry, seeking external validation from them that he was a good person.

He was very egotistically driven to looking physically good, as I myself was too, but I had been of the mindset to do so for myself whereas his goal had been to receive compliments and praises from other people.

Because of his charm and emotional manipulations, it had proven difficult to extricate myself from him and the marriage. He would hurt me then apologise profusely but would refuse to attend counselling with an intent to heal and repair our relationship as husband and wife. He had reached that point of no return where his lies had become his truths.

Yes, I had noticed certain characteristics, but it had been hard for me to understand that type of behaviour. Attending a Mental Health Training course at my workplace had given me a deeper understanding and insight into how mental health affects a person's behaviour.

It had saddened me to realise that our marital problems were swept under the carpet. It hadn't helped that he sought comfort and validation of himself from others whilst I slowly withdrew more and more into myself.

It had broken my heart to admit that I no longer trusted him, and I became cautiously careful of what I shared with him. We had on rare occasions still had some deep conversations and some intimate moments together and he had reiterated his promises and I had again believed him. For weeks and months at a time I lived on my hopeful expectations, only to feel let down again.

Whenever he felt vex, he would be extra controlling, especially if he were told something that he did not like or want to hear. He would sulk like a small child, pouting like somebody who was on the borderline of having a personality disorder. Of course, the prolonged sulking was part of his regime of manipulation to get his own way. His abusive and dysfunctional behaviours were stressful to bear, to say the least. The sulking alone felt like a form of mental and emotional abuse and torture. He appeared to take pleasure in choosing not to interact with me, creating in me a sense that I was his victim to be maliciously toyed with. I had been almost obsessively determined to stick by my marriage vows and so I stayed and suffered more incidences of his cruelty towards me. I told myself that I had made my bed so therefore I had to lie in it.

A part of me knew that I was illogically making excuses for his behaviour because I was keen to save my marriage and reluctant to let go of my love for him. His narcissistic manipulations manifested itself in the way he blamed me and everybody else, his rage, his not talking to me for long periods of time.

It had not been long before I felt my respect for him dwindling rapidly. He came across as mentally sick, immature and dangerous to be around. He appeared most happy when in the middle of social settings, seeming relatively normal under those circumstances. His Jekyll and Hyde personality became energetically draining and sometimes frightening too, causing me to feel unsafe and off balance. I tried to but there was no way that I could change him. For a long while I was his prey and victim and I had felt there was no hope in my escaping his demeaning clutches. It was like treading through quicksand and fighting a losing battle.

The stress of our marital situation caused us tons of stress. My blood pressure sky-rocketed to dangerous levels and he started to suffer from the effects of having an enlarged prostrate. In internalising the pain and hurt, we are more likely to suffer from stress related illnesses and our immune system decreases. At one point we were both ill but with some determination and a healthy eating regime, we had both been able to keep a work and life balance that was non-fatal to our wellbeing. I still felt that I needed to put in place some boundaries in order to protect myself so I had kept busy with work and organising social functions, supporting him with his mentoring and coaching courses, which were meant to focus his mind on being and doing good and better, but no matter what, he would not or could not change.

In becoming his wife, I had thought that I would be forever in a committed and intimate relationship with him. It appeared that he himself had suffered some type of trauma and needed to deal with those issues of his, head on. But he was not willing to communicate or face his issues at all. He would rather brush them under the carpet whilst burying his head in the sand. I had been more than willing to seek a definitive solution to save our marriage, but he was too consumed in holding on to the past. He was unable or unwilling to stand in his own truth and confront his demons. All his past intimate relationships had ended badly and yet still he was far too reluctant to look within himself to try to work out the reasons why that was so. He just had not cared enough to take that step. Or maybe he was just not capable of doing so.

He became verbally and physically abusive and despite my efforts in trying to educate him to change his patterns of thoughts and behaviours, by partaking in some mentoring and coaching courses, it had all been in vain. In thinking we could fix our problems without professional advice or help it had only served to increase the toxicity between us. My body was already showing signs that the stress of it all was affecting my health.

In due course I even began to wonder if he had ever genuinely loved me at all or had it all been a show for others to see and believe he was a good man and husband. His disrespect of me had cut me to the core. I grew to understand how he was gaslighting me – which is a form of psychological manipulation where he covertly targeted me and others with the intention of causing me to doubt myself and even my recollections of what I knew to be true but would still second guess myself. In due course his gaslighting made me question my own memories, perceptions and judgements. At its worst, it made me pause to discern what was reality and what was not.

Whenever we argued, he would be quite volatile and nasty, calling me a whore and worse. He would lie then insist that he had never said what he had said. His primary concern had been that we should look good together. Mine was that we should feel good together. I craved for us to have that normality of a loving union, but we found ourselves stuck in a negative rut as we both wanted different things and were heading in different directions.

I found myself responding to his abuse by becoming verbally abusive to him also. We were constantly shouting at each other and not listening to what each of us had to say. The frustration I felt with him was burdensome. I had grown weary of his lies, his dismissiveness and the way he would happily walk out of the room like a small child having a tantrum, slamming the door behind him.

I was hurting so badly inside and was silently depressed and feeling hopeless. His behaviour caused me to lose a few of my friendships with other people as he was determined in spreading lies to them about me, all so that he himself could shine bright. Both of us were not paying attention to the other's needs even though I tried not to be that person. He himself appeared not to care one way or the other. My desire to have and build a marriage based on good and positive energies was fast becoming a nightmare and a distant and unachievable goal.

At times it was confusing and draining the way he would play mind games with me. I could not see a future with him and yet I still hesitated, wondering what people would think of me if I left him when everybody else loved him. I had fallen out of love with him and could not imagine staying with him just to please and appease other people.

I prayed to God to help me to find a way out, an escape route that would preserve my dignity. I was still wishing for us to part on amicable terms without any drama or harmful repercussions. But I had known that he did not think the same way I did, and he was fond of playing the victim role, blaming everybody but himself for his mistakes. I used to cringe at the way he acted so fake in public and was the perfect narcissist behind closed doors. It is very ironic because years previously, when my daughter had first met him, the one thing she said that always stuck with me, was how she had verbalised that he was fake and in truth, that sums him up perfectly.

For my own sanity, I had no choice but to face the facts that he was a covert narcissist, always feeling that others had done him wrong, including me, but I also had to acknowledge and be accountable to myself for enabling that kind of behaviour and for not loving myself enough and therefore believing that I did not deserve more or better.

In this life here on earth, there is no man that comes before The Almighty. We need to be true to ourselves, always. There is nobody that should feel they have the right to shatter your dreams, your life, your light or your love that was given freely and with good intent. The time we have here, we should be living in love, peace and harmony. After everything I had experienced and suffered in my life, I was determined not to settle for anything less. We all have the right to seek and find happiness before we leave this life.

I have always believed that your home is your sanctuary and should be filled with love. Not just when it suits your mood or when other people are around.

We had some good times together and I was happy and grateful for that, but our relationship and legal union had come to an end, because truth be told, he had been wearing me down and he would gladly put other people before me, his wife, and his ungratefulness was just too hard to bear and live with. Our marriage ended because he would never change. I let him go because I had fallen out of love with him and because I needed to relearn how to love, respect and honour myself.

There are times we must ask ourselves why we continue to give people we love or loved, chances after chances even as they constantly dishonour you. Rather than sit and discuss our marital problems with each other, he had felt that it was appropriate to discuss our problems with other people.

He had blatantly dismissed all the opportunities I had offered to him to work on our problems and differences. Instead, he had disrespected our relationship, acting unfairly and ignorantly burying his head in the sand. He had been happier to seek validation from others so that he could feel better within himself, albeit temporarily, rather than to attempt to resolve the issues burning deep within.

Letting go of an intimate relationship does not mean that you have failed. It just means that you are releasing the shackles of something that did not work for you in order to make room for something that does or will in the future. It is always possible to find love again.

I had struggled to end that marriage as I had truly believed that we had something special to hold on to, but my declining emotional, physical, mental and spiritual health had told me a different story. For the sake of my personal and mental wellbeing, I had to find the courage and conviction to move forwards. I needed to find happiness instead of existing to make him happy, despite his unrealistic expectations and needs. No matter what I said or did, nothing was ever good enough for him and once I realised that it would never be any different to what it was, I had to step away and save myself. The time had come to stop giving away my empowerment so easily, especially to one who had not deserved or appreciated it.

I had chosen to stay for as long as I had, because I thought that I could manage the relationship between us. If I kept the conversation relevant to what he wanted to talk about, then all was fine with him.

But, if I ever dared to tell him that he was wrong or tried to change the subject, then all hell broke loose.

I had taken certain steps in attempting to preserve my sanity, like going swimming, to the sauna or to exercise classes. I kept myself busy with my work. I deliberately took on activities that kept me out of the house and which gave me a valid excuse to avoid being in his presence and having to endure his toxic behaviour. I had been determined to find meaning and purpose for myself and my life.

I found various ways in which to gift myself with self-love and selfcare, not wanting to be left stranded with a broken heart. I recognised that in putting all my energy into trying to help and change him, I was in fact causing severe harm to my inner spiritual self. Such manifestations of negative and soul-draining energy had never sat well with me.

His constant gaslighting of me had driven me crazy. Throughout the years he had worn me down, big time, and I had to give myself permission to forgive me, for not honouring myself and my wellbeing. My children's father was a narcissistic man like my husband, however Mr R was very handy and forthcoming to getting things done, like cleaning the car, and ensuring that sufficient oil and water was in it. He would do more maintenance jobs around the house, like putting up the curtain rails. He was a provider in terms of financially helping to run and keep the house, however, he was an abuser, so he too had to go after thirteen years of abusing me.

Whenever my husband was carrying on crazy and irrationally, I found it was best for me not to engage with him. I learnt not to take his verbal abuses and nasty name calling, personally. I literally trained myself not to indulge him by arguing with him because that was when things would get heated and intense. If I did not back down then the situation would escalate and end up in a physical fight, during which I would find myself throwing things at him, just to keep him away from me and to prevent him from causing me further physical harm.

The way he had treated me for so many years had left me feeling unworthy and devalued as a person and as a woman. I felt unheard. I felt invisible. It was not until I had started to study narcissistic personality disorders that I understood better that not only was I living with a narcissist, but that I could never help him to change. So, I had to get out of there, sooner rather than later.

I remember when I had found out that he had cheated on me, just before we had gotten engaged. I had ended up forgiving him for that hurtful indiscretion and after some time apart, I had taken him back.

He had been so comfortable in lying and had not shown even a little empathy for the way he had hurt me deeply. Eventually, it had not mattered whether I forgave him or not as it became irrelevant considering that he continued to demean me by calling me names, saying sorry, kissing and making up and then would repeat his misbehaviour all over again.

I had felt lost in my relationship with him. He hated being criticised which was his way of shutting down any kind of authentic conversations or communications to be had. He was egotistical and vain, always showing off his new suits, cars or house, whatever he felt defined him as a good and successful person. He lived his life like the whole world owed him something and at times he would fill whatever void he felt he had within him, with consuming vast amounts of alcohol.

It was 2020 and I had asked him to leave.

It is a sad reflection and reality of life that broken men (and women) show up with guarded hearts that cannot trust themselves or others and some become abusers and cheaters, hurting those they say they love. Hurt people hurt other people.

There are any number of reasons why broken people hurt others. It could be attributed to a lack of positive parenting, bad relationships, poor social conditions and non-nurturing environments. Many experience challenges in life and some are self-inflicted. So many find it difficult to form lasting and healthy relationships and lack the skills of expressing themselves in non-harmful and positive ways. There are those who are resentful of and intimidated by another's happiness and success.

Those who continuously hurt others usually have low self-esteem and insecurities they refuse to face head on.

So often women particularly are attracted to men thinking that they can fix them and when their lives are made miserable or unbearable, they remain, believing that if they become better that all will be well. This is so untrue.

It is so important for men and women to have good role models that they can look to and emulate. Therapy can be a good thing too.

Since his departure, I have felt free from his dysfunctional presence and behaviours. I have learnt to strengthen my personal boundaries whilst rebuilding my self-esteem. I will never put myself into another relationship where I am made to feel like a victim that deserves less than I do. I would rather be alone.

Remaining trapped within a toxic relationship damages your inner spirits. Your physical body and mind may try to deny it, but toxic people will only bring sadness, suffering and stress into your life, which ultimately can sometimes impact on your health and in drastic cases, your life.

Moving forwards, I will choose a healthy relationship, with myself and others and if it is my destiny, I will choose to be with a spiritually healthy, loving and kind man. I choose to live a mentally and emotionally healthy life, for me.

In December 2020, I had returned to Barbados. I had remained there into January of 2021, wanting to witness the full moon there. The spiritual meaning of the full moon is when Leo is symbolic of the birth of authenticity, as it represents the conscious self. It is where the heart recognises consciousness and where we combine our personality and soul energy in order to radiate love. This is the development of the ego and the realisation of self.

My needing to make the decision as to who I am and wanted to be, stemmed from my desire to *finally* draw that line in the sand. The time had arrived for me to learn to become whom I needed to be for me and not who others perceived me to be. I wanted closure from that unhealthy relationship which had been causing me so much hurt and harm to my wellbeing and general health.

Thy Father, I see that you are drawing a line in the sand, and I want to be standing on your side holding your hand. Let your Kingdom come and live. In peace I surrender my all, to the King.

Grief had brought us together and grief had torn us apart. In disconnecting from my former partner and husband, I had to pray to God to help me to find my salvation, my light, my self-love, my happiness and my peace of mind. I bent down on my knees to pray that there would be no returning to negativity, toxicity, always having to wear a false mask, of feeling unloved. I needed to learn how to reclaim responsibility of my own life so that once again I would be able to take care of myself. I had returned to Barbados in order to 'get my groove back' and to finally physically, emotionally and mentally, to draw that line in the sand, once and for all.

The Creator drew a line in the sand for all who believed in Him.

John 15: 18-23 – If the world hates you, keep in mind that it hated me first. If you belonged to the world, it would love you as its own. As it is, you do not belong to the world, but I have chosen you out of the world.

In the world in which they lived, people could either follow Him or 'be of the world'. There could be no straddling of that line. It was either one side or the other.

Having drawn my life-changing decisional line in the sand has meant that I am now free to thrive through my survival and that has led me to be thankful and grateful to be a part of this phenomenal Surviving Queens Anthology, alongside some tremendously inspirational and courageous women who have reminded me that our choices to survive has restored our beliefs in who we are.

All I can say is never say never, because we don't know what life can throw at us, so even though I have drawn a line in the sand at this moment of time and can see all the things that went wrong, I can also see the great things we did together and the love we once had.

I really don't know what help he needs, but all I can say I have exhausted all avenues of what I knew to help him heal and to learn how to love and to be kind to himself and for us to have a healthy loving relationship.

Is there room for reconciliation? Yes, there is room for reconciliation after a break-up. I am still waiting for that conversation to be had but I will not initiate it

Anything is possible if we could have an honest conversation and have therapy because when we split, we had no counselling, we had no professional guidance or support. Not living together could help us to build up that communication. I have no idea how or if this dialogue will start or if it could ever, as it could be very awkward but it the only way to resolve the situation, which is by communication.

In a relationship life is not stagnated. As the years go by, we grow, we change. Life is about evolving. We can't live the same day repeatedly, because changes happen and we must move with the times, and we need to move together, or one will be left behind and both persons will drift apart.

He would always criticise his previous partners and it was always their fault why they broke up and he would never take the blame for anything and would constantly test his boundaries like when he hit me, and I called the police, and he was arrested. He never did that to me again.

I know I should look out for these red flags in a relationship, however I thought I could assist him to change, but it wasn't about me, it was about his mindset and needing to find love in his own heart and to be consistent in his behaviour by doing good and not bad. I believed that when I got married, I was ready to be with someone for the rest of my life, however he played me with his falseness, he was wearing a mask and like myself I was not accustomed to being loved or seeing much affection like hugging and kissing between my mum and dad. Because of that, I didn't feel that there was any harm in not getting lots of hugs and kisses.

I did not pay attention to the red flags because I was in love and what do they say, love is blind, because I wanted this to work. It was both of our first marriages and getting married late I thought I had chosen a solid man, as this is what he portrayed. All I had wanted was a simple life, one of love, not an unhealthy relationship which was destroying my mind and my soul. I don't want a relationship with drama and pain. For me, the love needs to shine through, and I need a husband that supports me in my life and not one that brings me numbness where if I speak it causes arguments which made me become more increasingly unfulfilled and I wanted out.

When there's a storm there must be a calm, but I felt like the storm was hard to shift and I just longed for the calm vibration, the calm energy, the peace and when it came it hadn't lasted long. I wanted to feel free mentally and emotionally. I prayed every day for God to grant me peace and love and if my husband meant me no good, then I hoped he would please remove him from my space.

I couldn't do this myself, I needed help, not from people who just wanted news but those who would genuinely listen and help us to heal, but I felt I had no one I could really trust to help us move forward. That's why some people were in shock when they heard we had separated. Only God could do this for us.

Sometimes I don't think we realise when we bring bad traits from old relationships until its identified that the new relationship is showing behaviours like that of the old one. For example, struggling to communicate with things that upset me, showed me that he was not in touch with his emotions and was constantly irritated by things which was said that would trigger him off especially when he said something that was a lie and I corrected him, he would go into a mood and say I didn't say that, and I would say you did and off we would go again. Most of his previous relationships he left without coming to some resolution, so it would be hard for someone to move forward without solving previous relationship problems. Past relationships can affect new ones especially if you have had your heart broken, so it's good to talk about past relationships to your new partner and not hide the truth of what really happened, and you will find you can be more open and truthful with each other.

I believe healing is very important so that you do not allow another person to suffer, because developing a good relationship is very important to me, one built with love, caring, sharing and great communication. A healthy relationship is important to me as I believe that love helps you both to shine brighter.

I am and will forever be a Surviving Queen!

SARA MAYNARD

My name is Sara Maynard, and I am also known as Sarz to my closest friends and family. I am a 39-year-old mother of a beautiful twelve- year old daughter.

I am the Founder, CEO and Director of *Listen Uplift Vent CIC,* which is a community female empowerment organisation. I run a women's only group on social media called *LUV Ladies.* We also specialise in delivering staff diversity training in schools and we also facilitate workshops with the school children. I am experienced within the Administration field, working for the NHS.

I have learnt that sharing my personal and professional stories of survival and accomplishments achieved, helps to re-empower other women and helps me to understand my personal journey and growth. I would hope that when others read my story that they can recognise the inner strength and courage it has taken to share my truth honestly. It is important to let others know that the first step in fully loving yourself is in accepting all of who you are and will be and to acknowledge that your journey serves a purpose.

Because I grew up suffering in silence with issues of not being able to communicate and express my deepest thoughts adequately and positively and therefore felt unheard and misunderstood, I love this quote as it resonates with me on a deeper level: *'If I did something wrong, communicate. If I hurt your feelings, make me aware. If I did not listen well enough, tell me again in a way I will understand. If I am insensitive to your needs, to your desires or to your thoughts, tell me so I can consider them. But do not hold an attitude with me because you have not clearly expressed yourself. I am human, not a mind reader'.*

One of the things that I am proud of and thankful for, is that no matter how badly others have treated me, or how low I have felt and no matter the life struggles I go through and survive, I still retain a heart of gold and an abundance of love for self and for others. That is something that nobody can ever take away from me. In April 2021 I was proud and grateful to collect the keys for *Listen Uplift Vent CIC's* brand-new offices! It was the combination of having learnt to believe in myself and to know that I can achieve anything that I put my mind to.

Having the honour of being asked to be included in this awesome Anthology has shown and reminded me that I am and always will be a Surviving Queen!

My chapter is called 'Why Me?

CHAPTER 5

WHY ME?

SARA MAYNARD

W hy me? That was a question that I seemed to be asking myself constantly. I just could not work out why I kept finding myself embroiled in the same situations time and time again.

So, let me look back at my recollections to when I was younger.

Those memories of seeing my mom and dad fighting, well, to be more precise, seeing my dad being abusive to my mom as she struggled to defend herself from his physical and verbal attacks, are forever etched into my brain. Just his verbal abuse of her, swearing at her, yelling at her and insulting her, had left me feeling scared and wanting to just withdraw more into myself. The toxicity was devastatingly real and horrendous. I soon came to realise that domestic violence breeds the necessity for countless emergency department visits and had long term consequences on the victim's physical and mental health and even how they functioned in social gatherings.

There are many children who witness childhood domestic violence and emerge unscathed without experiencing any negative effects. In my case, I experienced both short and long term cognitive, behavioural and emotional effects. Living with abuse as younger children in those situations of domestic violence, I don't think that we respond to it as much as we absorb all the traumatic energies exhibited within our homes as we helplessly witness the violence between our parents. The impact of childhood domestic violence on impressionable young minds and our emotions can be devastating and debilitating.

My dad finally left when I was nine years of age and from that moment onwards, the relationship I had with him was not the same as before. That decision he made to leave us, this influenced me emotionally and mentally This I believe had a negative effect on my relationships and how I viewed men. Growing up I had always been a 'daddy's girl', so when he had not made the effort to continue to see me or be in my life, that had really hurt me and left me feeling tragically abandoned, rejected, unwanted and unloved.

I have no doubt that as a direct result of him leaving, it had triggered me into believing that I was unworthy of deserving more in life. His abandonment of me had caused me to grow up with a lack of positive motivation that affected various aspects of my life for many years to come. His sudden withdrawal of his fatherly love for me left me feeling constantly worthless and undeserving of anything good or positive happening to me or in my life.

I can recall my mom having to drop us off outside of his house and then swiftly drive off so that he would look after us whilst she went to work, but even now I can still sense how it all felt so forced, like he had to be reminded of his obligations and responsibilities as a dad, towards us.

It had been horribly hard for me emotionally to realise that he expected his young children to contact him even though his workplace was a mere five-minute walk from where we lived in our house. I would no longer deny that in suppressing my true feelings and sadness, I had developed ongoing anxieties, depression and emotional distress. My unspoken hurt would manifest itself in terms of my suffering headaches and trying to ignore that inner rage that always seemed to be threatening to explode at any moment, and it took its toll on my physical and mental health.

My brother had left home when I was fifteen but prior to him moving out, our sibling relationship had been quite volatile. He must have been seventeen when he left home, and I had recognised how angry he had been after our father had walked away from us. Over the years my relationship with my siblings have been up and down. My brother moved out and we hardly saw him over the next few years after that. I eventually moved in with him for a short while when me and my mom were not getting on. We have had our falling outs over the years like most siblings, but he is my next-door neighbour now and we have a good relationship. With both my dad and my brother gone, it had been just me, my mom and my sister, for many years, with very few male role models for us children to look to for guidance or support. I had an uncle that I was close to. He was the brother of my mom. My uncle had been like a father figure to me as I was growing up and I had loved him dearly. We are no longer close, and I am not sure why that is the case, but it still hurts me to this day, losing that closeness and bond that we had shared between us. My paternal grandfather had passed away. My other grandfather, my mom's dad, was living far away in Barbados.

All my life I have felt as if I am not enough. Family have never really demonstrated that they were willing or eager to make the effort. No aunties or uncles who call or text to check how I am doing or if I am okay. There are cousins whom I only ever see occasionally, one specifically, out of more than twenty.

When it comes to friendships, I feel that I have always gone out of my way for my friends, but very rarely do I get shown that same kind of love or attention back.

Any reason, no matter how big or small, I am made to feel as if I am not a nice person, no matter how much I may have done for them previously. This has always left me wondering, why me? Why am I not enough? What is it about me that people don't see me or hear me?

We are none of us perfect and we all make mistakes, but I question incessantly, why are my mistakes made to feel like they are the worst in the world? I often witness other people treat others in negative and bad ways but who are not made to feel the way I feel or am viewed or judged.

Those who say that they love me are so quick to condemn me and dismiss me as if I do not exist or matter. Over the years this has happened to me so many times and leaves me emotionally and mentally bruised and burdened with real issues of feeling rejected. This ongoing issue is one that I am still working on to this day.

The pain of feeling rejected is real. In the past it has caused me to feel an increase in suppressed and expressed anger, anxiety, depression, self-doubts, envy and sadness. At times it had affected my abilities to perform even the simplest of social, personal or intellectual tasks and there was a horrible feeling of lacking self-control.

My mental health certainly suffered, and I grew up feeling ashamed with an inbuilt grief at not being accepted by others.

I certainly recall the memories of the fear of being rejected which caused me to not know how to halt the lack of confidence to express myself or my needs. My fear of rejection evolved into being fearful of being abandoned all over again.

I had no idea of how to recognise any of the signs that being fearful of rejection causes, like giving too much of myself to others, and being too eager to please others. I had difficulties in trusting myself or others or even the intentions of other people towards me.

In hindsight, I question whether I was frightened of intimate relationships because I had a fear of love itself, especially since I felt I had no real knowledge of knowing what love was. Had I been cautious to show love or to love another because it would mean that I would have to be vulnerable with the possibility of getting hurt if someone I loved then caused me pain or left me? Being criticised or rejected often felt so overwhelming to me.

Rejection hurts deeply but it can also inflict damage to our psychological wellbeing that surpasses emotional pain as we all have a basic need to belong. Being rejected or abandoned throws us off balance and sometimes causes us to feel disconnected and isolated. Then, in not dealing with the effects of those emotions of being hurt, we then seek comfort, validation and company in all the wrong places. Reaching out from a place of feeling broken, we forget to value who we are and what we stand for as our main goal is finding ways, places and people to soothe our hurts. We actively are seeking to be accepted.

Rejection on an emotional level destroys our self-esteem. Feeling unwanted and unloved within an intimate relationship causes us to start finding faults in ourselves and we become convinced of a higher level of inadequacies of self. We blame ourselves and in so doing, we strip away any semblance of self-worth we may have previously felt. In our turmoil of feeling abandoned or neglected, we forget to consider that relationships may not continue or grow due to other factors, such as incompatibility, a lack of mutual chemistry, conflicting lifestyles and wanting and needing different things in life.

Have you ever recognised how being in a state of emotional rejection affects your ability to think clearly or to think or act logically? This is because rejection temporarily lowers our IQ (Intelligence Quotient), and we find it extremely difficult to retain short-term memories and to be clear and concise in our decision-making. In feeling rejected, we literally are rendered incapable of responding to reason.

There are ways we can learn to mend our psychological wounds that rejection inflicts upon us. It is possible to recover from the emotional pain that rejection causes. We can reverse the pain of rejection and prevent the cognitive and mental fallouts that occur and then show up in more positive and productive ways in our personal and professional lives. To do this, we must be prepared to acknowledge our emotional and mental wounds in order to soothe our pain, reduce our anger and aggression, to protect and preserve our self-esteem and bring into balance our need to belong.

Aged seventeen, I had thought I was so in love and that this first intimate relationship was going to last forever. In my heart, I had really believed that was going to be the case. He had seemed like the perfect guy to me and in my eyes, he was just so good looking, and I was convinced that everything about him, his personality and characteristics, was everything I had ever wanted or needed from a relationship with a partner. We were together for about two years and that had been my first experience of being in an abusive relationship.

Recently, I was asked how and when did the abuse start and I could not honestly answer the question because I honestly don't know when and how his abusive behaviours began. I don't know how. I don't know when and I don't even know why. All I know is that it happened, and that relationship became so threatening, explosive and painfully uncomfortable, that I had no other choice but to leave.

I will always remember the last situation that had happened before I had escaped. I had gone on holiday to Barbados as my uncle was getting married over there. One of my friends had written me a note before I had left and, as a joke, had decided to put a condom inside the letter.

He, my then partner, had been staying at the house whilst we, the family, were away abroad. The day after I returned home, I had gone into college. On returning home later that afternoon, with my friend who had written the letter, it had been obvious that my then partner had been looking through my bags and had found the note, with the condom in it, of course. He had then gone crazy, pushing and shoving me and my friend around, and at one point, he had pushed her into the bath. There had been so much frantic commotion and drama!

That incident of physical altercation had been the last straw for me, and I had decided that I needed to leave. It had become evident that his behaviour could easily escalate into a pattern of behaviour that would be controlling, coercive and physically threatening.

The traumatic stress I had experienced because of his behaviour had left me feeling fearful and depressively isolated. I had carried the shame and embarrassment of his aggressive misbehaviour on my shoulders for the longest time, which in turn had left me feeling anxious and depressed.

Following on from that toxic relationship, all my other relationships with men seemed to be so negative and far from loving or nurturing. I had no inkling really of how to self-regulate my emotions or how to adjust accordingly to protect myself from dire situations and circumstances.

I often wondered if abusers were possessed of the knowledge of how their maltreatment caused their targeted victims to feel isolated, fearful and mistrustful of others which can easily translate into psychological consequences that may manifest as educational difficulties, low self-esteem, low self-confidence, depression and trouble forming and maintaining healthy relationships, if they would still inflict abuse, violence and mistreatment upon their unfortunate victims.

Aged nineteen, I discovered I was pregnant. My best friend and I were expecting at the same time! I had been so happy and excited. Unfortunately, I had miscarried my first baby and that had been such a huge loss for me. I then had to watch my friend, who already had a child, blossoming with her growing belly until she had given birth. That had been so emotionally hard for me and again, I couldn't understand why me. I had felt so lonely in my sadness.

I am not sure for how long I may have been in shock, but I do remember feeling so devastated at my loss. For me personally, it had been more than a physical loss. There had been the sense of a profound loss of hope and positivity. I had felt so down and lost and with that came a sense of mental and emotional chaos. I had felt alone and isolated internally, mainly because the loss had felt so intense. At first, I had felt confused and resentfully sad at how those around me appeared to be moving forwards with their lives whilst I was stuck in processing and accepting my devastating loss.

It takes time to recover from a miscarriage and having experienced it, I can only advise that others who have also suffered a miscarriage take the time and space they need to recover fully and at their own pace. It may help you to seek out support from within a group setting, also.

It was not until a few years later, when I was aged twenty-five, that I finally settled down into another intimate relationship. Things had progressed quickly between us, and I had soon fallen pregnant with my baby girl.

But again, as with all my other personal and intimate relationships, that too soon became abusive. He may not have been physically abusive towards me, but his abuse was more of the mental and emotional kind, which is just as frightening and devastating. Emotional or psychological abuse often co-exists with other forms of abuse and is often the most difficult to both identify and accept as such. Verbal abuse is still an act of violence in the form of speech that ultimately strips away your self-esteem and self-confidence, reducing you to feeling hopeless and helpless. Suffering verbal abuse is being forcefully and aggressively criticised, insulted and demeaned by the abuser. It is universally accepted that the effects of suffering verbal abuse can be more impactful and long-lasting than physical abuse, in some instances.

When someone repeatedly uses words to demean, frighten or control another person, that is recognised as verbal abuse, and it can take its toll on your physical and mental health. As with physical abuse, verbal abuse is not your fault. The effects of verbal abuse are serious and can lead to depression, anxiety and fear. It can also trigger eating disorders, insomnia, self-harming and over-sensitivity.

Victims who are constantly verbally abused often ignore or misinterpret both the abuse and its effects on them because verbal abuse throws you off balance, making you feel unsure of yourself and your worthiness. Those feelings are mainly caused by verbally abusive mind-games such as brainwashing and gaslighting. Gaslighting is a form of psychological abuse where a person causes another person to question their sanity, perception of reality or memories. It leaves the abused feeling confused, anxious and unable to trust their thoughts, beliefs or reactions and responses.

Living in that type of home environment was not beneficial to me or my child and that was not the life I had wanted her to be growing up in, either. I had grown up in a similarly toxic atmosphere and I needed to be the instigator of change for her sake as well as for mine. I did not necessarily want to leave him but there was no way I could stay in that partnership the way it was. I had been scared that if I had stayed, I would eventually become emotionally unavailable for my daughter. I did not want the effects of existing within a toxic relationship to turn me into a self-centred toxic parent.

As time would prove, despite my leaving, it had made little difference to him, because for several years after, he had continued to abuse and harass me and would not allow me to live my life in peace. His actions and abusive patterns of behaviours caused me to be more concerned about how he would react, especially knowing that he would not accept that we were separated and no longer in a relationship with each other.

Severing that tie completely became so hard for me to do at times and I was forever questioning why? Why me? What had I done to deserve such depths of sadness and abuse? I just could not understand the reasons why. When you are experiencing and living within an abusive situation, it is so hard to gain a clear perspective.

Over the following years I had found it quite hard to separate from my daughter's dad and I constantly questioned myself if I had made the right decision in walking away from that relationship. My thoughts were stuck in wondering if I had given him a real chance at working at improving our relationship. There was six years difference between us, and I sometimes ponder if that had played a pivotal role in creating such conflicts between us.

Had my previous experiences of being in intimate and abusive relationships tainted my thoughts and patterns of behaviour in how I viewed men in general? I had to look within myself and at my actions and how they may have affected our relationship negatively.

Was he at a disadvantage because he was so young when we had created a child together? Had my eventual rejection of him made him feel unworthy and not worth fighting for?

I had no answers to those questions as I myself had not yet reached that point of recognising that I needed to start to learn how to love myself. I had no idea what love was meant to feel like.

When you are in the epicentre of experiencing domestic violence or abuse, denial can be a powerful and primitive defence mechanism as a way of coping and getting through each day.

Ten years later and the father of my daughter and I are now in a much better place as individuals and parents. We have forgiven each other for our past mistakes and are currently proactively and responsibly working on re-building our relationship and our co-parenting skills.

Back then it had felt as if I were mourning for the loss of what should have been considered as my ideal family unit of mutual care, nurturing, respect, peace, support and love. Staying within an intimate relationship with a toxic person or circumstances is potentially harmful to your emotional, mental and physical health and may negatively affect your child or children, also. The bottom line is to safely remove yourself from the abusive relationship or situation. Domestic violence is such a personal issue and in most cases is kept quiet as a shameful secret.

Abuse wears you down mentally and emotionally and you become co-dependent and too frightened to trust your thoughts and any belief in yourself diminishes rapidly. At times you feel you have little choice but to remain silent and or refuse to acknowledge the abuse of your being, in a desperate attempt to maintain what feels at the time like a much-needed relationship with your abuser.

Love was not something that I had truly witnessed whilst growing up. It had not been until I was about nineteen that I had seen 'love' for the first time, and it had not been on the television either. My ex-boyfriend's family were expressive in embracing each other quite openly and naturally, hugging one another and verbally expressing their love for each other, also. That type of behaviour had not been normal for me during my childhood or early adult years. I had only the referencing of having grown up in a dysfunctional family atmosphere to compare with and realised then that the environment of conflict and abuse I had known was in fact, not normal.

The lack of witnessing or even feeling that kind of love within the home as I grew up, meant that I had no idea of how to show it either and I do believe that lack of being free and capable of expressing myself in that way affected me deeply as I grew up so angry, feeling as if the whole world was against me. Most of the time I had this rage inside me that I could not always contain or even fully understand. I would take my frustrations out on those nearest and dearest to me and did not have the capacity or emotional maturity to comprehend why they then no longer wanted to be around me. I had no idea that my repressed childhood trauma would leave me having uncontrollable mood swings, anxiety, confusion and an intense physical hurt that felt as if it originated from the very core of my being. Intermittent explosive disorder is a lesser-known mental disorder that shows up as explosive episodes of unwarranted anger. Many refer to it as *'flying into a rage for no reason'*. Sometimes even whilst I was involuntarily releasing my rage onto others, a part of me had known that my irrational behaviour was disproportionate to the situation that had triggered it in the first place.

I had felt hard done by, misunderstood and rejected.

The continuation of the abusive situations started to affect all areas of my life, my friendships with other people, my work, my family. I grew so angry about life in general. I felt constantly frustrated and acted out as if I had the burden of carrying around the biggest chip on my heavy shoulders. I was convinced that the whole world was out to destroy me and that my lack of happiness was everyone else's fault and not mine.

It must have been around three years ago that I found myself feeling like I was in a desperately low place in my life. I was tired of allowing myself to be pulled into the same types of situations that left me feeling unworthy and unloved. I was tired of falling out with my family and those closest to me. There seemed no hope of me ever finding love and peace and I was still having to deal with the negative consequences of my daughter's father not leaving me alone. He would not or could not move on with his own life, which in turn meant that he made it almost impossible for me to move forwards in my life. I had felt harassed.

In all honesty, there were times when I just did not want to be here anymore!

There is a misconception that suicidal thoughts and suicide is a selfish act, but I would argue that it is the desperate action of someone who is in intense and hopeless pain. There is a vast difference between feeling sad and feeling hopelessly depressed. Depression leaves you feeling numb. You feel like a robot devoid of all human emotions. There is a depth of hollowness that nothing can possibly fill and make whole again. In moving forward, it would be great if we all stopped saying that someone *committed* suicide. Crimes are committed, rapes and murders are committed. Not suicide. It would be preferential and more understanding to say that someone *died by suicide*. None of us has the right to attach shame and blame to a person's desperation and hopelessness.

I was fed up having to feel like everything in my life had to be a battle. There were days and nights where it felt as if I had to fight to breathe, I was that exhausted emotionally and mentally. To me, my emotions often felt so intense, extreme and inappropriate but I could not control them as I was always feeling so sad and zombie-like, as if I were living in a dream, or more accurately, in a never-ending nightmare. For a long period of time, I could not fathom what it felt like to feel happy. My life had felt too complicated and complex in purely negative ways.

Having lived through domestic violence as a child and then being a victim to it myself as an adult, it was bound to have a detrimental and lasting impact on my mental health. There were times where I would deliberately self-sabotage and have suicidal thoughts. The consistent decline in my mental health meant that I constantly felt disassociated and detached from other people and uneasy and uncomfortable around others.

It had become clear to me that my experiences had been one of the main reasons why I had always found it so difficult to attract and maintain healthy intimate relationships. I had been fearful of being humiliated, yelled at and threatened by any partner I was involved with. Abusers will slap you around and then turn around and blame you, the victim, for their aggressive actions.

I have since discovered that women between the ages of 18-24 are the most typically abused by an intimate partner. Domestic victimisation is also correlated with a higher rate of depression and suicidal thoughts and tendencies.

As I lay there one night, contemplating and struggling to work out what I needed and wanted and if I even had the energy or motivation to do anything to resolve my circumstances for the better, I decided that I would create a private group on the social media platform, Facebook, so that I could build and offer a safe space for other women like me who must be feeling they had nowhere to go where they could speak freely without the fear of being judged for expressing their innermost feelings. It was something that I had felt was lacking in my life, particularly during those moments where everything around me felt hopeless and empty. In my despair I often felt others were being judgemental towards me and were more interested in telling me how they would feel instead of listening to how I was feeling.

With those thoughts swirling around in my head, I created the Facebook group which is called LUV – Listen, Uplift, Vent CIC.

My LUV group is mainly about empowering, educating and elevating through self-love. It is a safe space for women to come and share, knowing that they will be listened to and heard. Statistics show that the overwhelming world-wide burden of intimate partner or ex-partner violence is endured by women. That is not to say that women cannot also be aggressive and violent towards men, usually in self-defence, but the most common perpetrators of violence against women are men who are spouses, ex-partners or life-partners.

At the time that I created my group I was also attending various programmes that helped me to look within myself so that I could better understand who I was and wanted to be and to get more understanding into why I was the way I was, back then. I had no previous comprehension of how my past traumas and childhood had affected me and had taken such a huge toll on my mental health. My exploring and learning taught me why I was so defensive, hurt, frustrated and full of rage. I also learnt how to recognise how my unspoken feelings were showing up in ways that only hurt me and those I loved. I was constantly taking out my anger on others. I had little or no knowledge of how to deal with anything that happened to me. Instead of releasing it, I was holding on tight to everything negative and detrimental to my wellbeing. I was too busy looking externally for validation of my self-worth and clinging on to all the negative energies and anger around and within me. People do not fake depression, but I was so good at pretending that I was ok. I did not feel accepted by others as I felt no matter what I did it was always amplified, and I would always be cut off like I wasn't worthy. People around me would get treated worse and be quick to forgive others but I never received that same love.

There were times when I felt judged and belittled for trying to express how I truly felt inside. Those of us who have suffered abuse, mistreatments and domestic violence or abuse, are often told to snap out of the resultative depression we suffered from. That is so wrong as any mental health issue is not something that you can snap out of so easily. Depression is a chemical imbalance of the brain and to be told that you have nothing to be depressed about is in fact detrimental and trivialising the person and how they feel. Those times when I would spend days in bed, were days where I would be struggling mentally. I had no clarity of thoughts and my brain felt hazy and foggy.

In time, I learnt how to stop and pause. How to give myself permission to feel what I was feeling and then to decide how best to find a solution to that problem or issue, without coming across as so combative.

I started my LUV group in 2017 and now I am the CEO of a female empowerment organisation, helping other women to understand that true self-LUV is the best love! Our programmes are designed by women with lived experiences, to improve others self-confidence, mindsets, resilience and mental wellbeing. We provide techniques to support self-development, utilising professionals within those specific fields. We cover topics such as inner child healing, fitness and exercise, nutrition and its effects on wellbeing, mindfulness and meditation.

For me, it is about understanding that being abused is not your fault and knowing that personal growth is a continual process. Changing your mindset really can change your life and it has helped me to stop acting like or being defined as a victim. I remind myself every day to focus on all the positive and good things that I have done and achieved in life and that my self-judgement will not and does not have to serve or please everybody else. Compassion and forgiveness are key elements in my continued personal, mental and emotional growth

as a human being. I try to remember not to judge my past mistakes and experiences too harshly.

They were part of my life learning experiences and in forgiving myself and others I can move forwards in a positive and evolving way. It is so important to get others to understand that they are not in their traumatic crisis alone. Sometimes all they need to hear is for someone to tell them that they believe them, that they deserve better and to ask what they can do to help them.

LUV has been instrumental in helping me to be in a position where I can help other women to change their lives around and develop better understanding of my relationships with those dear to me. Me and my sister have always been close, but we also have butted heads many times over the years. What I love about us is that no matter what happens we can come back from it. My sister is my best friend. My mom is my ride or die, even when I felt that she did not like me, she had my back. During my years of going through abuse my mom was always my first person to call. I couldn't have got through what I have without her. I do not want my daughter to feel my pain of not feeling like she was enough. I tell my daughter every day I love her, I tell her how amazing she is, smart, beautiful. I ensure she is surrounded by family who love her dearly.

I now know that I have a divine purpose and mission in life, which includes uplifting and re-empowering others. It is important that as women with lived experiences, we do not just point people in the right direction but that we also walk with them. Our aim is to educate, empower and engage women and the community at large.

Now, I am no longer stuck in asking, why me!

MAXINE PALMER-HUNTER

My name is Maxine Palmer-Hunter, and I am an award-winning Educator and Health and Social Care Advocate. I have dedicated the last twenty-four years of my professional life towards implementing the elimination of injustice, inequality and discrimination against young people, men and women. I am also a trained L3 Counsellor and Mental Health Practitioner. In having to overcome various life challenges and adversities, I have had to learn how to mentally and emotionally peel away the protective mask I have worn in the past to safeguard my heart and maintain my sanity. Having survived numerous tragedies and incidents of varying abuse, I now stand courageous in my inner strength, resilience and honest transparency with the intention of offering insight, re-empowerment, support, encouragement and hope to others so they too will be able to overcome their personal traumas and heal from their past and/or present sufferings.

My love of learning directly resulted in the formation of my company RAISE Education and Training, which offers face to face and online courses including workshops to facilitate professional, personal and academic development for all whilst raising awareness, knowledge and self-confidence and enabling inspiration and offering ways to regain self-empowerment.

I am passionate about highlighting awareness around the rights of young people, men, women and children and as an advocate I have worked tirelessly in proximity with those displaying diverse and complex needs that are inclusive of: self-harming, Asperger Syndrome (AS), Autism, ADHD, FASD, drug and alcohol abuse, sexual exploitation and abuse, multiple personality disorder, mental ill health (such as Bipolar, Schizophrenia, depression and anxiety).

As the Founder of B.R.A.V.E. I offer support and encouragement to empower individuals and their families to overcome challenges and crisis resulting from sexual violence, trauma, emotional and physical abuse by way of a holistic cycle of recovery to wellness. In doing this my aim is to continue to raise awareness for the need to remove the stigma associated with mental illness.

I have had my written works published in the best-selling anthologies, 'Pain To Purpose', 'The New Woman' and 'The Book Of Inspiration For Women By Women'. I have also written a scene for a play called 'The Misogyny Trials', in collaboration with Shakti Women.

I have formed my own publishing company called Analia Publishing and my forthcoming trilogies of memoirs and self-help guidebooks will offer readers inspirational affirmations to be the best they can be as they are given the choice to find and develop their voices and my experiences may help someone and give them hope.

I have received awards and accolades for my work professionally and personally. They are inclusive of Outstanding Foster Care of the Year (2015), Foster Talk Pearl of Great Price and Woman of Power and Influence (Success Makers) (2015). The Motivational and Inspirational Woman Award (Hush) (2016), Teacher of the Year Award (Bexlive) (2017 and I was a finalist for the Carer of the Year Award (MBCC) (2017).

I am a contemporary modern wife, mother and grandmother bearing traditionalist values whose zest for life holds no bounds. My loves include all genres of music, reading, history, culture and travelling.

As a Surviving Queen, it is a privilege to be a part of this unique anthology.

My Surviving Queens Anthology chapter is called 'Nine Lives'.

CHAPTER 6

NINE LIVES

MAXINE PALMER-HUNTER

*'One day you will tell your story of how you overcame what you went through,
and it will be someone else's survival guide'*

— BRENE BROWN

What does it mean to me to be a survivor – is it one who remains alive after a critical event? Surviving and continuing to exist after a traumatic event and overcoming challenging situations that life throws at us all. Overcoming the obstacles that we may face from birth and into adulthood. To each of us, our experiences are unique and just as important as the next person's lived experiences.

I have been through many survival situations during my life which required resilience and involved a myriad of emotions in order to just get through.

I feel blessed that I have been given this opportunity to be an integral part of this unique Surviving Queens Anthology book so that I can finally have that safe space in which to highlight and explore specifically nine of the survival situations that I have personally had to go through. This is my chance to authentically acknowledge and analyse how I overcame those circumstances and how, more importantly, despite them having such a negative effect on my life and wellbeing, I have emerged triumphant after having my faith and self-confidence shaken and the impact it had on my physical, spiritual, mental and emotional wellbeing.

We some of us go through life experiencing so many negative and toxic things and people and because so many of us are taught to just get on with it, we do not realise how we are adversely affected until years later when the unhealed trauma manifests itself in so many unexpected ways, all to the detriment of our external and internal being.

Survival One involves my becoming a teenager inclusive of all the stereotypical emotions that accompanies those teen years and which nobody takes the time to explain to you. As a teenager, it's par for the course that you become so engrossed with your own thoughts, feeling lonely, alone, isolated and fearful of the unknown. Even with people around you, there is still that sense of detachment felt inside that is caused by your own emotive state of being and or the situations you find yourself hooked into.

As a teenager I recall silently crying out for someone to hear me, to listen to how alone I felt. There had been such a depth of anxiety felt from within me that I used to pray for someone to just take a minute to look deep into my eyes and to see my pain.

The hurt and secrecy of the abuse I had suffered was real and was beginning to feel more like an infected open wound that kept festering, one that refused to heal.

It was during moments like those that I had needed my mum and dad the most. I realised as I grew older that they each had their own personal issues to confront and deal with. Emotionally cold, it had always been difficult for them to express any emotional expressions or feelings either to each other or to their children. Mum had been desperately struggling to keep her family together whilst dad was hell-bent on running away from the commitments and responsibilities of having to care for a wife and children.

I had slowly de-graduated from being a consistent A-star student in school, whom the teachers had adored. Oh yes! I had been the 'teachers' pet', their favourite pupil. When I look back on my life, I think perhaps they may have seen the unspoken sadness within me reflected through my eyes and demeanour and had decided to take me under their wings, so to speak, to extend to me their professional care and nurturing. Because of them I had felt loved and had adored school. Before long, school had become my institutional outlet for escapism and for a few hours, at least, I was able to feel a sense of normality. Unbeknownst to me, my innate vulnerability had been evident for others to see. I had been quiet, withdrawn and filled with constant anxiety and a sense of dread.

The consistent abuse, bullying and harassment had eaten away at my soul. Having to pretend that I was fine had sapped and drained away my mental, physical and emotional energies. I had sought for solace in my books and with music and for a brief time, immersing myself into those activities had been my salvation.

I have heard many people say that being the middle child often means that they are overlooked or emotionally forgotten within the family dynamics, and so it had been the case with me. It had not helped that my siblings were displaying various unfavourable or harmful behaviours that not only affected them but the whole family, too.

I had been the quiet, discreet and humble child whose personality, characteristics and intelligence were illustrated through my reading abilities and my willingness to learn and study. I was happy to apply myself with learning new hobbies, like Aikido, attending dancing school, playing the guitar and the recorder and naturally exhibiting my attributes of caring for others.

Most of the time I had felt as if I were living in two completely different worlds and had to keep reminding myself to not let my mask fall to reveal my true feelings. I had so wanted to pretend that my life was just like the perfect and idyllic lives of those fictitious families portrayed and broadcasted through the television sets and resembling the characters I read about in books written by Enid Blyton and Margaret Blume.

One night, after being intimidated and harassed by a local lad in front of other people, where he had loudly made references to the size of my breasts and what he would like to do to me, I had felt the rising heat of acute humiliation and embarrassment. It had only served to remind me of the weighty burden of secret shame that I carried with me for having my boyfriend unceremoniously dump me for not agreeing to be intimate with him and not being able to stay out late. The shame of it had left me feeling like I was drowning in having failed to be who he wanted me to be. He had soon moved on to pastures new.

The internal turmoil I felt had been enhanced in knowing that even though I may have looked physically capable of passing for a sixteen-year-old, emotionally I had been a mess. I could feel the pressure of having to keep up with my schooling and all the unfair expectations placed on me, as it bubbled and quietly and forcefully built up inside me. I could sense that my mental health was beginning to seriously decline.

There had been such a rage inside of me, an anger that I could not possibly explain. My suppressed and fearfully silent anger manifested in ways that I disliked but could not prevent. I became sullen, agitated, feisty and defensive to those who dared to question me. Almost overnight, it seemed, my sweet and demure personality had drastically altered and then completely vanished. I felt like a raging bull in a China shop filled with delicate displays of fragile ornaments, just waiting to be crushed to pieces by the volcanic rage inside of me.

I learnt how to build and maintain a defensive wall around me, thinking it would protect me from being hurt by others but who was I kidding? It had only served to be temporary at best and fundamentally useless as it was still being chipped away repeatedly for many years to follow.

We all have our limits that we can bear, and my limit had come to an end the day that I had decided that I could not take any more and wanted to be free from everyone and everything. The bottomless depths of pain and hurt that I was feeling was just too much to bear and I hated how I had been unjustly forced into enduring situations that I had not asked to be involved in or a part of.

That evening I had taken a handful of paracetamols whilst in my bedroom. I recall feeling sleepy but thinking to myself, *"Wait a minute, I am still awake"*. I had felt sick and totally confused. And nobody had come to find me, to call out my name, to instruct me to come for my dinner. There had been nobody there to show that they cared *"See, you are a failure. You could not even properly kill yourself."* Nobody at all had cared enough! This attempt at trying to take my own life would be my secret. Who would care anyways? My feelings of being lost and alone did not matter! As the evening grew darker, my self-worth had diminished to nothingness. The following day I had replaced the 'mask of being happy' securely on my face and had reluctantly accepted that my particularly harrowing suicidal attempt was not meant to be.

Survival Two is paramount to when I became pregnant. It had been the height of summer and my pregnancy had not been an easy one. I was living in physical and emotional chaos, constantly laden down with anxiety, exhaustion and feeling ill. The nausea had only dissipated once I had reached the fourth month of pregnancy and lasted until the seventh month. I recall how I had craved McDonald's French fries and ice. I could not tolerate the smell of fish but had loved the smell of cigars, petrol and the Johnson's baby products.

During my eighth and ninth months, my body had suddenly and rapidly swollen. My ankles ached and my stomach was so huge that I could only sleep comfortably in one position. My blood pressure soared dangerously high. I could barely walk because the baby was resting heavily on my pelvis bone. It had been so painful and difficult to bear, at times.

At thirty-six weeks into my pregnancy, I had been admitted into the hospital after being diagnosed with pre-eclampsia, a condition that can lead to serious complications for both mothers and babies if it is not correctly monitored and treated. I was placed on bed rest and had felt scared for mine and my baby's lives.

Every day I had sung to my unborn son, rubbing and soothingly caressing my stomach to reassure him, to let him know that I his mother had his back, and to ease my loneliness and the pervasive sense of isolation I felt. I had to endure laying there immobile as I watched the other mothers on the ward safely deliver and take home their babies. I had felt hopeless waiting for it to be my turn.

My recovery from the various symptoms associated with having pre-eclampsia had been slow so the doctors had decided to induce me at thirty-eight weeks. *"I am so excited to finally meet my child"*, I remember thinking to myself.

I had been given pessaries which had led to me being in labour for three days. On day three of my long labour, surrounded by several staff members of the medical team looking after me and my baby, it had been declared that I was still only two centimetres dilated, despite having felt the intensity and forcefulness of the Braxton Hicks contractions.

I had been instructed to push but no matter how hard I tried, that baby was not budging. I remember my mum and my best friend being present in the room with me, with my dad, uncle and grandmother having passed through earlier with plates of food for me. Despite my feeling very hungry, I just could not eat anything.

With my swollen and painful legs fastened into the stirrups and my buttocks positioned to the edge of the bed, I had no time to feel any embarrassment as the additional pains had overtaken that sensation some time ago.

Seventeen long hours later, I was still only six centimetres dilated. The administration of the epidural had left me feeling paralysed from the waist down and both mine and the baby's heart rates were dropping. I had felt too weak to push to the point where they had decided to perform an emergency Caesarean Section to prevent the possibility of losing both of us. *"We are dying"*. That fleeting thought had flashed through my tired mind. The Anaesthetist had inserted a needle into my arm whilst asking me general questions in trying to distract me as they performed the operation to remove the baby from my reluctant womb.

In no time at all, I had awoken to see my mum standing by the side of my hospital bed, excitedly informing me, *"It's a boy!"*. She had made me laugh by telling me that in my delirious state the first words that I had uttered was to enquire if he was pretty.

My maternal instincts and curiosity meant that I could not wait to see and meet him. My baby was a beautiful, bonny baby boy who looked like a little Sumo wrestler, weighing in at 10.5lbs. No wonder I had not been able to push him out naturally.

I was just thankful that we were both ok, despite the need for me to remain in the hospital to further recover from excessive blood loss which had required a transfusion. I had also had to cope with healing and recovering from pre-eclampsia, sepsis and the trauma of giving birth to such a big baby. It had not been easy, but we were alive.

I had been determined to fully enjoy the arrival of my precious bundle of joy even whilst I was still attached to the intravenous drip machine. Initially, my baby had refused to suckle my breast milk and having him pulling on my stitches as he tried to suck away, had not been an ideal start to motherhood. His arrival had been frighteningly dramatic, but he and I had both survived to tell the tale of that lived experience and the trauma of what happened had stayed with me for years and had kept me bound by the spirit of fear that it would happen again.

Survival Three occurred during the school holidays on a lovely summer's day. The sun had been shining and it had felt scorching hot, with the children playing outside in their droves. I could hear the ice-cream van chiming further up the road and the loud, gleeful splashing of water as green lawns were being diligently mowed and beautified.

I remember on that day my ankles had been swollen and achy, but I had simply put it down to being overweight plus the heat of the day and had not given it much more thought or attention.

My friend had asked me to join her and her son in going to Drayton Manor theme park with my own son. I had not hesitated in agreeing, seeing as it was such a lovely, warm day. We had been fully engrossed in enjoying having so much fun and were in our element of laughing and trying out the different theme rides. My ankle had still been throbbing, but I had not wanted to spoil the fun for the others, so I had carried on regardless of the discomfort that I was feeling. We had eaten ice-creams, had lunch and sipped bottles of cold water to keep hydrated.

As the day progressed, the throbbing in my ankle had radiated into a searing pain that I could now feel in my leg. I was not sure what was happening and despite my friend's obvious concern, I had stubbornly forged ahead, determined not to sour the day. I had agreed to resting my leg for a short while and we climbed onto the cable cars where I could sit down for a spell. Even as I attempted to lift my leg to get onto the cable cars, a sharp pain had shot up my leg. Once sitting, it had felt as if somebody was placing a hot iron directly on top of my leg. My son had look worried in seeing me in such agony. I vaguely recall my friend shouting at the cable operators to bring us down quickly as something appeared to be terribly wrong with me and my leg. It had seemed to take forever for the cable car to slowly descend from us being suspended hundreds of feet in the air. Finally, we had reached the bottom of the wheel where I could painfully and tentatively climb down with the assistance of the staff there.

By this time, I had no choice but to admit to myself that something was seriously amiss. The anxiety and fear of not knowing what was wrong with me, were beginning to engulf and overwhelm me.

The kind staff there had offered to call an ambulance for me, but my friend had surmised that it would be quicker if she took me to the hospital herself. They had all helped me to limp back to where my friend had parked the car.

The thirty-minute journey towards the hospital had felt more like two hours. I had felt every bump and jerk of the car as my friend navigated her way through traffic. By then, the pain had escalated to a heightened peak that I had never experienced before.

Once we had arrived at the hospital, a wheelchair was retrieved for me to sit in. In witnessing the agony that I was clearly feeling, the medical staff had swiftly whisked me into a side cubicle. With each prod and poke my leg felt as if it were about to explode! *"Oh, it is suspected cellulitis"*, one of the doctors had casually stated. What the hell that was I had no idea. All I knew was that I needed the pain to stop immediately. They had then sent me down to have a scan taken of the leg.

"We have detected a large blood clot in your ankle and a piece of the clot has broken off and travelled up your leg and is lodged behind your upper thigh. You are a fortunate and lucky girl. One more day and it could easily have been a different story", they had informed me.

I had been admitted and kept in the hospital for two weeks, followed by six months of recovering at home from the dep vein thrombosis they had discovered on that day. But would you believe that I had then developed the same symptoms twice more after that incident? How unlucky can one person be?

The second time it had occurred was when I was thirty-five and I had just completed a vast amount of travelling, six flights in total, to different countries and states, all within a twelve-day period. I started to feel unwell and had noticed how my leg had swollen. On arriving at the hospital, that time they had discovered that a piece of the formed blood clot had broken away from inside my ankle and had travelled up into my stomach. I was treated immediately and given a large booster dosage of Warfarin, the blood thinning medication. It had hurt and had left my stomach bruised, but that had been such a small price to pay for having my life saved. It had been yet another close call for me.

The third time of suffering from a blood clot, aged thirty-nine, I had been working as the Head of the department and was in the middle of an Ofsted visit to the school. I had been busy studying and marking exam papers which had involved sitting for long periods. That familiar feeling of my ankle swelling, my chest feeling tight and my leg becoming more swollen and feeling hot had re-occurred. After the hospital had scanned my leg, they had found another clot located deep in my leg. I had been admitted as a patient and had remained there for four days and then had another six months of treatment at home to assist with my recovery and rehabilitation.

Survival Four had played itself out whilst I had been staying at a friend's house located in the countryside. I mean imagine standing in front of someone who was armed with a gun, whilst you pleaded for the other person's life, knowing that the potential shooter was out of their mind with an illogical rage that was going to be hard to diffuse. Let me take you back a little so that I can fully explain the situation. I had decided to take a short break in the countryside with a friend of mine and we had arranged to stay at the house where another friend had lived. We had been ever so grateful for their hospitality, certain that we were going to have a fabulous time there and with the chance to check out the surrounding areas.

Whilst we were there, I had noticed how my friend and the host had been outrageously flirting with each other. I had spoken to them both, asking that they stop as it was so disrespectful to the host's partner and to myself for having brought my female friend to their home. They had appeared to take note but unbeknownst to myself and the others present in the house, the blatant flirting had continued behind our backs, which I later found this out.

One evening we had all gone out for the night, including other friends and the partner. It had been a lovely, warm and fun evening spent, heavily influenced by the vast amounts of alcohol that was available and readily consumed. We had been enchanted with dancing to the music that spoke to our souls, the rhythmic beats causing our feet to tap in time to the music playing. Everyone had been in good spirits and feeling relaxed.

On arriving back to the home of our host, we had decided to retire to our beds. My friend had declared that she wanted a hot drink and the host had stated that he too was craving one. There had been something about that brief exchange that had left me feeling uneasy and even though I had been feeling so tired from drinking so much alcohol, I had made up my mind to speak to my friend, there and then.

"I do not know what is going on, but I do not feel comfortable, and I would prefer it if you did not spend time alone with him and would go to bed now, instead of staying and making that hot drink".

She had replied: "You have nothing to worry about. I am going to bed."

I had then drifted off into a deep stupor but had still been awoken by a loud noise. I had glanced over to notice that my friend was not in her bed. Hearing the noise again, a loud, piercing noise, I had leapt from my bed and ran to the lounge.

The scene that had assaulted my eyes was one that I will never forget. There in the room had been the host, his partner and my friend. The partner of the host was screaming and crying hysterically and had a gun pointed directly at my friend.

I tried desperately to work out what exactly had happened, but I could not understand the jumbled, sobbing words she was speaking. I could only guess that the host and my friend had been caught in a sexually compromised position.

Realising that I needed to be fully present within the situation unfolding before me, I had quickly sobered up and knew that I had to be the voice of reasoning.

An internal rage had boiled inside of me towards my friend for her silliness in creating this dangerous and potentially fatal situation and I had felt anger towards the host for his stupidity and lack of thought and respect for his partner. My anger had also extended to the host's partner for welding a weapon that had instilled such fear in me. I felt terrified as I stood in front of my friend, pleading for her not to be shot, begging for her life to be spared. The partner had kept on insisting that I move out of the way, but I could not do that for fear that more harm and irreparable damage would be caused. I had begged the partner to consider her future, her life and her children. I had pleaded with her to think about if it was worth it to pull the trigger. I had been so immobile with fear and felt extremely vulnerable and exposed as I had battled to bring calm and logic to a problem created by another person or persons.

If you are wondering why I had felt the need to step in front of my friend, it was because I had already felt a huge sense of guilt in having brought her there with me, to their marital home. Even though she had been partly to blame for the current situation, I had still not wished any harm to come to her. My guilt had pushed me forwards in wanting and needing to be the voice of reason.

After what felt like an eternity of time had passed, with her finger still poised over the trigger of the gun, the partner had calmed down. I had been left shaking like a leaf caught in the crossfires of a storm and I had been in shock. I could not believe what had just taken place.

I was so angry and disappointed with the misguided, foolish and disrespectful behaviours of the host and my friend and with what had occurred as a result of their selfish thoughts and behaviour.

Staring directly into the barrel of a loaded gun and not knowing if the adrenalin driving the irrational thinking of the person holding that gun, would ultimately take over and result in bloodshed, that had been extremely terrifying to me. Even now I still shudder to think of that gun being pointed at me and of what *could* have happened.

Survival Five is an illustration of how I survived being homeless.

"How have I ended up in this position with nowhere to live?" was a question I asked myself many times.

Having fled from a life dominated by domestic violence with only the one suitcase grasped firmly in my hand, everything had felt uncertain and unhinged.

A chance encounter with a stranger had given me courage and a way out to escape from that disruptive and abusive environment, and for that I will always be grateful. She had offered me the use of her sofa in her one-bedroom flat. It had not been ideal because she had already taken in another homeless woman who also had a new-born baby with her. The place was crowded but what choice did I have other than to gratefully accept her offer of respite and solace, far removed from being trapped in an abusive relationship. I had nowhere else to go and I had been too embarrassed to return home to my family's house.

Staying in the overcrowded accommodation had not been peaceful and the added fear of being kicked out was always there in the recesses of my mind. I had not known these people personally and our cultural differences had quickly become all too apparent. I had spent my days whilst living there working and aimlessly walking the streets until it had been time to consider going to bed to sleep. I had tried to limit my time spent around them to give them and myself space.

Something had still not felt right though and soon that dreaded feeling had manifested and reared its ugly head. My abuser had somehow found out where I was staying with my saviour and had charmed her with his narcissistic personality and now, she had resolved to plotting with him against me. I had felt bereft and devastated. I again had to resort to running away and found myself homeless again.

This time I had met a work mate who had recently started working at my place of work and having heard of my plight, she had invited me to stay with her and her sister.

Now would you believe my run of bad luck! Her sister became jealous of me and the relationship I had with her sister and soon enough, the sisterly relationship between the two of them had become fractured and fraught with tension. On top of that, the sister was bringing unsavoury characters around the house and encouraging and coercing them into harassing and intimidating me. The whole situation had become too messy, and I had ended up having to call my family members to help me. I had still felt too ashamed to let them know that I was homeless and was living from pay cheque to pay cheque. I had been physically abused and was on the verge of suffering a nervous and mental breakdown.

That night I had been moved to a house by someone I had only known for three weeks. The area had been over-ridden with addicts, drug dealers and prostitutes. My helping saviour had been lovely, but it soon transpired that she loved taking drugs too. Every night there had been the frightening sounds of shootings or beatings and it was deemed a no-go zone for anyone who did not live in the area. I was not allowed to venture out on my own and my friend and her partner would accompany me everywhere.

I had cried myself to sleep every night, wondering how I would survive living there and everything else that I had already suffered thus far. Sleep had abandoned me, and I had lain awake all night listening out for sounds that the door would be kicked in at any moment or for the constant piercing sounds of the sirens of the blue flashing lights of police cars and ambulances.

I had previously considered myself to be somewhat streetwise but now I was not so sure of myself. I had felt dragged into and catapulted into a world that was causing me to feel and quickly dampen down all sorts of emotions. It was a case of do I stay, or do I live on the streets?

When the house next door was raided by a swarm of armed police, I had known that it would only be a matter of time before the house I resided in would be next. So, with my one suitcase, I had taken to the streets once again, wandering the lonely streets aimlessly, contemplating where I could possibly sleep that night. Again, an individual had come to my rescue. Her one-bedroom apartment had been cramped but she had offered me the sofa and the others had shared the bed.

It had soon become apparent that she and the other woman were a couple. It had been the first time that I had been in proximity to someone involved in a same sex relationship. It had been fun living with them and going to their social scenes of choice and meeting their friends, including one friend who later became a well-known celebrity. Throughout my time spent with them, not once was there any hint of a sexual pass being made my way as they knew and respected that their lifestyle was not my thing.

The stress of not having a proper home to call my own was unreal and sometimes unbearable. I had been surrounded by people but had felt so alone. It had proven difficult to allow myself to let people in, to become close to me, because of the mistrust and paranoid thoughts that were forever swirling around in my head. Everybody appeared to be nice in the beginning but once you let them into your space, they would then show you who they really were.

My new mate had broken up with her lover and she had sunk into a deep depression. She had eventually given up her flat so that she could move back in with her parents. I could not afford to rent anywhere on my own and plus I was now pregnant and expecting a child. *Homeless, pregnant, penniless and broken.* Could things get any worse for me? I was still too embarrassed to inform my family of my dire situation. My life had felt too disorientated and upside down. I had pawned my jewellery so that I could buy a ticket to move to another city.

A childhood friend of mine had invited me to come and stay with her and her mum. At last, I had felt as if I had a nice home and family to go and stay with for a while, but that desired wish had been short lived. It had transpired that my friend had not sought permission from her mum if I could stay and her mum was already feeling the pressure and stress of having to work two jobs and to maintain her home. Their relationship was already fraught with tension, and I was surely another burden to them. I was poorly with the ongoing pregnancy, working but tired all the time and struggling physically, mentally and emotionally to understand the vastness of the chaos that was my life and existence.

I had still felt abandoned, even though the father of my baby had wanted us to make a life together but that had been impossible. I was scared and even more so after the mum had asked me to leave. Her daughter had been so sad and had pleaded with her mum to allow me to stay. I was mindful of how enormously stressed the mum was and I had so little fight left in me to plead with her, myself.

The only slight glimmer of hope that appeared was when after I had reached out to a relative, they had invited me to come and stay with them.

I had not mentioned that I was due to have a child. I had continued working. In no time at all, they had started to treat me badly, gaslighting and ostracising me, belittling me and preventing me from sharing in with their food or drink. I had cried myself to sleep and prayed earnestly to the Almighty to please save me and my unborn child from the wickedness that had been directed against me.

After spending six awful weeks in that house of horrors, I had finally called my parents, seeking refuge in their home. I had been utterly guilt-ridden and overwhelmed with shame, sadness and disappointment in myself. But I had nowhere else to live. Struggling to survive being homeless had been such a hard road to travel and to overcome.

Survival Six literally had me spinning out of control. Let me explain.

It had been a sunny day and I had just collected my son from school, and we were driving home. I had approached a junction to turn left, and the traffic lights had turned to red. I had stopped. The traffic lights had then turned to green and I was ready to pull out and to continue my journey home. I had the right of way at the traffic lights. Having positioned my vehicle, I had then moved the car forwards. Out of nowhere I had glimpsed a car hurtling towards my vehicle with another car fast approaching behind that first car. I had tried to swerve but it had been too late and the next thing that I remember is the first car crashing into us. Bang! Then immediately afterwards the second car had slammed into us. Bam! My head had jerked violently forwards, almost hitting the steering wheel. I swiftly grabbed hold of my son's trembling hands to comfort and reassure him. A third loud screeching noise meant that the second car had smashed into us again. *"What the ...! We must dead now!"* I thought in that moment of moving chaos and eerily silent stillness. I was acutely aware that the second impact had caused our car to spin out of control, like when you are at the fairground in one of those mechanical bumper cars and some stranger hurtles towards you with the intention of getting your bumper car to spin around and around until you can regain control. Trapped in my vehicle, I had one clammy hand gripping the seat in terror with my other hand holding onto my child. Even whilst trapped in the middle of trying to suppress my horror, I could see several other cars speeding towards us. *"Jesus, I beg you, please, to stop them before they too hit us!"* The persistent spinning of my car had felt like an eternity of a lifetime had passed and flashed before my eyes. Witnesses had later recalled how cars were swerving to safely pass us and how shocked they had been to see our car just spinning so scarily out of control in the middle of the busy road. Eventually the car had come to a sudden and abrupt stop by the kerbside. My son and I were in shock and aching all over our bodies. Even as I tentatively shook my head in disbelief, there had been a sharp pain felt in my head. The other drivers involved in the crash had emerged safe and unscathed. The driver of the first car had tried unsuccessfully to beat the red lights but the traffic lights I was at had already turned to green and the following second car had been unable to apply pressure to his brakes quickly enough and had ended up crashing into both cars.

Somebody had certainly been watching over us that day, otherwise how else had we survived that near fatal crash.

Survival Seven could easily have had me spiralling into a depth of darkness that would have been difficult to climb out of.

Being defrauded by a loved one certainly and unfortunately came at a price!

Imagine losing your life savings to someone whom you trusted and whom you had been offering help to on a temporary basis and with them being aware that your money was earmarked for life-changing events that I had so painstakingly worked so hard for.

I had scrimped and saved towards my plan of having IVF treatment, to buy a new car, make payments towards a business venture and to put a sizeable deposit down on a new house, a much longed for and desired larger home for my family.

Having picked myself up from the earlier traumas of my life, I had been thriving with creating a new life and lifestyle for myself. I had never wanted to be in that position to feel that vulnerable and homeless or hopeless ever again.

Through sheer hard work and resilience, things had been moving along nicely until the moment when I had been asked to help with a temporary loan to assist a loved one with a financial transaction. They had been waiting on funds from another source that had been provisionally confirmed but which would be too late in coming to help them with the transactions that were due almost immediately.

I had thought carefully about the request and had even spent time having a few meetings with them, highlighting the importance of receiving the lent money back as and when stated and mutually agreed upon. I had implicitly trusted their given word that the money would be returned to me within the month, by which time they would have received the promised funds from their other source. I had reasoned with myself that the things that I needed that money to pay for could wait another month as four weeks would not necessarily have a negative impact on my plans for that money.

Believing that I was being cautious and sensible, I had checked over and had been satisfied with all the evidence that my money would be repaid in full, and I had handed over the requested loan in three consecutive instalments.

To be honest, in hindsight, at the time that I was due to give them the last instalment, my gut instincts had been silently screaming that I should not go ahead with it, but I had chosen to ignore my inner voice and had continued to help them out financially.

Other loved ones had been strongly opposed to me lending out so much money, but I had stubbornly let it be known that it was my money to do with it as I please. I had no concrete reasons to disbelieve their promises, naively believing that they would not stoop so low as to try to deceive me.

It was only much later that I had learnt that they had indeed been paid the money from their other source, but that they had chosen to spend it instead of repaying me the loan they had so readily taken from me.

What then followed, had been a seven-year battle of trying to rectify and resolve their betrayal, physical abuse and the involvement of the police authorities. Not to mention the resulting estrangement of relationships, a decline in my mental health and the loss of my dreams.

I had no idea how or when I would ever get over such a huge betrayal of trust perpetrated by those who had professed to have love for me.

The eventual price I had paid through this crisis, had been highly costly in more ways than one, indeed.

Survival Eight had almost proved to be the death of me.

It had always been a dream of mine to travel to Hawaii, ever since I had watched those Elvis Presley movies with him frolicking and singing and dancing away in Honolulu.

When the opportunity had finally arose for me to go, I had been so ecstatically happy and had felt blessed beyond measure.

I had spent blissful days exploring the island of Omaha, sitting on Waikiki beach and watching the beautiful sunsets, reminiscing about the historical events of Pearl Harbour and meeting and becoming acquainted with the lovely people I had met on the island.

One day, my cousin and I, along with some fellow travellers, had decided to visit the Polynesian Cultural Centre, which had incorporated activities sourced from around the world, a museum, a restaurant in which to eat a meal and a show.

It had been another enjoyable day and we had agreed to have lunch whilst we watched the show. They had served up a lovely buffet style meal. I had walked up to the buffet station and had chosen to place a variety of foods onto my plate, before returning to my seat.

I do recall cutting into a piece of beef which had felt quite tough under the blade of my knife and fork, so I had proceeded to cut it into smaller pieces. My mind and attention had been focused on watching the show and I had absent-mindedly chewed the piece of beef in my mouth. The show had been glorious to watch with the parade of singers and dancers in their vibrant array of stunning costumes of various colours and there had been a comedian on stage too.

I had felt immediately when the tough piece of beef had become stuck in my airway. *"Cough, Maxine, cough!"* someone had instructed me. The meat was not budging at all. I could feel my airways and throat closing. I had jumped up from my seat, spluttering and flaring my arms in a panic. I was desperately trying to expel the words *"Help me!"* from my blocked throat but no words came forth. My companions were frantically thumping me on the back. The staff had come running out from all directions to help me and even the performers on stage had stopped performing because of the commotion my almost dying was creating. I was still gasping for much needed air as over five hundred patrons were sat with mouths agape, watching me struggling to breathe. I pointed to my throat and indicated to them that I could not breathe. I could feel all the blood draining from me as if my life were ebbing away painfully and slowly. *"I am going to die right here in Hawaii"* I had thought to myself, consumed with a disbelieving sadness. *"Please God hear me. Do not let me die like this".* That tiny piece of meat lodged tight in my oesophagus was threatening to end my life here on earth, in this foreign island.

Is that how death feels when your life feels like it is draining away? I felt weak and even in my despair I could still hear people crying and sobbing at my distressing dilemma.

Suddenly, I had felt two strong arms grasping me from behind and pressing firmly into my rib cage. The first attempt had yielded nothing, but the second attempt had caused that wretched piece of tough meat to come flying out of my open mouth!

I was still in deep shock when the paramedics had arrived. I was visibly shaken and still crying. I could not believe that I had woken up that morning in a beautiful part of the world and then hours later I had been fighting for my life, for survival.

The hero who had ultimately saved my life had been a gentleman from the United States of America, who had been a voluntary medic. He had told me later how he, like the other people who had witnessed my choking and had watched the drama unfold, had quickly realised that what my companions were trying to do was not working and that he could clearly see my life slipping away swiftly but almost like in slow motion at the same time. He had raced over to try to save my life and he had done so brilliantly.

Survival Nine had preceded my turning fifty and my serious and life-threatening brush with death, due to contracting the dreaded Covid-19 virus.

I had been so excited at turning fifty. I had grown internally in so many positive and marvellous ways and had felt that this new chapter of my life would be the one where all that happened before would now fade away in my memories and bring me peace of mind and manifest in my being blessed with the fruition of my having survived all that I had.

It had been unfortunate timing that the global pandemic that was infecting and affecting the whole world was threatening to hinder my plans. I had been dutifully and conscientiously shielding and isolating myself within the confines of my home for the previous four months and then sadly, one of my dearest friends had died. My extended period of isolation had come to a swift and abrupt end as I had attended her funeral and had then partaken in a few celebratory birthday dinner gatherings. After that, I was once again back in my home, shielding myself for another three long months.

Shortly thereafter, one day I had awoken with a sore throat and noticed a change in my body temperature. I had immediately assumed that it was due to the treatments I had undergone the day before, inclusive of some acupressure, acupuncture and reflexology treatments with a Chinese practitioner. I had put my general state of feeling slightly unwell down to the toxins being dispelled from my body as part of the process of having had those recent treatments. Over the following few days, I had then developed a headache and all my joints had begun to ache.

What followed next was a feeling of dizziness that seemed acute and sudden, but I had thought that with a few days of rest that I would soon be feeling better and that the symptoms would all pass in due course. By the third day, I was shivering, simultaneously feeling hot then cold. The heavy achiness in my joints and bones had worsened. I soon discovered that I had no sense of smell. I had considered that maybe where I had not yet received my flu jab that maybe I was suffering with a bad bout of the flu. My appointment to have the flu vaccination had been postponed for over two months due to the onset of the pandemic and the consequent shortage of available doctor appointments. I had only ever had the flu twice in my life and so I had accredited how I was feeling to having caught the flu again.

The dizziness was so bad that if I went upstairs to use the bathroom, I could not manage to return downstairs. I would need to lay down in my bed, struggling to breathe. It had felt as if my lungs were permanently filled with fluid. My sleeping pattern became erratic as I could barely breathe properly, and I was frightened of possibly dying in my sleep.

Unbeknownst to me, I was in fact dying, my insides being ravaged by the Covid-19 virus.

With each passing day, I found myself drenched in sweat. I could not eat or drink anything at all despite my feeling hungry. I was slowly but surely becoming delirious with dehydration, and it had been during that time that I had 'seen' my dad, who had in fact passed away several years prior in 2016. I also 'saw and heard' a toddler by the name of Elizabeth, calling out to me, calling me nanny and mummy simultaneously. She was playing hide and seek and kept hiding behind the television. My school mate's father, who had been murdered over forty years ago, kept appearing in front of me and I saw myself lying down in a white coffin lined with pure white satin sheets, and being pulled out of the coffin by hands belonging to a person whose face was obscure.

Other visions of mine included me looking around and seeing the sun shining, with stunning waterfalls and flowers of vibrant colours gently blowing in the breeze. There were people dressed in white, sitting together grouped in numerous clusters. Everybody there was happy and appeared relaxed. The ambience had felt so peaceful.

Suddenly I had felt unseen hands linking with mine and raised voices singing *'Ring-a-ring-a-roses, a pocket full of posies'*, and then just as suddenly the singing had stopped abruptly. *'Maxine, what are you doing here?'* As I had looked up, the perceived hearing of those voices had, I realised, belonged to two of my best friends who had passed away in 2009 and 2020. I had seen a flicker of pleasure cross their faces but that had quickly changed to an expression of annoyance. *'You have to go back'*, they had informed me. *'But you called me'*, I had replied. *'No! You need to go back. It is not your time. You have more work to do.'* I had then felt invisible hands pushing me forwards whilst someone was holding me around my waist to prevent me from going back. I looked up and saw many hands pushing me, but I could not see their faces.

I was lying in the hospital bed, struggling to breathe and dangerously dehydrated. I had been administered with oxygen and was unable to talk or walk, feeling paralysed with a growing sense of fear. It had been a very anxious and petrifying time for myself and my family, not knowing whether I would make it out of that hospital alive. All I could do was to silently pray.

My family and loved ones had already been told that had I not been admitted when I had been, that one more day at home being so seriously ill would have meant that Covid-19 and pneumonia would have been the end of me and my life here on earth and I would have undoubtedly transitioned to another world or realm of the Universe, one which I had not been prepared for or ready to spiritually go to. *I Survived.*

In reading my accounts of the various examples of just nine of the survival situations that I have miraculously emerged from − multiple deep vein thrombosis, choking, suicidal attempts, Covid-19, pneumonia, car accident, facing a loaded gun, homelessness, pregnancy, childbirth and financial, physical, mental and emotional abuse and domestic violence − I pray that you will have received the messages of how hopeful life can be no matter how hopeless it may feel at times. In writing about my survival experiences, I am amazed and thankful that I am here to speak about and to share my stories of a life lived. Each example shared here has brought forth a range of emotions for me, inclusive of sadness, anger, bitterness, anxiety, feeling low, a sense of loss, shock, uncertainty, numbness, disbelief and amazement. The fundamental emotion that combines and binds all these emotions, is the one of *fear*.

Fear had initially bound me, filling me with anxiety but it has also led to me to becoming stronger within. Has that fear just always been the mask I wore to hide my self-doubts and low self-esteem?

I started my journey into revisiting those *Nine Lives* experiences, feeling scared of the unknown but I found that as I grew wiser in my understanding of each one, my so-called fears became more susceptible to rational thoughts and processes of thinking with clarity. I learnt better coping strategies to deal with whatever I was experiencing. Being a survivor does not mean that all that you experience is not to be viewed as valuable and important lessons to be learnt, but it does serve its purpose in helping you to understand and appreciate how much you have grown and how far you have come.

I had not allowed or given myself permission to heal from the many traumas that I had encountered, suffered and overcome in life, which in turn had left me feeling tormented for many years and at times, with the additional baggage of having self-destructive thoughts and behaviours. Those patterns of behaviour had only proven to be detrimental to my wellbeing. I had systematically coped by masking my hidden feelings and allowing my vulnerable self to be constantly hidden. It was not until I was in my late forties that I had felt ready and able to take stock and reflect upon on all that I had been through.

My life had been shaped by each situation that I had suffered, each one leaving a toxic residue that had only been chipping away at my inner core of self-worth until such time that I knew I had to finally deal with it all. After a moment or two of self-pity, I had learnt how to forgive myself and others and I had meditated my way to wellness. Affirming daily the reasons for my still being here and of being worthy of that, has been invaluable to me and my inner healing process.

I unreservedly give thanks and my eternal gratitude to the Almighty for cradling me in His loving arms and for my guardian angels who continue to watch over me.

One thing that we must never forget as survivors, and one which I apply daily in my life, is to always remember to focus on how far we have come and risen from the ashes and depths of darkness of a life once experienced and lived.

I have overcome so many things and not just circumstances directly attacking me. I have healed from situations that were meant to bring me to my death. There have been many times that I have felt that I could not possibly go on for much longer. Each time I raised myself again, I grew internally and spiritually stronger to face another day.

You too will experience that euphoria of not giving up and knowing that you have it in you to face one more day.

'Where there is no struggle, there is no strength' – Oprah Winfrey. I am so proud and blessed to be a survivor and a Surviving Queen.

ANCHILA KAMALA

My name is Anchila Kamala, and I am a single mother with one son.

I like to laugh a lot and I am always determined to be and feel happy, no matter what. My friends love that about me because they say I make them feel happy also and that is what I like.

I love to travel and meet new people. Travelling brings about a love for researching, which I really like doing.

I am the type of woman who knows how to love with the whole of my heart, but in saying that, I would still rather be alone than with the wrong kind of people. Those who are loved by me consider themselves to be fortunate, but do not ever take advantage of my love, generosity and kindness because once you have broken that trust I place in you, I will quite comfortably walk away as I detest lies. I pride myself on being an honest person.

I am a System Analyst by profession. When I graduated from University, I had the opportunity to analyse a computer system at the Global Agency Company. They were using Excel for their accounting activities and purposes. I had the task of analysing it and then proposed a database system for them. I worked with Programmers to create a database system and the completed project was extremely successful. One of the main issues was to resolve the problem encountered so that the business owners could then see the business status at any time, especially the financial statements. In applying my accounting skills, I had helped to make that a possibility.

I live in Rwamishenye Bukoba Kagera in Tanzania.

It is a privilege to have been included in this wonderful and inspiring Surviving Queens Anthology book.

I wanted to share my story to show others that anything that you put your mind towards achieving, is possible.

My chapter is called 'My Life'.

CHAPTER 7

MY LIFE

ANCHILA KAMALA

My name is Anchila Kamala, and I was born thirty-four years ago at Kashasha Village, Misenyi District, in the Kagera region of Tanzania, Africa.

The day I was born, my mother did not make it to the hospital, so she had delivered me right there in the banana farm, close to the hospital but without a doctor being present. I had arrived looking healthy and without any obvious complications.

As a young baby I kept getting sick all the time, so I had truly been my mom's little baby and she had made sure that I was with her all the time, even taking me with her whenever she had to travel.

She had taught me how to cook and clean efficiently and diligently.

I was only fourteen years old when my mother died. I had cried a lot and felt extremely sad, not knowing how I would live without her. I had missed her so much, but my dad had given me hope and although he had not physically been by my side during that tragic time, he had at least ensured that he was with us on the weekends. He had been working as a Civil Engineer in the town. He was a very responsible man, working hard to make sure that we had everything that we needed.

Six short months after my mother had died, my dad had also passed away.

Losing a parent or parents at such a young age is devastating. It is a loss that leaves you drowning in pain and if you are not careful, can have you doubting the meaning of life and focusing on the things you have missed out on and could have had if your mother or father or both, were still there prior to my parents passing away, I and my family had been extremely happy. Our parents provided well for us all and we had everything that we needed. After my parents had died, I had felt a shift in completing my chores around the house as it suddenly felt more of a responsibility than a pleasure, as before. I had lost that feeling of happiness living in the village because I no longer had the time or freedom to play like all the other children of my age group did. Feeling somewhat sad and disheartened I had started to fail in my exams at school.

It had not been easy for me to overcome everything that I was going through at that time, but I had learnt how to appreciate my life and the people in it, and I had grown to be increasingly happier after some time.

My parents had been victims of the HIV/AIDS virus. My mother had passed away due to kidney failure and my father died of complications related to diabetes.

My older brothers and sisters were grown up, some attending colleges and the others were away working in the town, so therefore it had only been me and my younger brother who had remained at home in the village.

Aged fourteen I had become the head of the household! Even being so young I still had to ensure that my younger brother and I were okay and thanks to how my mother had taught me to cook and clean house, I was able to prepare and cook our meals, do the dishes, wash our clothes and maintain the cleanliness of our home. I had even won a Cleanliness Award at school during my grade seven graduation.

There was an organisation called Partage, whose goals were to help orphans. They had registered us with them and had helped to pay for our school fees once I had joined the secondary school. The organisation ensured that we were provided with our basic needs and that we had access to a good foundation of education. They recognised that as orphans and vulnerable children that we needed to preserve our dignity and equality with our peers at school.

My journey to the secondary school involved my having to walk ten kilometres every day to and from school and I had made that journey for two years. After two years, I was then transferred to the boarding school which was called The Rugambwa Secondary School. The Partage organisation had continued to offer me assistance, giving me the opportunity to learn about electronics at their workshops and they were paying me an allowance. I had determinedly saved my allowance for three whole years and had used my savings to attend college to study for my certificate in computer science at the Ruaha University College, where I had achieved a Distinction before joining the Degree in Computer Science course with the help of a Government scholarship.

After completing my studies at college in 2012, I had tried my best to secure a job, but I had not succeeded in doing so. In 2013, I joined a company as a Project Manager. The company dealt with land development, and they would buy under-developed land, survey it and then sell those plots in the city of Dar es Salaam. I was being paid for selling plots of land and was working to the highest level, almost as if I were an official partner in the company.

At the end of 2014, my boss had become extremely ill and had been suffering from depression. He had then had a massive heart attack and passed away. After my boss had died, I could not get another job for several years.

It had been in 2014 that I had dreamt that I was getting married, and I had shared the details of the dream with my family. They had been fully aware of how I would see things in my dreams and then whatever I had dreamt about would happen.

My ability to dream about things that would ultimately happen makes some people think that I am a wizard. When I was at the college, I had dreamt that one of my friends was going to be discontinued from the college. I had told her about the dream and when my dream or vision had turned out to be true, my friend had swiftly grown to hate and resent me, and our friendship had not survived the sharing of my dream with her.

In November of that same year, 2014, I had married a British man named JR. He had travelled to Tanzania specifically to look for a woman to marry and to take as his wife. I had been ready for marriage, and we had tied the knot in the traditional African way at my brother's house.

During the few days we had spent together, I had already become pregnant with his child. He had then returned to England, promising to come back in two months, but he had never come back to me, even now. We had continued communicating through telephone calls.

In 2015 my son was born, and I had named him Hotep Mugabi. I had felt so happy to be a mother and being a mother is the best and most rewarding thing that has happened to me during my whole life.

The love I have for my son is limitless and I will do anything for him to make sure that he is happy. He is healthy and awesome. He is now five years old and has never met his dad, but he does speak to him on the telephone. I am also grateful that my son was fortunate enough to have had the opportunity to meet his grandmother when she had visited us from England. Even though she had not stayed for long, we were able to go to the beach with her to spend a few precious moments of quality time there with her. We had visited a few spiritual places with her too and may God continue to bless her for creating and gifting those memories to my son, her grandson, Hotep.

Life as a single parent is not easy for me and the lack of sufficient finances makes it more difficult, at times. My son often asks many questions about his dad, and I do not have all the answers that he seeks. As his mother, I do my best to ensure that he is receiving a good education by using what little financial resources that I have.

In the year of 2018, I had finally secured a job as a Data Processor with a company called EDI Global. It had been a temporary position but at least I had work and was able to pay my bills and my son's school fees. The company always calls me when there is an opportunity for work as they only employ people when a vacancy becomes available for a project regarding data collection.

It was in 2017 that I had first been diagnosed with suffering from Bipolar Disorder and I have been admitted to the Muhimbili hospital on three separate occasions, the first being in November 2017, the second time was in the April of 2020 and the third time was in August 2020.

Bipolar Disorder used to be referred to as Manic Depression and I do suffer with having episodes of depression when I feel down and lethargic. When I am suffering through an episode of this disorder, I feel sick and do not want to get dressed, eat or sleep and I tend to use bad language and verbally abuse people but after receiving my treatment, I have no recollection of anything I may have said or done. Having Bipolar Disorder means that my moods will switch from being intensely happy and manic to extremely melancholic and sad. In between though, my moods will be normal, like any other person's daily state of emotional moods. Having Bipolar means that my uncharacteristic periods of anger and aggression may sometimes manifest itself in my feeling confused and unfocused and easily distracted. I often feel on edge and easily irritated during an episode.

Stress is a common factor in triggering a Bipolar episode. There is no 'cure' for this condition but with medications and the implementation of various coping strategies in place, I am equipped to managing my mood episodes effectively, to live a normal and functional life.

I had known about the Covid-19 virus two months before it was initially discovered or began in China. My dreams had revealed its nature and location to me. I had then reported it to the Government.

They had not taken me seriously and dismissed my warnings, until it had happened in their country. From that moment, they had then begun to take me seriously and to believe what information I had shared with them. I had proposed that we should be using traditional herbs to cure the infectious Covid-19 virus, especially using the steam method, because I had been a victim of contracting the virus but had used the herbal steam to cure myself and it had worked well. The President had supported my idea one hundred percent and had made a public announcement to the citizens of his country who had agreed to use this herbal steam method. The Government had called this treatment NYUNGU. There had been no enforced lockdown in my country of Tanzania. We had overcome the threat of Covid-19 by not allowing fear and panic to cloud our judgements and with the usage of NYUNGU steam treatments.

MIND POWER

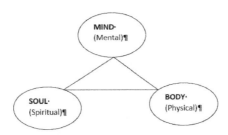

The Holistic Triangle represents the necessity of maintaining the balance of your Mind, Body and Soul. The triangle is the most structurally sound shape in the universe with each arm of the triangle being connected to and supporting the others. For the triangle to remain equilateral, the Mind, Body and Soul all need to be in optimal condition so that it is possible to anchor your ultimate potentials and happiness daily, no matter what.

If you think of your brain as hardware and your mind as the software, when the mind habitually thinks something, the brain develops neural pathways that create thought patterns and behavioural cycles. This means your mind can rewire your brain as you become conscious of your instinctual and habitual thoughts and behaviours. Becoming conscious of your thoughts and behaviours is the first step towards a healthier mind, body and soul.

Mindfulness is the practice of constantly observing, reflecting on and positively directing your thoughts. Being mindful means intentionally overriding your automatically negative thoughts with thoughts of positivity and love. In this way, you can be accountable and take responsibility for your experiences of life, to be aware of how you affect others and to use your time and energy to become the best and most productive version of yourself.

Being proactively mindful means slowing down to think before you speak. It means taking a moment to ask yourself why you are feeling something and how you should respond. Mindfulness allows you to be less reactive, anxious and defensive, so that you can live more compassionately. Our cultures train us to prioritise thinking and talking quickly and efficiently which is why many people struggle with mindfulness.

Mindfulness allows us to visualise how our thoughts become the energy that ultimately creates our lives lived. When we become aware of our thoughts and typical thought patterns, only then do we hold power over them. Mindfulness – the mental state of focusing on being intensely aware – allows us to develop self-love, self-respect and to move beyond judgement towards understanding and empathy. Where others see solid walls, you will see windows!

Mindfulness is the mental state of focusing on awareness of being present in the moments whilst calmly acknowledging and accepting your internal feelings, thoughts and bodily sensations and can be very therapeutic.

Emotions are the great enemy of logic which leads us to absorb trauma and stress – mental illness, which in turn then diverts us from choosing the better pathway to beating and overcoming the odds and any life obstacles or adversities that we may be faced with. We need to build a foundation of inner strength so that we can then uplift ourselves as well as others, mentally. Instead of aiming to mask our problems, we must face them by erasing the stigma that sill surrounds the issues of mental illness. When we spend time worrying in isolation, our health deteriorates, and our energy is depleted which then creates a great opportunity for ourselves to be attacked and invaded with negativity and toxins.

Spirituality – our souls are the undying immaterial essence of our persons that is contained within but not restricted to the body. The soul is the subconscious birthing centre for the personality and energy we manifest into the physical world. Our souls know our true purposes, that which we were incarnated on earth to learn during our individual lifetimes. Our souls are where the drive that urges us to seek out truths originates from and the source from which we grow from the physical experiences we encounter in this world. Spirituality is energy. It is an invisible and powerful force that lives within all of us and impacts us from day to day.

Our thoughts create emotions that either cleanses and strengthens our energy or they pollute and weaken it. This dichotomy is referred to as being either high vibration (Heaven) or low vibration (Hell).

Positive emotions such as love, compassion, kindness and joy, allows us to feel energised and creative whilst low emotions such as anger, sadness and jealousy leaves us feeling tired and lacking in energy.

Emotional energy is constantly generated by our bodies, heavily influenced by our thoughts, experiences and the current state of health of our minds. Energy is the language of the universe and we can learn to use it to communicate with the world we occupy around us. Whenever we have a negative experience, the vibration of our energy weakens and over time this can result in blockages. To help our energies to flow again requires an understanding of the body's Chakra system, the way in which energy affects humans and how to release negative energy.

Our thoughts move along wavelengths that are faster than sound or light. When we keep our energy vibrations high and positive, the Law of Attraction states that *like attracts like* and this will work in our favour, meaning that the energetic frequency we emit will attract a similar energy back to us. When we are inspired our consciousness expands and heightens our sensory awareness so therefore remaining inspired and motivated are crucial to our daily lives and helps us to focus on our future goals.

Thinking about the so-called *'Judgement Day'* can induce unnecessary stress but the truth is that we are the greatest judge of ourselves and possess the ability to create our own fate. There is no person standing there with a sword in their hand and held aloft towards the sky, observing or monitoring every human error so that they can immediately *'wield the sword of justice'*. Within the universe there is a general rule known as the Law of Cause and Effect. Energy is not lost in space and every action has a consequence and a counteraction, so the energy we put into what we do, sooner or later it will return to us. When making decisions, we need to think them through carefully and with perspective, especially when those decisions concern other people, also.

Justice or the physical law of energy, once sent somewhere will return with the same strength and in the opposite direction and does exist and functions, whether we believe in it or not. So, for example, if your intention is to seek revenge on another person, the only thing that will happen is that you will be causing harm to yourself. Each of us bears the responsibility of our actions to the universe and there is no such thing as any person's actions remaining unscathed from due consequences. Whatever the situation may be, try to remember that every trial is given to you along with the strength to overcome it. Also, gratitude is the highest form of prayer and the most effective way of attracting more of the good things you may desire or want.

Peace of mind can only occur if you carry peace and love in your heart, so with this in mind, it is important to try to clear any feelings of aggression, conflict, hatred or fear. If you harbour any of these negative emotions within your heart, try to approach the person or the situation with a pure heart.

Life itself is the greatest miracle so we must be thankful and take every single day we have breath, as a miracle itself. Even when we are suffering or experiencing traumas, when everything feels doomed and hopeless, there is always hope. Our difficult life experiences are one way of helping us to learn to believe in miracles and the support of angelic beings.

During those times when we may be going through difficult and unusual situations which may not necessarily be dangerous to yourself or a loved one and might just be a case of reacting spiritually or internally, it is important to be aware that we are never truly alone in this world. There are always invisible forces there to support and help us at any time. Miracles happen when they are expected and believed in, so do not allow yourself to be overwhelmed with doubts that it is possible for a miracle to manifest in your life.

Our bodies are our temples. The first meal of each day is essential for us to begin our day right.

The breakfast meal can give you energy for the morning and contributes to the overall hydration of your body. It is an important meal as it largely determines your dietary balance for the day ahead. When implemented correctly, eating a healthy breakfast can improve your concentration and performance at work and provides you with the nutrients to give you strength and endurance when partaking in any physical activities.

A good way to determine the amount of sleep you need is to go to bed at your usual times without setting the alarm. Allow yourself to wake up naturally, as and when your body is ready to. Whatever is revealed by doing this, that is your personal arena for you to assess the number of hours sleep you require. Once you have worked that out it will be easier to monitor and sense when you are going into sleep debt or sleep deprivation, wellness is all about having the tools to deal with stress, having wisdom about how your body is affected by your environment and knowing what exercises and foods are going to provide you with the optimum energy you require. Wellness is not as simple as eating healthily and regularly. It is much more than that. Wellness means taking control of your general health and happiness and that process will be different for each person.

Humans have only been sedentary (inactive) for a small part of the history of our species. Our bodies were designed to move. Without movement most people will begin to develop health issues and problems, physically and mentally. When we increase our levels of activity, the brain sends a signal to the body to use that energy that is stored in our fat cells from the unused calories we have consumed. In creating a habit of exercising, our metabolism which stimulates the process of turning fat into energy, will commence working at a much faster rate. Regular exercising contributes to a higher resting metabolic rate, allowing us to burn more fat throughout the course of the day, even when not exercising.

Most body fat is turned into energy when we are active, move around and digest our food. The body also burns a higher volume of fat if we have more muscle mass which means building muscles can help us to lose weight. Plus, the endorphins released during exercise makes us feel good, lowers our stress levels, reduces inflammation and improves our motivation to do more. When you exercise consistently and even when you keep it simple, the transformation of your body, mind, emotions and energy will be evident.

The human body needs adequate water, nutrients, movement, rest, sleep and positive relationships with others for it to function at its best. If we neglect our physical health, the body begins to deteriorate, little by little and certain systems will malfunction to alert us to the need to pay attention to how we treat ourselves. Neglecting our mental health over time can also lead to physical illness. Being physically fit without working to maintain the health of your mind and soul will never allow you to reach your optimum level of good health.

Nutrition is the fuel that allows your brain to compute and gives your body the green light to perform well. Exercise and nutrition are equally important within our daily lifestyles. Our body's systems are constantly interacting with each other, and they require nutrition and movement to function properly.

When embarking on your personal journey of self-discovery, it is not uncommon to spend time worrying about how you look. Wellness is about the energy in your body and the way you *feel,* not how you look. There are many 'beautiful' people who struggle with maintaining wellness of health. Taking care of your body boosts your energy levels and your mood and yes, it can improve your physical appearance as well. External beauty is just a side effect of wellness.

Aging is an exciting and empowering process and is nothing to fear or be ashamed of. We must learn to dismantle the myth that aging is something to be prevented as it is something to be celebrated! The habits we have today and throughout our lives affects the way in which we age. It is no secret that nutrition and exercising plays a major part in the aging process. With exercise, nutrition is delivered to our cells that aids in the skin retaining its elasticity. As we age, we lose muscle mass at a faster rate which means that our resting metabolic rate also diminishes. Including a regular routine of exercise such as yoga into our lifestyles, means we can enjoy better health and appear more youthful as we grow older. Yoga and swimming are easy on the joints too. Practicing meditation and using powerful mental techniques to keep your mind sharp and alert means you will become wiser with age and it helps in improving brain function. Research indicates that we can become smarter with age if we adopt healthy habits.

There is no reason why today should not be the day that you begin to develop those healthier habits for your own wellbeing.

I strive to maintain my personal and mental wellbeing because I am a phenomenal Surviving Queen!

KIMOLAKAY

KimolaKay

My name is KimolaKay and I am 55 years-old and a proud mother of two beautiful young adults.

I pride myself as a professional and I am a Graduate of the Chartered Institute of Personnel Development, having achieved my Degree in Human Resource Management. I have worked within the National Health Service (NHS) for over 28 years. People are my passion, hence my chosen career path.

In creating my business, I am also the Founder of *Kimmys Nibbles Catering Service,* which is predominantly a bespoke service that provides home-made sandwiches. This business has now expanded to be inclusive of catering for and providing authentic Caribbean dishes to small businesses and larger corporate companies alike, as there was a huge increased demand for my services.

My family heritage is from Guyana, South America and I am one of nine siblings, five of whom, including myself, reside in the UK.

My adult life to date has been quite turbulent and the last six years has been dominated by the impact of having endured various incidences of domestic violence and those experiences have proven to be prevalent as to the reason I am now embarking on this personal journey with the unique and great opportunity to be a part of the *Surviving Queens*

Anthology project, with having my chapter incorporated into this amazing and powerfully inspiring anthology book.

My inclusive chapter is about the violent domestic abuse I endured during an intimate relationship spanning five years from 2012 to 2016.

My only advice to anyone going through any type of domestic abuse is to seek help.

It is not your shame to hold, so break the silence and be free. I did. My Surviving Queens Anthology chapter is called 'Rose Petal'.

CHAPTER 8

ROSE PETAL

KIMOLAKAY

What is love? Who is love?

I have two beautiful children whom I love unconditionally but that deep preciousness I feel for them always serves to remind me that I also have two major failed relationships behind me, plus a few encounters that were perhaps not the best situations I could have found myself in.

The question that I often ask of myself is, 'Will I ever learn?' Maybe I will and maybe I won't. The real question for me is, 'Am I afraid of growing old and being all alone once my children have finally fled the nest?'

Standing in front of the bathroom mirror, I look at my reflection and examine my face, trying to look past the external shell of my being and deeper into my mind. I let out a deep sigh, loudly this time and shrug my shoulders. This time the small movement of my tensed muscles causes very little pain in my left shoulder but still causes my thoughts to wonder there again, and even though it has been five years since that awful and eventful night, it still feels like it had all happened yesterday.

What was I thinking and what on earth had made me even go there?

As I ease myself down to sit on the edge of the enamel bath, tears of shame roll down my face. I reach for the face cloth with the intention of wiping away the hot salty tears, but I am still with numbness as I grip the piece of cloth tightly in my hand. I am unsure for how long I had sat there but it must have been a while as I allowed the tears to flow freely, wetting my cheeks as they fell further down and dripped off the end of my chin. I could sense that I was unthinkingly staring into space, into nothingness. Eventually I had stood up, composed myself and headed downstairs to the kitchen as that space was my sanctuary and where I felt safe.

So now, here I sit at the dining table staring at the fridge and I can clearly hear the echo of my inner voice telling me, *'Rose, do not do it'*. But why the hell shouldn't I? I mean, what the hell else did I have to look forward to? It had been a Saturday afternoon with no kids around and I had been all alone in that big house. Dinner was already cooked, and the house was spotlessly clean. The children's school clothes were washed, dried and ironed, hanging up ready for Monday morning.

My mind begins to wander again, sitting there all alone, reluctant to think about it but feeling powerless to stop myself from doing so.

A narcissist. Just imagine I had never even heard of that word before meeting him and now I could recite every frigging characteristic of a narc, plus I have the scars to prove it. I swiftly file in the back of my mind a mental note to myself to not ever get to know anyone when you are feeling depressed, stressed or feeling low and disenchanted with life. You will most definitely attract a narcissist who will appear in your life, clothed in all his false glory, ready to pounce and drain all the energy from every living cell in your body and yes, that is what happened to me.

Just imagine for a minute the usually happy-go-lucky-me, flaunting her single self after a recent break-up, and just beginning to get my life back on track after the sudden and devastating death of my beloved father followed shortly thereafter by my dear sister, just a fortnight later. That alone had been enough to tip any sane person over the edge.

The year of 2008 had not been kind to me at all and then I had met *him*. He had initially been kind, funny, a real charmer and a humorous banterer, just like me. I thought I had hit the jackpot with someone who had finally understood me and had made me feel alive and hopeful, again. Little did I know that what was ahead for me with that relationship would end up being my worst nightmare and a horrific and complete living hell.

Ok, time to pause and hit the Chards, also known as Chardonnay, as there is no way that I could relive this tumultuous period of my life without my trusted liquid friend. When you have been stuck in a rut for a while you become susceptible and receptive to anything that appears a little different that suddenly waltzes into your life and shows you the affection you had been silently craving, creating the foundations for a whirlwind romance to flourish. I shake my head as I pour myself a large glass of wine, almost forcing myself to go back in time to when it had all begun.

He had been catering for the New Year's Eve party that I was attending and the person responsible for picking him up couldn't go, so I had finished getting ready and had then reluctantly driven the three miles from my house to collect Freddie and the food. We had chatted and laughed because even though it had been the first time that I was meeting him in person, we had spoken on the telephone and via text messenger for at least three months and to be honest, I had been curious about meeting him as he had seemed a likeable, cheeky chappie. It had been purely platonic, so no harm done there. The party had been good. We had laughed and joked around for most of the evening, and I hadn't even noticed when he had left. I had known practically everyone there so my time had been taken up with being kept busy in the kitchen serving the foods, chatting and dancing like there was no tomorrow. I have always been known as the dancer amongst our crew of female friends.

Freddie and I had spoken the next day and for several days after that. In all honesty, I don't even know when the friendship had grown into a relationship, but it had and then it was summer, and we had started to get even closer. He lived in the countryside, so we hadn't seen much of each other for the first year or so. His family lived locally though, nearer to my area, and whenever he came down to visit them, he and I would end up spending most of that time together. We talked, laughed and drank, getting to know each other better and before I knew what was happening, I had found myself in a full-blown relationship with him and he had practically moved himself into my home.

It had not been a case of my wanting to keep what we had going between us a secret, it had simply been that I was enjoying spending time with him, just the two of us, without any outside interference or influences. For that reason alone, I had not been in the habit of bringing up my relationship with him to any other person. I had just wanted more time to quietly enjoy getting to know him some more and he getting to know and understand more of me and who I was as a person.

I would sometimes make a detour and stop off at his mum's house on my way home from work to spend an hour or two with him during the times when he would come down to visit his family and me. Then I would head home to collect 'Tonka', (my affectionate name for my son), who would be waiting for me at my mother's home, which was literally only five minutes away.

I remember when Freddie had asked me who knew about us and I had responded by telling him that no-one did really, apart from my two children.

There had then followed a lengthy discussion about why nobody knew. It felt slightly like I was being interrogated by him as he wanted to know if I was ashamed of him, to which I had replied that of course I was not ashamed of him, in any shape or form. A few nights later I happened to be scrolling on social media when a notification had appeared asking me to respond and accept that I was now in a relationship with Freddie Krueger. I had sat there staring at that notification for what felt like forever with my shaking finger hovering over the keys of my laptop, unsure of what to do, so instead I had picked up the telephone and called him.

Despising the trembling I could hear in my voice I had nervously asked him why he had sent that notification, to which he had responded that he wanted everyone to know that we were together as a couple. I had sighed heavily before expressing to him my hesitancy and in not being sure that was what I wanted just yet. *"Well, I do! I do not want to hide it anymore"*, had been his reply. *"It is not hiding it is just being private"* I told him. *"What is there to be private about? We are both adults"* he had counteracted. *"I know that, but I am not ready yet for all of that"*.

He had sounded angry and quite petulant, to be truthful, but I had stood my ground and disagreed with him about making our relationship public knowledge just yet. If only I could have kept my inner strength up during the years that followed then maybe, just maybe, things might have ended differently.

We had continued chatting for another fifteen minutes or so and once we had ended our conversation, I had then prepared myself for bed.

I did not hear from Freddie at all the following day until I had again picked up the telephone and rung him that evening. He had sounded off and distant during our brief conversation and I realised it was because I had not accepted that notification he had sent. He had ended the call saying that he had someone visiting him and that he would call me back later. He never did call me that night and after awaking the next morning, I had reluctantly logged on and accepted that damn notification request.

Within a few seconds of my having done so, the telephone rang, and it was him on the line, his voice back to normal now, like nothing had happened. I had not been overly elated but had felt relieved that we were back to how things had originally been between us.

That should have been my first red flag warning sign!

A few weeks later I started to notice how he was not as attentive as he had been before. He was still treating me well and we were getting on, but something was amiss, but again I had just shrugged the feeling of unease away.

My unspoken discomfort had continued with the way he began taking little things for granted whenever he was at my house. He had stopped cleaning up after himself in the kitchen, bathroom and bedroom. I had challenged him about his lack of consideration in cleaning up after himself and it was like he was looking straight through me, as if I were not there, standing directly in front of him. He had continued to stare past me as if he had not heard me. That should have been another red flag warning sign to me, but I had been too tired to even say anything else to him and instead I had gone and cleared everything up myself.

After about a year had passed, Freddie had started to make comments about the clothes I was wearing to work, disdainfully questioning me about who I thought I was dressing to impress. His hurtful remarks had left me feeling shocked and somewhat confused as I was still dressing the same way I always did for work. I am a professional and that is expressed in the business attire I wore for work purposes.

I can recall, with a tinge of embarrassment, how during a lunch break, one of my work colleagues had asked me if I was ok. When I had asked her why she thought I was not, she had replied that it was because something about me had changed significantly. Her comments had bothered me for the rest of that day because she had been correct in her observations. I had already felt myself changing but I still couldn't quite put my finger on the how or why of it. I had suspected for some time that being so busy at work and then having to go home to my children and Freddie, to cook, clean and be a partner to him, was taking a toll on me, physically, mentally and emotionally. I knew for sure that my children were not the cause of my problems but Freddie himself had become a problem, but by that time I had felt that I was already too deep into the relationship and in over my head.

Over time Freddie had me drinking every night, two, possibly three bottles of Chards every evening, which meant I was not getting to bed to sleep before two in the mornings during the week.

Around that time, I had felt a massive need, a longing even, to talk to someone but by then most of my closest friends had distanced themselves from us as had my family members.

Why was there no-one available for me to talk to?

His friends, immediate family members and associates were the only people that still called and visited. I had felt so desperately alone and frighteningly isolated. I would still visit my mum at her house but had felt reluctant and unable to talk to her about how I was feeling. I could sense that she was becoming increasingly worried about me, but she was elderly, and I had not wanted to worry or burden her with my problems or concerns. I hadn't felt comfortable speaking to my sisters either as it seemed as if they too had no time for me, anymore. I had seen on social media how they were often going out together, doing things as sisters but not including me. Our relationship therefore had grown distant and strained.

What I had failed to realise at the time was that they had all noticed the way Freddie behaved towards me and how he spoke down to me. They had also noticed how withdrawn I had become over the past months, not to mention the vast amount of weight that I had lost. Unfortunately, I hadn't taken note of all of that, or had I?

I hadn't fully been aware or sensed the increasing and effective ways that Freddie had manipulated me and our relationship so that I was left alone and without the company and support of my previous friends, inclusive of my family.

The loneliness I had felt in being in a relationship with Freddie was real but unacknowledged by me. It is the type of loneliness that is so often underestimated and dismissed as not being that bad to bear. There were times I used to ask myself misleading questions like, if things were awful with him, how much worse would they be without him?

Freddie did not have a job and whilst I was busy at work, he would spend all day lounging around and making a mess and generally just doing nothing at all.

He had always been extremely close to his mum and sister, and they would buy him clothes and give him money and sometimes they would give him other stuff like toiletries and food shopping.

One morning after having had my shower, I had used a little of the Body Butter lotion that his sister had given to him. He had entered the bathroom and seen me using it. He had immediately and violently grabbed it out of my hand, shouting at me that it had been given to him by his sister. I had responded by telling him that I was only using it to cream my hands. The next thing I remember after he had snatched it out of my hands, was him viciously striking me across my face, screaming at me that I should not touch his things!

I had stood there frozen and in complete shock, hugging my burning cheek where he had hit me. Tears were streaming down my face. All I kept thinking was that it was only a bloody tub of cream and that he had been living in my house for almost two years now and he was carrying on like a mad man about my having used a little of his body cream that his sister had given him!

Almost immediately after having hit me, he had approached me, telling me how sorry he was and that he didn't know what had come over him. I had stepped away from him and exited the bathroom, still reeling from the shocking reality that he had raised his hand and struck me. Luckily for me, my children had not been home and had gone to see their Dad for the weekend, but that had also meant that I was now alone in the house, with him.

Not knowing what I should do with myself, I had quickly dressed and went downstairs into the kitchen where I had started to prepare and cook a meal. For the next few hours, the house had been completely silent as I tended to the chores that needed doing. I had even emptied out all the cupboards to clean and pretty much found jobs to do that hadn't really needed doing, just so that I could keep busy. My mind kept replaying repeatedly what had happened upstairs in the bathroom.

I must have done something wrong I reasoned. I made a mental note to myself never to touch anything belonging to him, ever again.

But it was my home. I lived there. I paid the bills. I did all the cleaning and cooking. In my mind I could hear that inner voice urging me to tell him to leave but I had felt too scared to verbalise any of that to him. I had kept out of his way and avoided having to communicate with him. I had prayed for Sunday to arrive so that my children would return home to me.

Much later that same evening, he had come over to me to speak to me, apologising profusely for what he had done and telling me that it would never happen again. He again repeated that he hadn't known what had come over him. He had told me to sit down and had bought over a basin of water and had proceeded to wash my feet. Stupidly, I had forgiven him, not knowing that that first time would be one of many times that he would physically abuse me.

Things had appeared to be good for several months after that initial incident and he had reverted to being the attentive man I had originally thought him to be. He started to clean up after himself and when I returned home from work, most evenings he had dinner prepared and ready on the stove.

I had thought and believed that he was truly remorseful for what he had done and that he had changed for the better.

Freddie was a very frequent user of social media and had numerous virtual friends and many of those were women. He would flirt outrageously with them, both openly and privately in their inboxes. He even used to use my laptop when I was at work, which wasn't a problem for me as I would sometimes sit with him when he was there bantering with his social media friends.

Alone at home one weekend after he had left to go back to the countryside, I had needed to use the laptop. After logging into the social media site his account had come up, so yes, I do not deny it, I had looked and was horrified as I had thought that he had not had anything to hide, seeing as I would be sat next to him and could see what he was doing online.

My horror was because of the numerous pictures of various women's private parts and tons of sordid messages between him and them. Just as I was looking through them, he himself had logged on from his home and was continuing to have these sexually explicit conversations with these women.

I had felt so shocked and terribly disappointed but still, I had carried on looking and reading and screen-shotting them for future evidence, which I still have to this day. Maybe I should not have looked, but once seen I could not then unsee them.

On his return to London, I had confronted him about the nasty pictures and messages he had on his social media account in his private messaging inbox. He had shouted at me and we had argued about his online behaviour.

He had then gone out and returned a few hours later, drunk and persistent, aggressively raising his voice at me.

In the next instant I found myself laid out on the floor, bruised and hurting all over my body. It had taken me a while to get back up onto my unsteady feet. I had made my way to my son's room and laid down on top of his bed. My son had been away at the time.

The next morning, I could not move. He had entered the bedroom to see me lying there in agony and had taken me to the hospital.

What the hell was I going to do now?

I was so scared of Freddie and his possible reaction to me telling the doctors the truth of what had happened to me, that I had lied to the doctors and told them that I had fallen down the stairs. I had left the hospital on that occasion suffering with the pain of having sustained a few cracked ribs from the beating he had inflicted on me the night before.

Obviously, I had to then use that same lie for my children and my work as I could barely walk and had to take four weeks off from work to heal and recover fully.

I kept berating myself as to why I hadn't had the strength or the courage to just tell someone, anyone. Why did I feel that I had no other choice but to suffer in shameful and fearful silence? Despite my profound sense of trepidation, I had stayed and did nothing to help myself. Freddie had completely and utterly broken me down to nothing and I was just too frightened to let anyone know just how desperately sad, lonely, battered and afraid I felt.

Around that time my daughter had moved out due to an incident that had happened on the day before my birthday when Freddie had physically fought with her boyfriend inside my house. I had again been too weak to see through Freddie's manipulative and narcissistic patterns of behaviours to stand up for my daughter and as a result I had almost lost her because of my failure to see clearly what was in fact happening. My lacking in any inner strength, will power and sense of self-worth meant that I had wrongly put him and his violently unjustified ways above my child. I had nothing left internally and absolutely nobody that I could turn to for help or moral support. I was spiralling down into a deep depression and feeling like a nervous wreck. I had been in a very dark place indeed. Inside I was screaming to God to please help me. I screamed silently for anyone to come and help me.

I had known instinctively that nobody was going to come and rescue me. I was all alone.

I had gone from being a happy-go-lucky woman to having no self-esteem or self-confidence. I couldn't even bring myself to look at my reflection in a mirror as I had come to hate the person staring blankly back at me.

Yet still I kept telling myself that somehow, I had to soldier on. I had my son living with me under those threatening circumstances and awful violent domestic conditions. I knew in my heart that he must have heard the fights between Freddie and me although he had never visually witnessed them. But just to be sure, I would tell him that whatever happened in our home should remain at home. I now know that was the wrong thing for me to have instructed him to do but the shame I felt was overwhelmingly suffocating and oppressive. Telling my son not to say anything was symbolic of my own inability to speak up.

Freddie would constantly call me at work and if I didn't answer he wouldn't believe that I had been in a meeting and therefore couldn't answer my phone. And when I did answer, he would threaten to come to my place of work and embarrass me in front of everyone there. Being abused and controlled by him had been horrendous. He had caused me to feel persistently emotionally and mentally drained.

I was vaguely aware that people were talking about me, how I looked then compared to how I used to look. Going out proved to be a terrible ordeal as he would openly humiliate me in front of people, especially if he didn't get his own way. It had not mattered if we were on the bus, the train, in the car or stood in the middle of a busy street. He hadn't cared and would willingly shout and scream profanities at me.

One time he had even forced me to drive to the petrol station to fill a can with petrol which he had then kept in the conservatory for over two weeks before fetching it and pouring the contents over me whilst I slept. He had woken me up, threatening to set me alight as he stood over me, menacingly flicking the lighter that he had grasped in his hand.

We had attended his sister's birthday party which had been held in a club. The evening had been going relatively well until Freddie had drunk too much and had then insisted that he was ready to leave. The cloakroom had been full on our arrival, so we had put our coats on the seats in the booth where we had been sitting. Unfortunately, my car keys had fallen out of my jacket pocket and rolled into the middle of the seat. It had taken me a short while before I had located the keys but by that time Freddie had been getting very impatient and had started to shout at me, in front of everyone. By the time I had found the keys, his anger had grown out of control, and he had aggressively dragged me out of the club, shoving me all the way down the road.

There had been a friend of mine there that night, who had witnessed his appalling behaviour. She had been so shocked that she could not even speak.

We were not taking the correct route home, but I had said nothing as I soon recognised that he was in fact driving to go see the crack guy to buy drugs from him.

Luckily, or not, depending which perspective you viewed it, the police had appeared out of nowhere and stopped the car. As he had been the one driving, they had escorted him to the police station and my car had been impounded.

Freddie had told me all about his life before we had started dating, so I had known that he had previously been on drugs, but everybody deserves a second chance in life, so I had totally believed him when he said that he had been to rehab and had been clean and free from drugs for several years. That had been one of the reasons that he had been living in the countryside instead of in London, he had explained.

But what I had not known was that he was back on the gear, or maybe I had been naïve to the fact that he had never really stopped using drugs.

By then he had been openly smoking it inside my home at night and forcing me to take him to buy it, too. Whenever he had money that is what he would spend it on.

How did my life come to this?

Feeling too frightened to go home after finishing work, instead of taking the bus from the train station on my way home, I would walk the forty-five minutes journey because it meant that it would take me longer to reach my front door and I never knew what mood I would find him in or if I would be beaten and slapped around that evening.

In the summer of 2016, my children were going away on holiday without me. I had left my home with my son, carrying his suitcase, to go to my daughter's home and I had then waited with them until they had left to go to the airport before I had made my way back home. I was gone for maybe a few hours and on returning to the house I was unceremoniously dragged inside and beaten because I had stayed with my children until the taxi had arrived to pick them up, so that I could wave them off. Freddie had beaten me, pulled out large chunks of my hair and broken a few more ribs, all because I had taken longer than he had liked before coming back home to him.

After he had severely beaten me, I had to go to the hospital again because my injuries were so bad. On that occasion I had told them that I had been mugged and attacked whilst I was on my way home. Having to create such lies to cover up what was really happening behind closed doors, had been an awful way to live, but that is exactly what my life had been reduced to. That had been the longest two weeks of my life until my precious children had returned home. Again, I had to take time off work, stuck in the same house with Freddie, having recycled the same bullshit lies to my employees.

The day when my two babies came home, I had felt elated. I had gone to collect my son early that Saturday morning because Freddie and I were due to go out that evening and I had to drop my son back later that same night as he was attending a party with his sister. I hadn't managed to spend much time with my son that day but had been looking forward to collecting him again on the Sunday afternoon and hearing all about his holiday trip to Jamaica.

Later that evening Freddie and I had gotten dressed and made our way to the BBQ. One of his friends was also going to be there and I had informed Freddie that under no circumstances was I driving his friend home. We had both agreed that was fine, but during the function he had told me that I was to give her a lift home. I hadn't been best pleased but in trying to avoid making a scene, I had reluctantly agreed to give her a lift home.

After dropping her home, he had wanted me to divert off-route so that he could buy some gear. I had refused to do that and had reminded him that he had promised me that he would no longer do drugs anymore. A few weeks earlier, after he had beaten me, I had told him that if he continued with taking the drugs, that he and I would not be together anymore.

The night we had left the BBQ he had been drinking and I had consumed a few drinks too and I had wanted to go straight home.

That night for me would prove to be the beginning of the end as he had then proceeded to beat me even whilst I was driving the car along the A40, and he hadn't stopped viciously hitting me until I had stopped the car in front of the house. He had displayed such a rage against me that I was surprised that I hadn't crashed the car.

Through the fogginess of all the pain I was feeling, I had instinctively known that had I got out of the car that night, that I would probably not survive the night. The beatings were getting more severe each time he laid his hands on me in anger, rage and jealousy. He was literally out of control with his savageness, and I was in fear of my life as I could feel the rising of abject terror gripping me.

When I had pulled up outside of my house, he had gotten out of the car and I had immediately spun the car around and sped off down the road, driving at high speeds until I had reached the relative safety of the police station. To this day I don't know how I got there. All I remember is banging on the station door, bare-footed, bleeding and then collapsing onto the floor when they had swung open those heavy doors to grant me entry into the police station.

I had stood slumped there inside the police station, unsteady on my shaking legs, and desperately trying to explain to them what had happened. I knew that I was not making much sense as my lips were so badly swollen and painful, and my words sounded incoherent to my own ears.

"What's wrong with your shoulder?" one of the policemen had asked me.

He had then asked me to try stand up straight so that he could get a better look at my shoulder. As I straightened best as I could, I could see where my left arm was just hanging there. It wasn't until he had finally mentioned my shoulder that I had begun to feel the searing pain in my collarbone. My mouth was bloody, and I had a massive, painful black eye.

As I stood there with the policemen, Freddie kept calling me on my mobile. I had passed the phone to the policeman to answer, but Freddie had immediately hung up his phone.

The police had then called for an ambulance which arrived to take me to the hospital, the same hospital that I been to twice already because of him having beaten me previously.

I had been admitted into the hospital where they had hooked me up to an intravenous drip, but I had been released the following day. I had sustained a fractured collarbone and severe bruising to my eye, mouth and body. Following the strict advice of the police, I was not allowed to go home as Freddie's whereabouts were still unknown and he was still at large. The police themselves were fearful for my safety. He had finally been arrested later that day.

As if the last forty-eight hours had not been traumatic enough, on my return to my house I walked into what I can only describe as resembling a mini war zone. He had maliciously, intentionally and spitefully thrown several raw eggs against the walls, ceilings and over the furniture as well as the food that he had cooked the previous day. The yellow yolks of the broken eggs had congealed where they had landed, and parts of the gelatinous egg yolks were still slowly dripping wet and cascading down the walls to land onto the wooden floors of the living room and kitchen. The cooked particles of food and the raw eggs had combined to produce a smell that hit the back of my throat the minute I had stepped inside. As I stood there immobile, feeling numb, I couldn't work out in my brain what on earth to make of it all. I could sense and feel his vengeful wrath leaping off the walls at me. Looking at the terrible mess around me, I had felt violated and attacked all over again. The state of the rooms truly represented the state of my life and my emotional and mental state of mind – everything was a huge, frightful and chaotic mess!

Freddie was remanded in custody and sentenced a month later.

He had received a measly eighteen months' sentence whilst I had to endure needing corrective surgery to my left collarbone where the bone was protruding up and out of its original and rightful position. During that major surgery, they had to shave off two inches of my collarbone and the rest of the collarbone had been pushed back into place with the use of metal pins.

I have never laid eyes on that man again since that day and I pray that I never will.

That fateful night after the police had left and my daughter had returned to her home, I had laid in bed, unable to ignore or bear the terrible pains that I was feeling all over my body.

The only person that I wanted to speak to about my ordeal was Liz.

Liz is different from anyone that I have known in all my life. I had tried to talk to her before about what I was suffering and to be honest, I think she had an inkling but had gently made it obvious that she would be there for me when I felt I could open up to her and besides, I think she didn't want me to feel like she was prying into my private life. Unbeknownst to me, Liz had been subtly distancing herself from Freddie in an attempt to show me that she knew something was dreadfully wrong. She had been careful in trying to convey to me that she didn't want to alert him to the fact that she had an idea of what was happening in case he took it out on me with his violence, but she was also trying to show me that she was there for me whenever I felt safe or ready to confide in her.

That night I had picked up my mobile phone and called her. Immediately on hearing her voice I had broken down and through my floods of tears I had tried my best to explain my anguish, fears and what I had endured so recently. Being such a gentle, loving and insightful individual, she had understood totally.

Liz had explained that she was in fact away for that weekend in another city, with her sister, but that on her way home the following morning, she would come to see me.

Unbeknownst to me, Liz hadn't slept that night as she had been so worried about me and had left the hotel the following morning a few hours earlier than she had originally planned to. Knowing how much she cares and the depth of compassion she feels, I can only imagine how long those hours driving down the motorway from Birmingham to London must have felt for her.

I had drifted off to sleep that night after speaking to Liz for almost an hour. I had slept well in the knowledge that Liz would fix everything once she arrived in the morning.

The effects of the pain medications that I had taken that night had meant that I had overslept. It had been the sound of the doorbell ringing that had awoken me. My various injuries and cuts inflicted into my flesh meant that it had taken me awhile to get up from the bed and to make my way downstairs to open the front door. As soon as I saw Liz standing there, I had collapsed into her welcoming arms, sobbing like a baby, for what seemed like an eternity.

My dear friend and her sister had stayed with me for the best part of that day. Liz's sister had kindly offered to start cleaning up the vast mess that Freddie had caused, which in turn had given Liz and I the much-needed space and time I had been so craving for me to talk to her, to unburden myself to her.

Just as I had expected, Liz had known what to say and do to comfort me and to just listen! Just her presence alone had given me courage and confidence. She has a background of being a Counsellor for many years, but she had not treated me like a client but as a friend and sister. She had taken charge where she needed to, to help me, and by the time she and her sister had left, I had felt calm for the first time in years.

One of my sisters had telephoned me the night before but I had not picked up the telephone. After speaking with Liz, I found the courage to dial her number and call her back. I had sheepishly related to her what had happened. I had also asked her not to tell anyone else, especially our mum as I hadn't wanted to worry her. I still had not felt ready to receive visitors, but my sister and I had kept in contact by the telephone and spoke every day.

The next day I had contacted my employers and for the first time I had told them the truth about why I was unable to come into work. I had explained to them what had transpired the night before and summarised the history of what I had been subjected to by an abusive partner. Work had been incredibly supportive and had not intruded my privacy by asking too many questions, which had made it easier for me to cope with revealing my situation and circumstances to them.

My daughter had visited me every day, bringing me foods to eat and had also had to assist me with bathing myself as I am left-handed, and it was my left shoulder and collar bone that had been so severely damaged. I couldn't even brush my teeth properly let alone to dress myself, do any housework or shopping.

It had become rather noticeable that neither Freddie or I had been active on social media, and I had been inundated with a considerable number of messages, which I had ignored. I was far from ready to explain to people what had happened and why. My phone would ring, buzz and bleep constantly and I ignored those incoming calls too. Shame and embarrassment kept me silent and incapable of interacting with people.

Despite finally being free from Freddie's threats and physical and mental abuse and violence, I had still felt trapped and imprisoned in my mind. The memories of his narcissistic bullying had left deep scars that I was finding hard to dislodge or forget.

Days and weeks went by, and Liz was all I needed. She had a way about her that made it so easy for me to talk to her and to learn how to come to terms with my horrendous ordeal. We had spoken daily, and she had driven halfway across London to spend time with me and to take me to my hospital appointments, knowing I could not drive with my damaged shoulder and collar bone.

The physical pains of my injuries were slowly subsiding, but the mental and emotional torture was still so rife in my thoughts and mind. I could not help replaying it all repeatedly, no matter how hard I tried not to. I could feel myself sinking further and further into darkness as

I relived every slap, punch, kick and verbal abuse he had ever inflicted upon me.

How was this possible, that I was still stuck in that mindset? I should have been feeling better and free, but I could not face seeing or speaking to anyone else.

My facial bruises had almost disappeared so I informed my daughter that it was time to bring 'Tonka' back home, so that I could explain to him what had happened. He had been staying with his father since that horrific incident. My daughter had taken one look at me and told me that he could not see me like that, not in that state. She had then rung his dad, explaining what had happened and asked him to collect his son from her house so that he would not be traumatised in seeing me in that terrible and fragile state.

It had been a few months later and although I was still absent from being on social media, I had begun to respond to a few of the messages I had received. I had felt overwhelmed by the support, cards, flowers and even food parcels that I had been receiving. My shattered spirits had begun to lift a little, but I had still felt vulnerable and emotionally and mentally fragile.

I had been having weekly sessions of physiotherapy at the hospital and attending fortnightly appointments at the fracture clinic. It was during one of the appointments with the Consultant at the fracture clinic that he had informed me that I was making good progress but that alas, I would never regain the full use of my left arm. He had explained that I would need an operation in order to make the best usage with the left arm. Being left-handed, I used that arm far more than I did my right arm. The bone that was sticking out was becoming a physical hindrance to my recovery and wellbeing.

I had returned to work in the November and had felt grateful for the total support from my colleagues. I had also commenced counselling, supplied from my place of work and those sessions appeared to be going well. I felt I was becoming more confident in talking about the violence and hurt inflicted on me by that narcissistic, Freddie. It may have been that where he had been locked up, I had not felt scared of him anymore. I had, however, still felt embarrassed and ashamed that I had allowed him to continually disrespect me and abuse me, but I no longer felt frightened.

In time, I started to accept offers from friends to go out socially. I must admit that I was nervous as the places I frequented, people there knew me and were now aware of what had happened to me. However, they all embraced me, men and women alike, which helped to make me feel less nervous, so that in time I felt I could talk freely about my experiences in being a surviving victim of a brutal and manipulative narcissist.

In speaking with other people, I soon came to realise that I was not alone in my experiences of domestic violence and that so many others had been through similar situations. I was shocked to discover what some people had themselves endured.

More than two years had passed, and it was the summer of 2019.

Speaking about what I had survived had given me a sense of inner strength and determination. In sharing my story, I learnt that the abuse I had suffered was not my shame to hold onto. I had been a victim of somebody else's brutality and aggression. I also learnt that I had the choice not to continue to be a victim.

I had contacted a friend of mine who hosted a Saturday morning show on the radio. The topics she covered varied from week to week. She had known what I had been through so I had asked her if I could be a guest on her show as I felt it was time for me to speak out about the domestic violence I had suffered and survived. She and I had spoken in detail for approximately twenty minutes, and she had explained to me the format of the show and we had gone through the types of questions that both she and her co-host would ask me during the interview. I knew it would be tough, but I had made great progress in healing from within and I was no longer that fragile and scared person, cowering from the vicious blows of a bullying coward. I had evolved from victim to survivor, and was now personally, mentally, emotionally and spiritually blooming and radiating from the inside out, to be honest. I was no longer afraid to look at myself in the mirror. I was no longer ashamed of the reflection looking back at me.

It had felt like the right time to put the record straight as Freddie was now out of prison and busy telling untruths about what had really transpired during our relationship and about what had taken place that awful night which had finally signalled an end to my suffering at his brutal hands and vicious misbehaviours.

If sharing my story reached and helped even one person, that, as far as I was concerned, meant the process and continued progression of my personal healing was worth it.

Saturday 14th of September 2019 had felt like it had come around so quickly and I had felt as nervous as hell. My heart was pounding heavily in my chest as I drove to the studio. On arriving there, I had been warmly welcomed and we had taken photos that were to be uploaded onto various social media platforms after the interview had been completed.

The interview had gone extremely well, and I had articulated myself in a way that could be understood by the listeners of the show. The part of me that remembered every detail of what I had suffered wanted to rebuke the questions as being too intrusive but the healing part of me knew that those questions had been necessary, and I had responded and answered them all to the best of my ability. There had been questions from the listeners too and so much support and encouragement. I had left the studio feeling overwhelmed. That night the interview had been uploaded onto the internet social media platforms and I had received so many calls, inbox messages and texts from friends and strangers, all telling me of their plights and asking me for advice.

I had done it! I had spoken out and shared my story and it had felt great and liberating to finally feel safe and courageous enough to do it. To date, over nine hundred people have listened to that radio interview, people from all over the world.

Since that first interview, I have been a guest speaker at an event about domestic violence, once again speaking about the cause and effects of domestic violence and now I am able to write about a portion of my story as part of the Surviving Queens Anthology book. God is good!

It has taken some time and numerous painful experiences of violence and abuse inflicted upon me, but I have finally been able to break my silence and be free.

If I can do that, so can you. There were times I had forgotten my truth, but I have always been a Queen and now I am a phenomenal and blessed Surviving Queen!

MAUREEN ELIZABETH WORRELL AKA JAH SISTAR

My name is Maureen Elizabeth Worrell and particularly on social media platforms and as a multiple award-winning Author, I am also known as Jah siSTAR.

I am a daughter, mother, grand-mother, stepmother, step-grand-mother, sister, aunt, cousin and friend to my beloveds.

I am also a multiple award-winning Author, Counsellor (Dip.Couns CBT BABCP), Therapist, Non-Generic Book Manuscript Editor, Inspira-tional Speaker and Writing Therapist.

I have been a Counsellor for over thirty years and counsel those who have been impacted into adulthood by childhood sexual abuse, domestic violence, rape, molestation, depression, eating disorders and depression.

I have personally edited numerous books for clients that have been published and several have then achieved award-winning statuses. I take great pride in my work as a Non-Generic Editor as writing is my passion and one of my gifts to the world is to help other silent victims and survivors who have endured unspeakable hardships, trauma, abuse and life challenges, to guide them through the processes of having their voices heard through their written words.

I am also a Senior Peer Practitioner for the Free Your Mind Charity— a multiple award-winning organisation that specialises in proffering counselling services to children impacted by domestic abuse and domestic violence.

As a survivor of childhood domestic violence and childhood sexual abuse and rape, I share my story and lived experiences with the intention and aim to helping others to realise that they are not alone and that their voices silenced by fear and verbal threats are worthy of being heard.

I specialise in helping those who were once fearful of stepping into their inner courage to tap into their desire for regaining their self-worth and purpose in life, by having their silenced voices heard through their written narratives. Writing has always been my greatest passion and helping others to help themselves into emotional, mental and spiritual wellness, has always been my true purpose in life.

To this end, it is why I created and founded my own company – *MW Counselling and Consultancy* – which offers a unique and bespoke service that facilitates in providing safe spaces for those requiring or wanting to know how to have their voiceless traumas turned into having their voices heard through their written and published narratives.

In 2005 I somehow found my personal courage to share the first part of my life story in my multiple award-winning (450 pages) published book which is called *'The Journey of I & I'*.

I am currently editing the second in my trilogy of Journey books – titled *'The Definition of I & I'* and aim to have this published by the end of 2021, as I am also currently working on editing several books for male and female clients.

My numerous awards are inclusive of: REEBA Outstanding Achievement Award, Back2Black BAFTA Inspirational Award, BEFTA Best Author Award, Lift Effects Extraordinary Lady Speaks Inspirational Star Awards, REEBA Counsellor of the Year Award, Leadership Minds Ambassadors International Most Creative Female Author of the Year Award, Author of Colour BEXLIVE Award.

Despite living with limited mobility and various debilitating health issues and being a survivor of cancer, I awake each morning giving Thanks for life and for each breath that I am blessed to inhale and exhale.

My journey of inner healing and living authentically with inner peace is a continued process and progress of my life here on earth. I strive to live in and with gratitude as each day to me is a reminder that I am blessed to be here in honouring my Ancestors and loved ones who have passed.

Every day as soon as I awake, I give thanks and praises to The Higher Powers and The Universe for my blessings.

'Set peace of mind as your goal and strive towards achieving that goal on a daily basis' ©

The title of my Surviving Queens Anthology chapter is: 'The Definition of I & I'.

CHAPTER 9

THE DEFINITION OF I & I

MAUREEN ELIZABETH WORRELL

It is sometimes said that violence and abuse are a private crisis. Violence and/or abuse of any kind thrives on the victim being or feeling isolated, threatened, alone, vulnerable and unworthy.

Is this due to the nature of what they suffer? It had to have had something to do with the lack of support and the shame and guilt that surrounds the victimisation of girls and boys, and adults, for that matter.

The numerous years of endured childhood sexual abuse and the agitated distress and stress of the prolonged domestic violence and sexual abuse had proven to have a long-term effect on my general health in emotional, mental, spiritual and physical ways.

I had often wondered, as a very young adult especially, if all abuse victims asked themselves how they could ever learn to love their own bodies after having experienced sexual abuse and invasive molestation and rape.

For so long I had hated my body. I had resented it.

At times, I had deeply despised my body. Was all that body hair *really* necessary?

What was it with all those frigging prominent curves that only served to draw unwanted attention from all those immoral, debauched and evil males?

I had spent many a year not forgiving my body for blossoming into womanhood, with breasts and curves.

Was this nature's cruel way of giving abused females a constant reminder of why their bodies were attractive to those males with horrible thoughts that turned into wicked deeds of molestation, abuse and rape?

I had dressed down all the time, wearing black and baggy clothes that had made me look far older and larger than I was. I had so desperately *wanted* to look dowdy and unattractive. Oversized clothing had become my best external asset and tool of protection.

On the very rare occasions when I had ventured out of my comfort zone to wear bright colours, I had felt so uncomfortable and *exposed.* Wearing a lovely shade of sky blue or a beautiful red dress, had made me feel like I was deliberately asking for unwanted attention, especially from men. Dressed in bright colours, I could feel the difference of how men looked at me, literally licking their lips as their sexual fantasies took shape in their perverted and sick minds.

I used to throw away all the belts that came with any clothing I wore because belts only drew attention to your waist and womanly curves and I had preferred that the materials just draped loosely over my whole body, from my neck downwards to my ankles.

To this day, I don't buy clothing with belts. I have one coat with a belt, but even then, I never use the belt for it. Another long-term and learnt-to-live-with remnant from my abused past.

Somehow, in my sub-consciousness, I had learnt to trust the myth that being abused or assaulted was the fault of the girl or the woman. Just as with when males are abused, they are groomed to believe they are the ones at fault.

As a sexually harassed fifteen-year-old, I was still not quite sure if the feelings of illogical guilt [for being a female] or the disgust and suppressed rage at what I had endured [for being a female] would totally vanish but as a teenager, rapidly approaching adulthood, that burden was laid heavily on my shoulders and truth be told, was entrenched in the very core of who I was or defined myself to be as a human being and girl and woman.

As an abused and molested teenager, I had had no time, reason or cause to have ever *celebrated* being a girl, a female: for just being me.

Being the target of so many instances of attempted or actual molestation leaves you feeling like you have lost a great deal of your personal integrity because the fundamental wish or desire to be respected is absent. The abusers leave you feeling worthless and deserving of anything bad that you encounter in your life. I often felt as if they had all, in turn, reached into the depths of my soul and stolen something precious from me, something that could never be replaced or repaired.

It got to the point where even a simple glance from those perverts had left me feeling helpless and dirty, because I had not had the luxury of being in control of how others saw me or thought of me.

The things that they, those depraved and sadistic sex abusers say, is often so offensive, but they don't seem to realise that. Either that or they simply don't care. Their twisted egos are obviously far bigger than their grasp of common sense or emotional intelligence. Or in regards for a basic sense of respect for girls or women, in general.

"Me a look fe a live-in child minder fe come mind me picknie dem during de week whilst me a work. Me will pay good money fe de job. What yu seh? Yu interested?"

Really?!

No, I mean, **_really!!_**

Who in their right mind would ask a fifteen-year-old girl that kind of question? More so after you know that you have tried to grab and touch and molest that same child on numerous occasions already?

Such idiots who beggared belief at their foolish audacity!

During that point in time, I had become more and more withdrawn. I was afraid that people would be able to 'see' the extent of the humiliating degradation of what had happened to me.

I had been so determined to be as invisible as I possibly could. I wanted to just blend quietly into the beige walls. I wanted to see and observe from a safe place but not to be seen or noticed, at all.

I had had no idea back then that my *permanent* sadness was most probably due to chronic depression.

The unwarranted attention from those perverts was obnoxious and nauseating and I had felt consistently suffocated by it, harassed and under emotional and physical attack. That sense of male dominated aggression had seemed to permeate under my skin and had caused me to feel that I was of so little value as a human being, as a person.

I had a plan though.

It had been a plan borne out of desperation, but it was a plan all the same.

It was a plan of mega proportions and consequences, if executed well.

I had, for a short while, decided to starve myself as a way of gaining back some of the control that I had felt had been wrenched from me for years now. Starving myself was going to be my coping mechanism, to shrink and be less visible in a physical sense.

But such extreme measures in our house had not gone unnoticed, ironically, as my beloved mother was a staunch believer that she lovingly fed us and that we ate as a way of her showing and giving us nurturing and love.

"Come, eat up yu food. Yu nah left de table till you finish."

So, in a relatively short time, my clever plan had evolved and had involved me going to the other extreme.

I would eat to get *fat.*

If I was fat then I would be unattractive and less likely to catch the attention of ANY male, good or bad, decent or indecent.

My fat would be my ultimate protection. The fatter I became the more protected I would be. Excessive weight gain would be my way of avoiding being seen as an abused victim or a girl to be abused and molested.

Now, **this** plan proved to be far easier to put into action and maintain.

Trust me to have taken the more difficult route to eventually finding the solution to my problems!

I found that if I cut down on all the sports I did – like netball, athletics, tennis, hockey and swimming – that the weight gained was at a faster pace and stayed on longer. Became more permanent far more quickly. In my weakest moments, I had berated myself quite severely whenever I had found that I was missing playing or taking part in some of my favourite sports, like tennis, athletics and netball. In the beginning of my quest for gaining excessive amounts of weight, I had felt pangs of envy as I had stood by and watched some of my classmates running around the court scoring goals in a netball match or practising their backhand on the tennis courts.

Tennis had been the most difficult sport for me to walk away from as I had and still do, love tennis.

But I had already made up my young mind to just go all out and eventually withdraw from and quit all sports.

That had not been so easy to achieve as the Sports Teachers at my secondary school would only accept so many excuses from me of not feeling well enough to partake, week in and week out.

I can recall, with a slight tinge of guilt, the definite look of disappointment on the face of my Tennis Coach as I had seemingly acted as if I had lost all interest in playing the wonderful game of tennis. I had won a couple of tennis trophies already as part of the school tennis team that had taken part in a few matches against other local, secondary schools.

The disappointment in myself and the angst that I must have been feeling must have been considerable as I can still remember that it had been a Sunday afternoon when I had surreptitiously taken down my tennis trophies from my chest of drawers and then hidden them in the bottom drawer under my winter jumpers. If they were out of sight, then surely my dilemma and thoughts of regrets would ease far more swiftly and less painfully, or so I told myself.

I had always been a skinny child but all that had changed once I started in on this new over-eating plan of mine.

"What a way dat picknie marga eh? Yu woulda neva beleev sey she can nyam a food like any big woman."

I hadn't slept properly at night for so many years already, so it had not been unusual for me to be first up and about in the house, in the mornings.

With my need to put my new eating to get fat plans into action, I would stealthily go to the kitchen and have my breakfast before the others had even thought about waking up.

By the time they were up and ready for breakfast, no-one had had a clue that I had eaten already so I would sit and have my breakfast with them, as was the norm. They had not suspected a thing because in my devious but necessary cleverness, I had already washed up the bowl or the plate that I had secretly used to eat my first breakfast from.

So, it transpired that most mornings I would make myself an egg sandwich for example and then, a couple of hours later, I would have a large bowl of cornmeal porridge, prepared and cooked by my beloved mother.

Some mornings I would have a bowl of cereal, eaten furtively in the kitchen with the door firmly closed, not even bothering to heat up the milk, and then I would sit with my family, without any self- acknowledged qualms, and eat a plate of fried eggs, sausages, toast, and baked beans, within the same hour.

I was on a serious, life-long and secret mission and proceeded to using every penny from my pocket money, to spend on sweets. I would hoard them away in my bedroom and munch on them throughout the day – dipping the liquorice into the sherbet powder and then afterwards munching on nuggets of sweet and sticky fudge.

Whenever my beloved mother had finished cooking dinner, I would go into the kitchen, open the pot and help myself to a piece of meat, knowing full well that she would be serving dinner any time soon. Sometimes she would hear me entering the kitchen and her voice would echo loudly and accusingly up the flight of stairs as she queried: *"A weh yu a do inna de pot, gurl-child? I hope a nuh de likkle meat yu a trouble yu know!"*

"Nah Mum. Just tasting de gravy!" says I, almost choking on a piece of braised and succulent chicken leg, quickly followed by a mouthful or two of rice and peas from the other pot on top of the stove.

At school, I had still taken part in P.E. but hadn't put as much effort into the lessons as I previously had done. Sometimes I would complain to the P.E. Teacher that I was feeling unwell and would have permission to return to the dressing room or to sit at the side of the pitch as the other girls battled it out on the fields in a game of hockey, rounders or tennis.

Food, *any* kind of food, became my ultimate comfort.

If I was sad, I craved food. When I was not so sad, I craved food.

I couldn't even type here 'when I was happy, I craved food' because to say I was ever happy, would be a lie.

Every day was like living under a heavy, dark cloud that just wouldn't shift.

The more I ate, the more I was convinced that eventually I would think less about the abuse and molestation.

The more I ate, the more I became convinced that I would be incapable to feel anything, emotionally, physically or mentally.

Eating was a great way for me to push down and suppress my feelings, so in no time at all, I was eating so much that even my baggy clothes began to feel somewhat tight across my stomach, breasts and hips.

Still, I was not deterred. I continued to over-eat.

"Her nose lovely and straight and yu nuh see how har eye dem pretty and she a go have one lovely figure when she finish grow, watch and see"

How damaged was I, to now think back at how such a compliment, from an Aunt of mine, had filled me with panic and resentment and anger? All I could think to myself on hearing those words were, if she, as a woman, thought me attractive, what say the male, sexual perverts then?

As a direct result, I had immediately increased my consumption of fattening foods.

I'm not entirely sure if my family noticed my weight gain at first but I don't recall anything significant being said to me at all. My beloved Mother had continued with her daily routines of feeding us breakfast, lunch and dinner, often preparing and giving us special treats on a Saturday or Sunday evenings.

I had no-one to challenge me about my negative thoughts, so I figured that no-one cared and more so, that my thoughts were normal.

I had no doubt fallen into that well-established victimised mindset, but I simply had not known how else to think differently and especially since I had always felt as if I had a sign emblazoned on my back saying, *'self-destructive because I am a sexually abused victim'* I was mindfully adamant that I did not want any unwanted attention from those who wanted only to harm me and at the same time, even though they were unaware, I had felt ignored by my parents and siblings. Or to be fair, I had felt that my horrific predicament and subsequent feelings, were ignored.

Knowing that they didn't know, hadn't helped me or my situation, in the slightest.

I still felt ignored, because nobody noticed my hurt and the daily pains that I was struggling through and with.

My self-inflicted and rapidly addictive eating disorder became another secret that I held close to me. I guarded it with a determined anxiousness and guilt that only I could possibly understand and control at that point and during all the ensuing years. Amid it all, I had really felt that I was in control of this. I had tenaciously clung on to that 'fact' – it was I who was in control.

Desperate times and circumstances seeps into your reality and encourages delusion and illusions!

Eating to deliberately gain weight, or to be more precise, body fat, had not exactly helped with my low self-esteem or extreme lack of self-confidence. The combination of those toxic behaviours and thoughts and my distressing and damaging experiences, had only served to increase my depression and suicidal thoughts, but ironically, at that time, I had not been in the right frame of mind to recognise or realise the connection. The more depressed and saddened I had felt, the more I ate.

During the initial commencement of my plans to over-eat, there were some days when I would literally binge on foods until I felt ill and wanted to throw up. Some days I did throw up.

I over-ate because I was so unhappy and wanted to be *not* seen by anyone and in so doing, the act of over-eating itself, presented me with feelings of fleeting guilt for being so reliant on food to provide me with a sense of happiness and control in my life. I had felt resentful at believing that that had been my one and only choice, yet I had been determined to continue with this destructive, secret and hidden regime, because I felt I had no other alternative.

The moment I had swallowed the last mouthful, the guilt of disgust with myself would kick in and I would end up feeling so bad. That emotionally momentary moment of disappointment in myself and the anger at myself lasted no more than a few seconds. It took longer for me to realise and acknowledge that the very brief euphoria of eating to suppress my negative feelings lasted for even less than that. It was almost like it went from satisfaction to guilt-ridden devastation in a blink of an eye.

I think the guilt part stemmed from knowing in my heart that I was bingeing purely out of needing to not feel anything, good or bad, happy or sad, positive or negative.

To me, food literally represented my best friend and my worst enemy.

When you rely on food purely as a source to suppress your emotions you can't even really say that you tasted or enjoyed eating the food, either.

Over-eating under those circumstances was certainly not an enjoyment.

It became a *chore,* a means to an end, because I was on a mission, albeit a self-destructive one, to achieve my goals to become fat and ugly and unattractive and invisible. *To become safe from harm. To lessen the internal pains and hurts. To suppress my having to feel any emotions.*

I don't think I even took the time to properly chew the food at all.

As I stuffed my body with all those unhealthy foods and drinks, I recall feeling a plethora of confusing and painful emotions, which I quickly learnt to suppress. For me, food became synonymous with sensations of guilt, disgust, disappointment, discomfort and of feeling over-whelmed and powerless.

I stuck with this unhealthy and toxic eating regime for many years, with only the **intensity** of it varying as time went on. For the first few years, although I had put on a lot of weight, in my mind it had not been enough or swift enough.

The mere glance from a male would have me reaching for a large bar of chocolate.

A touch, whether intentional or unintentional, from a male, would be worthy of me gorging on a huge bowl of ice-cream – or two or three.

Finding myself in a place where I had been forced to remember or think about the abuse and molestation, literally had me craving for fried foods and takeaways, washed down with a few cans of sugar-loaded fizzy drinks.

In consuming such unhealthy comfort foods, under those circumstances and for those specific reasons, there was always that momentary but very fleeting 'high' of euphoria in consumption. But trust me, when I say it was momentary, that is exactly what I mean. By the time I had swallowed the offensive piece of fried chicken or chocolate bar, a profound feeling of guilt had set in pretty much immediately. Binge eating is such a crazy cycle of comfort and guilt, so you eat more to try to make that feeling of comfort last a second or two longer.

I often found ways to eat alone so that I wouldn't be judged by my family or by anyone else, for that matter. The consequential isolation that caused me was just another thing I had to accept and put up with.

On the rare days when I hadn't eaten too much, I would make sure that what I did put in my mouth had the highest number of calories or the highest volume of saturated fat in it.

Bingeing with a bit of intelligence, I used to tell myself, sarcastically.

My bad and unhealthy eating habits multiplied and became far worse after I had come through the gallbladder and gall stones removal operation.

At the time, I had used the excuse of feeling down due to the pain of recovery from the operation and from the stitches and staples becoming infected and the wound being so painful. I had told myself that over-eating helped me to overcome the pain, but of course, in my morbid reality, the real excuse for it had been my silent internal raging and incomprehension as to 'why me?'. Why had I been singled out for childhood sexual abuse and molestation and why had I been left feeling worthless and neglected because of the ongoing childhood domestic abuse and violence, occurring day in and day out.

I had found huge comfort in eating in that manner because my enforced silence meant that that was my only avenue to shout out to my loved ones that I was suffering silently and painfully and hurting **really** bad.

This destructive relationship I had developed with food eventually brought me crashing down to my knees with intermittent bouts of depression and suicidal thoughts.

I ate because I was sad and binge eating made me more depressed. Happy days, eh?

In hindsight of course, many painful years down the line, I had realised that the 'trigger' for my over-eating was of course due to sadness, anger, stress and many other bad and negative emotions.

Even whilst I sat and contemplated a way out of this awful, consuming and addictive cycle, I would be scoffing down a mars bar or three.

I hardly allowed myself to experience hunger because as soon as my mind or thoughts touched on an indecent incident or memories of my past experiences, my very first and last thoughts was always food, more to the point, the consumption of foods. I had readily and eagerly accepted the vast misconceptions that food would offer me the comfort that I had so craved. Unfortunately, when bingeing, you don't immediately think of a salad or a glass of water. No, your mind immediately springs to thoughts of fizzy drinks and cans of ice- cold coca cola or a piece of chicken leg or a nice piece of deep-fried snapper [fish], lathered in sauce and washed down with thick slices of hard dough bread slathered thickly with butter. Or if the cravings were mainly one of wanting sweet stuff, I would be reaching for the tub of ice-cream or the bars of milk chocolate – 'fruit and nut' and 'bounty bars' were my original favourites at that time. I quickly lost my 'shy-ness' and 'trepidation' in asking for 'seconds' around the dinner table and what with the keen and happy responses from my parents to yes, eat if you want it, I had the green light to eat more and more.

On those bingeing occasions where I had eaten until I had felt as if my stomach would burst, I had felt ill and bloated and so uncomfortable to the point of feeling an ache or actual pain in the pit of my stomach, yet still I had carried on, because I had unquestionably accepted that pain as deserving of the unworthy person that I had considered myself to be, that the abuse had taught me I was.

The self-inflicted pain that I now felt, through over-eating, was my deserved punishment for being an abuse victim, of being so unworthy.

I had been so convinced of this for so many unhappy, torturous and wasted years.

In the middle of all of this, I was still struggling to cope and come to terms with the constant bickering and arguing that was going on with my parents almost every single day. Somehow, too, it had become the norm that I was constantly put in the middle of their bickering and arguments. There were times when they were hardly speaking to each other and both or either of them felt it was acceptable to use me as a go-between, to bridge that gap of stubborn unforgiveness or resentment that they allowed to grow between them. Until, of course, they suddenly decided all was well between them again and they were once again smiling, laughing and joking around together. Until the next time – and then the vicious cycle of repeated patterns of behaviours would commence again!

Fortunately, the domestic *physical violence* had all but ceased, which was a huge relief but the continued cussing from my beloved father still left me feeling so anxious and on edge all the time. At any moment, I was convinced that his ranting or explosive temper would escalate into physical harm being meted out once again, so I could never really relax with any confident convictions that all hell would not soon break out in our household, all over again.

I found myself constantly and nervously listening to what words and how my mother spoke or responded to his comments or arguments.

Even back then I was aware that I had developed this fear of her using the *wrong* tone of voice, no matter whether she had done so unintentionally or not.

In my *need* to want to protect her from further harm, I had been exceptionally afraid that she would say something to set him off again.

I hated myself for doing it and resented the fact that I felt I had to.

Knowing full well that my beloved Mother was such a mild mannered and softly spoken woman, did very little to help to assuage my concerns and fears.

Besides, there had been times when my beloved Father felt righteous in feeling offended or peeved at a whisper, much less an even slightly rebellious or confrontational tone of voice.

As I continued to eat away my emotions in order to suppress all feelings, all I could really do, was to pray for peace and no more violence.

Had I ever really been given the chance or the permission to just be an innocent and care-free child?

I lived my young childhood days and nights, always feeling as if I had to look out for and after everybody else in our household. Always feeling as if I was caught in the middle of their misconstrued communications or lack of communications and their fighting and cussing and bickering.

Being so unhappy myself I had made a point of always trying to make sure that my siblings were happy and content and protected from hearing or seeing everything negative or abusive that was taking place in our home.

I readily took on the mantel of being the 'bossy' one to my siblings. I had 'bossed' and cajoled them into enjoying their childhoods as children, as my beloved brother and sister. I had forcibly encouraged them to play more than they worked, in terms of housework. Not to say that I had discouraged them from taking responsibility for their appointed chores but very often it was far easier and less hassle to either help them with it or to just go ahead and do it myself. It had been far easier and less stressful to change and redress the bed with clean sheets rather than to have to tell my beloved sister three times to do it and still find it had not been done. It had made more sense to me to just go ahead and sometimes tidy my beloved brother's room instead of having to listen to him being angrily told to do it more than once in a single day and he not listening and then me thinking that this situation would escalate into him getting a beating: so, as his sister and self-appointed family peace-maker, I had considered it had been no problem to just change his bed sheets and sweep out his room. We had no access to a hoover in those days. We therefore used to have to use the long-handled broom to sweep out the rooms and passageways and the short-handled broom and dustpan to sweep the numerous stairs in our three-storey house.

"Yu jussa spoil dat bwoy hevery time yu jump up and clean him dutty room fe him" my beloved Mother would scold me.

My beloved Mother was correct, of course, but a word of thanks would have been nice to hear, still, I used to mumble to myself. Always the *silent* rebel, that was me.

There were rare moments where we, as siblings, had managed to steal a few precious moments of just being children. Children with seemingly not a care in the world.

I loved remembering those times we had played in the garden: running up and down the long concrete pathway as we raced against each other, inspired after having had the rare treat of watching another athletics programme on the precious television in the downstairs living room.

Our beloved brother would always arrogantly deem us a 'head start'. Despite this advantage he had afforded for us, he had always overtaken and beat us in those races, still.

My beloved sister and I would glance at each other and without the need for spoken words, we would somehow agree to 'cheat' and sneak forward a step or two for the next race, just to try and beat him in the next race contest.

Our deviousness had not helped us though. He had still raced against us and came first, every single time.

My beloved sister couldn't understand it and would sulk a little, well, quite a lot. *'Maybe if we change and wear different shoes Sis, we can win next time, eh?'*

Bless her.

Or the times when we would securely attach a long piece of thick rope from one fence to the other and throw a huge sheet over it and use it as a 'net' over which to play a game or two of tennis.

This had been one of my favourite games. I loved tennis. Watching or playing it, I just loved tennis.

"I will be Arthur Ashe this time" I had declared with a childishly enthusiastic determination.

"How can you be Arthur Ashe? You aren't a man, silly" my beloved brother had responded, with a hint of patronisation in his voice.

"Does that really matter? I want to be Arthur Ashe. He's my favourite player so I'm gonna be him."

If my brother rolled his eyes at me one more time, I was going to slap him, I swear.

"Well, why don't you be that woman player; you know the one. Oh, what's her name again? Martina .... Martina.... Errmm, Martina something."

"You mean, Martina Navratilova?"

"Yea! That's the one! See, you even know her name, so you can be her."

"Yea, but she's white though" my beloved little sister had piped up.

"Hush up you. If you gonna insist I be a woman tennis player then I will be Althea Gibson, then." said I, feeling I had trumped my beloved bigger Bro.

My beloved brother was bent over, creasing up with laughter.

"Why, what's so funny? Is she white too or what?" my beloved sister had queried with a serious look on her perplexed face.

"That's cool but you do know she's dead though, right?" asked my beloved brother, through his hysterical cackling.

"Sis, please stop going on about white this or that. I want to be Althea Gibson cos she was the first black woman to play tennis professionally and she won one of those tennis grand slam titles. And it doesn't matter if she dead or alive. When we watched that documentary about her, I already told you I liked her."

"Oh. So, she's black, then." My beloved little Sis was testing my patience and beginning to annoy me now.

"She is a black woman yes. A black, female, tennis player. She was really good in her day, you know."

"OK. So, we have a black man playing a black woman, yes? Can we start now then?"

I have no idea who told this child that she was funny. Her sarcasm belonged in a league of its own.

Being her 'elders', we turned to give her a stern look. She had no idea how we both, my beloved brother and I, took our tennis 'matches' seriously and with racquets firmly gripped in our hands, we became so competitive like we were playing at Wimbledon or something.

"Are you going to referee this match properly or what? You remember how the scoring goes right?" I could see that my beloved brother had obviously felt bored with the jokes now that our tennis personas had been decided.

"They are actually called an umpire not a referee and yes, I certainly do remember how the scoring goes!"

I had to chuckle quietly to myself. There was no point arguing with this stubborn and feisty child.

"OK. Let's play. Mr Arthur Ashe to serve first." When she wanted to, she could take her role-plays seriously, to the point of exasperated annoyance.

Our game begins.

My brother serves first and hits the small, firm, fluffy, lime-green, yellow tennis ball and it smashes into the net. His second attempt flies up and high over the net but lands way past the service line, drawn out in white chalk on the concrete garden path.

As we each are walking to the opposite sides of the 'court' we are stopped in our tracks as our beloved little sister announces:

"15-0 to Miss Worrell .... Oh, sorry, I mean Miss Gibson."

I was by now laughing so much that I couldn't even be bothered to remind her that she should really say the score accordingly, as to who happened to be serving at the time.

Just thinking back on those precious, fleetingly joyous memories, reminds me that between the three of us, together, we had had some lovely times just playing and being around each other. No doubt, in hindsight, it's what kept me somewhat sane, I bet.

One of my beloved brother's favourite games was giving us piggyback rides up and down the garden as he raced against the clock [we took it in turns to time him] from one end down to the bottom of our garden and back up again.

I'm not sure how this game came about but my beloved little sister and I would take it in turns to jump on his back and off he would charge down the 'track', as he had referred to it.

"Start the time now!" he would shout as he took off, running like a hare on steroids.

We can't have helped much as we giggled hysterically every time and how we never fell off is a mystery to me.

Well, there was one time I had fallen off as he had almost come to the end of his running, with me clinging precariously with my arms around his neck, long legs dangling wildly and trying desperately to keep them fixed firmly around his waist. I must be honest and admit that I had been laughing as my beloved sister had been screeching at him to hurry up in order to beat his previously set time. Had she been under the impression his setting a faster time would go down in history and into the record-breaking books or something? His exaggerated running motions and my laughing combined had caused my arms around his neck to loosen their grip.

His panting had turned into a desperate gasping for breath and still I had been oblivious and had carried on laughing and urging him to run faster with my beloved sister screaming at the top of her voice at him that he was nearly there and to keep going.

Just as he had stepped over the 'finishing line', he had tapped my arm in a gesture for me to get off and in my excitement, I had released my arms but not my legs and over and down I went, landing with a thud onto my left knee. I must have landed on a piece of sharp stone or broken piece of glass or something, because the concrete turned crimson red, almost immediately.

Shock is a good thing as I had not felt the sharp pain straight away.

"Oh Jesus! Look what you made me do! Get up! Let me have a look at it, Sis" I still hadn't been at all worried at this point. It was just a little cut, right?

"Lawd! I can see bone! You in big trouble now."

Trust my beloved sister to be so *dramatic*. How many times had we fallen and scraped our elbows or knees before this? *Really*! No need to be exaggerating and scaring our beloved brother with threats of getting into trouble with our parents.

I threw her one of them 'cut-eye' looks and went to stand up and immediately collapsed back onto the ground.

My left leg felt weak and the pain on trying to stand up had been immense. Oh, jeez! Someone was definitely gonna get tell off or beat tonight.

"I can't stand on me leg, Bro," I whined, hot salty tears now rolling down my cheeks.

"Go get Mum or Dad!" my beloved brother instructed my beloved sister, a look of fearful panic in his beautiful, large, dark brown eyes.

"Me? Are you crazy? You go get them. This aint got nothing to do with me."

My poor, beloved brother. He had looked so scared and worried.

He shot a withering glance at our beloved sister and ran over to where I was still sat prone on the cold, concrete floor.

The red blood just kept spurting out and now and I could begin to feel the sharp stabbing pains in my knee, even more.

I recall my beloved brother gently trying to straighten out my bent leg to get a better look at the cut on my knee and on seeing it for the first time, his face turned an ashen grey colour.

"Ouch! That bloody hurts when you move it like that!"

"Keep still will you! It looks deep, but I can't really tell with all that blood."

What do you mean, keep still? Were you not the one who had a hold of my poor injured leg and was twisting and turning and bending it at all angles?

"Listen! You need to go and get Mum or Dad now! This is serious and I aint joking around no more. Just tell Mum she's fallen over and cut her knee, ok?"

"What? You mean lie?"

"Just move it and go will you! Jesus! You are enough to test the patience of a saint, I swear."

By this time the shock of adrenalin had worn off and I was crying in agony for real now. Part of me was panicking a bit because even I could see that the cut was deep and long. I was almost morbidly fascinated at seeing the shiny white of my knee bone – or was it the tendon – protruding through my dark chocolate skin. The edges of the cut looked nasty – jagged, dirty and almost black.

I was also anxious and worried about my beloved Mother's reaction as I knew full well how the slightest thing could inexplicably send her into a tailspin of fretting and non-negotiable worrying, inclusive of heart palpitations and all, either perceived or real.

I couldn't think too deeply or concern myself about my beloved brother getting into trouble, with our father more than our mother, but at the same time I was prepared to go along with his untruth about my falling over, if he didn't make it into a long elaborate lie and just kept it simple. I was a terrible liar at the best of times and the mere thought of trying to remember details of a lie brought me out in a nervous and hot and itchy sweat.

"I'm so sorry Sis. It was an accident man. It doesn't look broken though, right? It's just the pain of the cut itself why you can't stand up right? Jesus! How comes there's so much blood? Is that white bit really the bone or just tissue? Jeez man. What we gonna do now?"

My poor head was spinning and my whole leg had felt as if it was on fire.

Did my beloved Bro really think I had the time or energy, in my present agonising predicament, to be thinking of answering his questions?

A part of me had been praying that my beloved sister had taken the coward's way out and not told either of our parents. The very thought of all the ensuing fuss and reprimands was almost too much to bear or even think about.

I just wanted to sit there quietly a little longer and wallow in some self-pity and release the tears of pain. I wasn't sure which would be worse: my mother's intense fretting and panicking or my father's unspoken concern and worry manifesting itself into an irate and uncontrollable anger, with shouting and cussing with verbal threats of *"Unuh mussi want two licks a unuh backside!"*

Just then my beloved sister came back out into the garden. Upon noticing that I had not moved, she had looked scared and uncertain.

"They coming? What they say? Did you remember to say she had fallen and not mentioned that I was giving her a piggy-back ride?"

Through my agonised wailing, I was sure that I had heard her say that she hadn't told them, or was that just wishful thinking on my part?

"What?" our beloved brother had screamed in utter disbelief.

"I said, I did not tell them. Are you deaf?" "But a weh de backside yu a ..."

Oh-oh. My beloved brother must have really been scared or pissed off, or both. He was chatting **patois** now.

"Tell him Liz. Tell him not to have a go at me. He can go tell them if he wants. I aint going to cos I aint gonna be the one to get shouted at, thank you very much."

"Well, they aint gonna shout at YOU, are they? Honestly. You never do as you're told."

She stood her ground, her bottom lip pushed out in vexation, arms folded akimbo across her flat chest, the look in her saucer-sized, dark eyes, challenging our beloved brother to *dare* to say another word to her.

"She's right Bro. I can't be dealing with the fuss and cussing either. Just help me up please and we can clean it ourselves and put a plaster on it. It be fine, I'm sure."

"Plaster? You gonna be needing more than a plaster. Look at the size of that cut. And its plenty blood pouring out there, too."

"The time you making useless comments, just go and get some water will ya? And then afterwards go upstairs and see if you can find some bandages and plasters"

"Please ..." he had added as an afterthought.

"OK."

And off she ran, returning once more with a small bowl of warm water into which she had dropped a clean flannel.

"I put a little Dettol in it. You know, for the germs and stuff when you clean it."

"Thanks" replied our beloved brother as he took the bowl from her.

Suddenly my beloved little sister had bent down and threw her arms around my neck and hugged me tight, almost causing me to lose my balance, not to mention almost cutting off my airway.

"What on earth is the matter with you? You almost made me topple over, you know."

"Well, I just wanted you to know that I love you Sis, you know, just in case you bleed to death and die, innit."

"Oh, for goodness sake! Stop being such a drama queen and go get some more of the stuff you been asked to get, will ya."

"But aint you gonna tell me you love me too, then?" "Are you serious? Really?"

"Yea. Course I'm bloody serious. I love ya, innit."

I really had wanted to laugh out loud, but I could tell by that look on her face, she had not been joking. She had wanted or needed me to say it, to tell her that 'I love you'. I had to swallow a couple of times because I could feel the hysteria rising in my throat. *"I love you too, Sis."*

"Thanks. Love you too, Bruv."

She had then run off again to go search for the bandages and towels.

My beloved brother and I could only look at each other and shake our heads, with smiles on our faces. She was a nuisance at times, but she was our beloved younger sister and we loved her dearly, despite her tendencies for sarcasm, stubbornness and feistiness.

"This might sting a little bit ok. Sorry. Looks like bits of dirt in there too."

As he had squeezed the excess water out of the flannel and proceeded to wipe away the blood, I had thought I was going to pass out.

"Sorry. Its gonna hurt though, Sis."

"Look! Just pour the water on it so it washes the cut out will ya? It might not hurt so much then, anyways." I had probably sounded quite rude in my response, but pain has no patience or gratitude.

"Oh OK. Here goes then."

Impatience and pain do not go hand in hand, trust me. But I had to bite my tongue and bear it. It seemed to take an age for him to clean away the blood and the minute bits of grit floating around in the blood-filled wound.

"Ssshh! Here it is. Be quiet though cos Mum was on her way in to go check the pot of soup she is cooking, but I told her I would do it for her. She is still out front, helping Dad fix whatever he is fixing on that car of his."

We still had time to giggle as we all knew that Mum 'helping' Dad with fixing his car, really meant just passing his tools to him. Bless her. She knew nothing about cars at all.

"Hang on. You better dry it before putting that bandage on it. Looks horrible man. Is that bone or tissue then?"

"Errmm ... you wanna go bring me a clean, dry towel please?" says my beloved brother, with remarkable restraint.

"Yea. Sure. One sec."

As they carried on drying and patting down my gaping wound, I had been silently praying they would hurry up. My backside was getting numb sitting on the cold, concrete ground and I could feel my body begin to shake and tremble.

"That looks clean and dry enough to wrap now, yea? What you think?"

"Yea. I suppose so. Just make sure to put couple of those big plasters over the cut first. That way, the bandage won't stick to the dried blood."

"OK. If I put the plasters on, you can then wrap the bandage around, right?"

What was this? A medical teaching lesson with me as their guinea pig?

They at last had stood up and surveyed their handy work. I must admit they had done a good job. It looked neat and the bandage had felt secure. I couldn't see any blood seeping through the bandaging either.

"Can you stand up now, Sis?"

I could, with their help and did so. It still hurt to put weight on the left leg, but I could hobble along and that was at least something and therefore fine.

My beloved brother had run around like a frightened chicken getting rid of the evidence of the blood-red water and the backing he had torn off the backs of the plasters.

"You have to be careful when you sit down though, otherwise the bandage will show and they will see it and start asking questions."

That was a good point and with the help of my beloved sister, I had hopped my way up the many flights of stairs like a tipsy frog with one good leg, all the way to the top floor of the house to our bedroom and changed into a pair of navy-blue trousers and a black top.

It was then that we had noticed how the blood had seeped into the hem of my dress and had already dried into a yucky, brown colour. We had looked at each other and 'telepathically' agreed that it was easier to get rid of the dress rather than to draw attention to ourselves with trying to wash out the already dried blood stains.

I grabbed a black carrier bag from the kitchen cupboard, wrapped the stained dress in it and threw it in the kitchen bin, making sure to cover the bag with my dress in it, with other rubbish piled on top of it.

It had taken ages for the gaping and painful wound to eventually close and heal properly and had hurt like hell for several days.

During the night and having to share a double bed with my beloved sister, I had had to resort to placing a pillow, lengthways, between her legs and mine, as she had had this awful habit of flinging out her legs and arms whilst sleeping and as luck would have it, she very often would kick me on my cut knee, causing me to cry out in a muffled scream. She had not once woken up, the little so and so, to even say a simple 'sorry'. She had just carried on sleeping in blissful ignorance. Like I just said, the little so and so.

My parents had never suspected a thing.

It was years and years later when the truth had been revealed to them during one of our moments of reminiscing about our childhood, with our parents. They had laughed at the audacity of us kids hiding it from them, and Mum had wondered aloud why we had not told them at the time it had happened.

I know my beloved mother very well and that fleeting look of worry that had skimmed across her face was a result of my beloved mother having placed herself back in time to that very moment of which we had just shared with her. That look of fretting had been brief as she had quickly realised or *remembered* that it had been so many years ago now and more importantly, that we were obviously OK.

It had also been a look that represented her own memories of the past. I had half expected her to make a reference to how things had been for her back then and of how she had felt during those intensely chaotic and painful years. But she had not. That moment, for my beloved mother, would come later.

And trust me, when I tell you all that I have also always known my beloved father very well too. After we had finished the telling and sharing of this particular story with our parents, interspersed with giggling and raucous laughter from all of us, our beloved father had piped up with: *"Unuh lucky me neva did know cyar a two bitch lick me woulda gi unuh ...."*

Yes. **Now** imagine us three, despite being grown arse adults at that point in time, creasing up with hysterical laughter and almost falling off our chairs. We had laughed so much till we had tears running down our faces. So funny. Hilarious.

Despite all of that, as children, we had still gravitated towards playing piggy-back rides after a short reprieve of getting over the shock of that incident in the garden.

Despite the pains incurred through our playing, those carefree moments were welcomed reprieves from the pain of being inappropri-ately touched or grabbed. For a few minutes I could almost forget the horrors of always being sexually harassed.

When the truth is finally verbalised and recognised, it is then that all victims and survivors can begin their recovery and Healing journeys.

Far too often secrecy prevails in such a negative manner, and it is then that our stories of devastating trauma will reveal itself not as a shared spoken account but rather as a negative impactful symptom.

Perpetrators, abusers, rapists, cannot live with the truth. Survivors cannot live without it.

We, as the present generation, must be willing and courageous enough to face these issues head on in order to protect that part of us which is scarred and traumatised and more so for our future generations.

As I mentioned earlier, my inner healing will always be an ongoing, progressive process and journey of personal growth and being a small part of this Surviving Queens Anthology is another aspect of my personal journey towards further emotional, mental and spiritual healing and wellness. Having the privilege of being inspired by and standing shoulder to shoulder with my siSTARs, has served to remind me that not only am I a joyous survivor of my lived experiences, but that I am also one of those beautiful, inspirational and humbled Surviving Queens.

CHAPTER 10

POEMS BY JANNETTE BARRETT AKA MS. LYRICIST B~

REGRESSION OF DEPRESSION

This feeling of gravity is pulling the essence right out of me and making me uncertain of what's real anymore.

I'm struggling with my breathing. I'm struggling with my sleeping and I can't seem to get up or off the floor.

My stomach feels as though it's in a deep pit, making me sick and anxious all the time. I'm suspiciously paranoid of the pills they gave me because none of them are helpful in clearing my mind.

I know my family are lying to cover the shame and some of them are spying on me and saying I am to blame.

They don't know what to say to me and I cannot abide their pity. But even more importantly, I will not digest hypocrisy.

This feeling of gravity is pulling the essence right out of me and making me uncertain of what's real anymore.

It's like a freight train was driven through my head and into my brain, to block my thought processes and make me feel insane.

I visualise my scattered memories strewn across a track. I try to piece them together as I travel in my mind, but I always get lost and don't know the way back.

I want people to stop asking me how I am, then leaving me to figure it out without a plan. Nothing makes sense to me. My life is such a tragedy.

I need someone to walk with me. The lies are catching up, but I can't admit what happened to me.

This feeling of gravity is pulling the essence right out of me and making me uncertain of what's real anymore.

Everything feels heavy and laboured like lead. I'm living like a hermit, peeing in a bucket by my bed. I ain't brushed my teeth or even washed for days because to get out of my room feels like a trip through a maze.

The sun sheds its light on my windowpane, penetrating my curtains, but I still lay here lame. Paralysed in my demise I scream and shout at the sun. 'Why don't you just intensify your heat upon my sheet, vaporize and disintegrate me, my life on earth is done'.

This feeling of gravity is pulling the essence right out of me and I'm as scared as can be that if it doesn't stop, I'll stay in my room not eating or drinking, not washing or sleeping, just stay here decaying until I rot.

BRAIN FOG PLEA

Before I tried to sleep again, I willed my brain to speak. I asked, no, I pleaded 'Please brain, a friend is what I seek'.

There's something foreign in my brain that doesn't seem to connect with me and no matter what I do or say, it goes against me every day. It makes my body pollute itself then makes my body fight. It makes me lie and lie and I know that can't be right. It's always pounding in my head, knocking against my skull. It's like it wants to hurt me or even wants me dead.

I shake and sweat, itch then scratch in my attempts to resist but find myself ranting instead and clenching tight my fists. I pull my hair and bit my nails, rocking back and forth. I will not drink. I will not drink. No further will I sink.

Back into my brain fog where everything feels dreamy and nothing seems to matter much if nobody wants to get in touch. Liar! My denial is crazy. This is down to me.

If I can speak then I can ask so I'll ask, that's what I'll do. I know I can't do that face to face and may still have to do it at my pace, but I must think of how, today. I'll write a note, leave it on the table, saying 'Help me please, I am not stable'. Gosh, I don't feel able.

There I go again, talking my way out of it. I just need to do it and see. I don't need to make a brain plea; my brain is me. I'm talking sense right now. Don't think, not now, just think how.

I must step back into reality, or I'll never get over my past hurting me.

LOOK AT US ALL NOW

Look at us all now! With our eyes so bright, our smiles real, in control of our destinations because we stopped our procrastinations.

Yes, we all walked with scorched feet upon roads and paths riddled with potholes. Slept at night with minds wide open, no dams to block the floods of depression.

Oh, the anticipations and fluctuations of our what ifs, maybe's and could haves. It's going to be okay. Look at us all now.

All those doubtful words swirling in our brains, we squeezed them out to free us from pain. Those stresses so tight and daily tension fights against pretending. It's ending.

We've broken free, you and me, from the shackles that bound us. We're making our own master key, the one that will open any lock of every door on our freedom journey.

Woweee!! Isn't that crazy? When we consider where we came from, what we endured and what we survived? What some of us tried to do! Sisters, aren't you glad you're still alive?

Did you like me, have the feeling of oblivion? Did you look from inside of a hole, out at life, seeing people in their splendour, but wanting your life to be over?

Look at us now! Planning, visualising, fulfilling tasks, because we all removed our masks and faced ourselves and everything else.

Placing the ink upon the page, this magical phase will catapult us to heights only dreamed of before. Our past will rule us no more. We've all told our truths as we felt it, hopefully transporting others so they too can begin to heal from it by contemplating theirs.

Oh, the hairs at the back of my neck stand in salute and applause. We've found our purpose and our cause.

Be proud my sisters of your scorched feet. Our scars bear witness of our battles, the ones we rose up and out from.

The world can be a beautiful place without us thinking about the negative ugliness from some of our fellow human race and it is ours now to behold.

So, take that master key out of its mould and step forward in wholeness my sisters and Queens, you are indeed Empresses now. We have the knowledge, we have the resilience, we have the passions to succeed. We have our WHY! We have our HOW!

We are done saying if, maybe or can't. We are saying RIGHT NOW!

TAKE YOUR STANCE

Time to stand and fight, it's time to get over
Time to make things right, supporting each other
Even if we're scared, we cannot stay under
Take your stance today to break away from
Troubles at your door, troubles from within
Trauma to your heart, please don't make them win
Don't make them win
Time to take control, step into your power
Skills depression stole, will pull you together
Write or speak it out, this is your hour
Look how far you've come from your yesterdays
Troubles at your door, troubles from within
Traumas to your heart, please don't make them win
Don't make them win. Don't make them win. Don't make
    them win!

PERSONAL TESTIMONIES AND DEDICATIONS - SURVIVING QUEENS ANTHOLOGY AUTHORS

CORNITA TAYLOR - ABORTED BUT NOT DEAD

My name is Cornita Taylor and I am part of the Surviving Queens Anthology. My chapter is about my story of when I was nineteen years of age and in a domestic abusive relationship. I am now telling my truth as I have a voice and am breaking the silence and the curse, and I speak for those ladies who feel they do not have a voice. I am not a victim. I am a survivor.

I would like to thank Andrea Maynard-Brade and Maureen Elizabeth Worrell for giving me this opportunity to tell and share MY story.

I was very nervous writing my chapter but they both supported and encouraged me, especially on days when I felt unable to write anything. Their understanding motivated me to do more. I salute you both and may God continue to bless you.

My Surviving Queens Anthology chapter is dedicated to my Aunty Kathleen, who is no longer with us. This wonderful woman had been my strength when she was alive and even though she is no longer here, she remains so. Aunty Kathleen always taught me to do what is right and to be true to myself. She was my rock even when I didn't want her to be. I think about what she would do if she was in my situation. She showed me the strength of her character even during those times when she herself was feeling scared from within.

I dedicate my chapter and this book to her because we all need to hear voices that come from a place of internal and external love and if you cannot speak for yourself, there is always someone who can and will speak out for you and your silent experiences of life.

Thank you, Aunty Kathleen. I will never forget you for as long as I live. Thank you for being there for me. XX

MAE TERESA - MY PATH TO DIVINE EMPOWERMENT

My name is Mae Teresa and my written chapter in the Surviving Queens Anthology is to help men and women and my encouragement to you is to find out who you are on this journey of life. I would like to take this opportunity to thank Andrea and Maureen for introducing me to a phenomenal group of women who have empowered, encouraged and overcome. Your vision, Andrea, felt powerful and necessary from the beginning to the end. Thank you.

I am so grateful that Maureen encouraged me into writing a chapter for the Surviving Queens Anthology book. You have inspired me and encouraged me to look at words in a different way. Words to describe feelings and emotions. You are a great Editor and throughout your own personal losses and illnesses you never failed to be in contact to encourage and empower. I am thankful to God for Him leading us to each other and I look forward to continuing working with you as you stand with me to finish the work I have started, the three books in one that I have within me. May God continue to watch over you and guide you in helping abused, lost and battered women. Many thanks to you Maureen and blessings upon blessings and I hope that you, the readers, enjoy reading my chapter.

My journey is nothing without taking the opportunity to acknowledge a few key people in my life such as my mum, brother, family, best friend and especially my daughter, whom I lovingly refer to as 'my Sargent Major'. My daughter has stood firmly beside me from day one and accompanied me to all my hospital appointments, never leaving my side on the day of my surgery. She has encouraged me, taught me how to re-empower myself and has lovingly and without hesitation pushed me into doing and completing all I needed to do for my necessary recovery and healing, inclusive of physical exercises. My daughter has selflessly put her career on hold so that she could nurse me through the traumatic and sometimes devastating effects of my surgery and treatments. I could not have asked for more of or from her. I would also like to acknowledge Sharon Franklin and Maureen Elizabeth Worrell, who have both guided me through this challenging journey of becoming a published writer and during the horrendous Covid-19 pandemic. I did not have a clue as to where or how to start my writing journey, but I believe that God has blessed me with the right individuals to help me overcome any doubts, insecurities and fears about acknowledging and owning my truth, the authentic truth of how life's challenging obstacles has ultimately helped me to grow into the person that I am today. Last but certainly not least, I thank the Almighty God who has deemed me worthy of His love to blessedly fill me with the Holy Spirit as my divine guide towards completion of my Surviving Queens Anthology chapter and very soon, my book of my personal journey to achieve wellness.

JANNETTE BARRETT - THE SECRET LINING OF MY HIDDEN SUITCASE

Even though I am a multiple published author already, I am so grateful to Andrea Maynard-Brade for inviting me to be a part of this fantastic Surviving Queens Anthology. On my own I couldn't find the strength to write and reveal the deepest, intricate and intimate details of my life and various traumas, but with the encouragement and support of Andrea to share my chapter within this Anthology, I am so very grateful for her belief in me, in asking me to be a part of this wonderful journey with so many other great and uplifting Queens, who have also shared their deepest survival stories. I could not have completed this overwhelming challenge on my own. For that, I will be forever appreciative and humbled for her act of sisterhood.

This is my heartfelt review of Maureen Elizabeth Worrell's Editorial expertise of my written chapter. It is a rare but beautiful find when you connect with someone that truly gets your inner mind. Maureen, our Editor, has that inbuilt quality. I wrote my feelings as they came and Maureen saw the reality of them and connected with my emotions and therefore, she was able to add light to my writing, enhancing its visibility to the reader. A reader who hasn't experienced my kind of trauma needs to be able to see where I am coming from as it's a difficult task to get everything across in writing when you are returning to the pain of its effects and impact. Maureen, who is a fantastic Editor and an accredited and multiple award- winning Author in her own right, could see the path I was on and gave my words more clarity and depth, harmonizing my voice. I cannot thank her enough for assisting me to finally release the secrets hidden within the lining of my suitcase.

I don't know you, but I believe that we are of ONE VOICE! To know someone personally is to know their truths.

So, I dedicate my Surviving Queens Anthology chapter to you because you are about to read and to learn more about the core and the essence of ME!

You have purchased this book for a reason, and I pray and hope that whilst reading the narratives written on these pages, that your inner strength increases, your questions are answered and above all, that you take your stance to overcome.

Within these pages, we are ONE VOICE, and that voice is a resounding voice of Victory!

ANDREA MAYNARD-BRADE - KNOWING WHEN TO DRAW A LINE IN THE SAND

My name is Andrea Maynard-Brade and I am the visionary leader behind the Surviving Queens Anthology.

You will have read the chapters from some phenomenal women and their dynamic stories. I would like to thank them all for their support in being a part of this wonderful journey we have embarked upon as Surviving Queens and as sisters united.

My chapter is called 'Knowing When To Draw A Line In The Sand' and I wrote this chapter because we women need to know when to bail out and when the relationship has ended. We need to follow our intuitions. We need to follow our hearts and our minds. We need to trust that we know when things are not right. We need to learn to know when to draw that line in the sand.

I dedicate my Surviving Queens Anthology chapter to all women who are struggling and not knowing which way to turn and contemplating whether they should stay or leave. This is a time of decisions without procrastination now.

I dedicate this book to all my friends and family who have stood by my side with unconditional love and support and who have treated me with the utmost respect and love.

A special dedication is extended to my daughter Sara Maynard who has been there in more ways than I can write about here, even though she has been experiencing and overcoming her own struggles.

To Maureen Chiverton, who has kept me laughing and has kept my spirits uplifted, I thank you.

I would like to thank my cousin, Deborah Lovell, who keeps me grounded.

Queen Zora in Gambia, Maxine Palmer-Hunter and Claire Tabonnor, who have demonstrated how friends for life show up and remain in my life. I thank you all.

I dedicate this amazing book to The Most-High Creator, who has instilled in me this vision and for answering my prayers with His divine guidance.

Finally, I dedicate this unique book to Maureen Elizabeth Worrell, the Editor, who has also been a rock for me throughout the whole process. Even though she was dealing with her own tribulations and health issues, she never once wavered, complained or had a negative word to say about anything or anyone. She is a Surviving Queen of pure love and integrity. Thank you.

Blessings in abundance.

SARA MAYNARD - WHY ME?

My name is Sara Maynard, and I am an Author in the Surviving Queens Anthology book.

My chapter is called 'Why Me?'

I have struggled a lot over the years with many different things and the question always came back to asking myself why me?

I never quite understood why I had to deal with so many struggles, but I am at a point now where I am mentally and emotionally stronger. I have a deeper understanding and able to speak my truth and I really hope that whoever reads my chapter is blessed to take strength from it, grow from it and understand that self-LUV is the best love.

I am a surviving Queen!

I dedicate my Surviving Queens Anthology chapter to my beautiful daughter. I pray that she does not need to go through life questioning herself, her Self-LUV or her self-esteem.

I also dedicate my chapter to the LUV Ladies. Without this group and your continued support, I am not sure that I would have truly found my voice, the inner strength to speak honestly or the courage to be ME!

Thank you to Maureen Elizabeth Worrell for helping me to create such a great chapter and for everything you have helped me with during this process.

Last but certainly not least, I would like to dedicate my chapter to my wonderful mom, Andrea Maynard Brade, who made writing this chapter of my life journey possible and for always being there by my side.

I hope that all women reading my chapter gain inner strength and understanding and recognize that Self-LUV is their best LOVE.

MAXINE PALMER-HUNTER - NINE LIVES

My name is Maxine Palmer-Hunter, and I am one of the co-Authors in the Surviving Queens Anthology book. My chapter is called 'Nine Lives' and I have written snippets of experiences that I have gone through during my lifetime. Some of those experiences have left me living with trauma for many years, which in turn has imprisoned me physically and emotionally in different ways.

What I have realised is that if I had loved myself more, some of the experiences and situations that I went through would not have happened. But we learn and what I wanted to do with sharing my chapter was to let the readers know that no matter what you go through or are experiencing, whether it is in your past or now, you will overcome. You need to become powerful in your own existence and remove the victim mentality. Although my journey is still in recovery, renewal, revive and rise, I have stepped into my greatness and eventually you can too. Do not be a prisoner of your past I would like to dedicate my Surviving Queens Anthology chapter to all the readers who can resonate with my life experiences. Be the kind of person you want in your life, one that is loyal and forever has your back. There is always a light at the end. Trust the process and trust that timing is everything. I dedicate my chapter to all of you

The Almighty – whenever my faith wavered, you always came to me at the right times.

My Son, you are a constant light in my life, one who has aided my strength to carry on and have the privilege to experience growth as a Mum.

To my Mother, Thank you for giving me life. My Grandmothers Your legacy shines bright.

To my Husband, Thank you for your unconditional love, grounding and support.

My Roots – Who loved me in my past, my present and in my future. Thank you.

My sisters – I thank you all for being the voice of reason, a sea of love, listening ear and unwavering support.

For my Grandchildren, know that I got you and will always be your 'go-to' person.

Julie, Chantelle, Tracey and Andrea My Darlings For you SIEP Queens. Thank you for loving me.

Maureen, you saved my life and contributed to my path of healing, transparency, and restoration.

Avril, you are a diamond epitome of a true friend. Andrea, I thank you for this opportunity and your love.

To my Surviving Queens, I thank you for sharing this valuable platform with me.

Finally, to all my life experiences – I MADE IT!

ANCHILA KAMALA - MY LIFE

My name is Anchila Kamala.

I am part of the Surviving Queens Anthology, and my inclusive chapter is called 'My Life' and details part of my life journey of how I overcame certain obstacles I had to face along the way.

I feel proud to have this platform to explain my challenges of abuse and suffering as I did not have a very joyful childhood, but I am a survivor.

I am so grateful and want to thank Andrea Maynard-Brade for giving me this chance to share my story. In reading my story you will better understand the kind of person I am.

I would also like to dedicate my Surviving Queens Anthology chapter to my lovely, encouraging and supportive mother-in-law, Andrea Maynard-Brade. You gave me the chance to tell the story of my life even though I am no longer in a relationship with your son.

You are always there for me as a mother, and I thank you so much for everything that you have done for me. You keep doing for me and my son, Hotep, and I am so grateful as you make me feel that I am not an orphan anymore.

KIMOLAKAY - ROSE PETAL

My name, for the purposes of my Surviving Queens Anthology chapter, is KimolaKay.

I was given the opportunity to join the Surviving Queens by a dear friend of mine, Maureen Elizabeth Worrell.

This opportunity has given me a positive platform to raise awareness about domestic violence and the ensuing horrible situations you can find yourself in because of it.

My chapter details what I went through over a five-year period by the hands of a narcissist.

By the grace of God, I am no longer in that place of suffering. I am a survivor. I am a surviving Queen.

You too can break the silence and be free. I did.

I dedicate my Surviving Queens Anthology chapter to the strongest woman I know, my Mother, who is the foundation of my family. Her knowledge, integrity and inner strength of character was second to none. The love she had for her children and family was endless and is still felt today, even though she has now transitioned. May you always rest in perfect peace, Mum.

To my beloved children, Petrona and Cameron.

Petrona, you are beautiful inside and out, you are strong, fierce and intelligent beyond your years. Continue to rise and shine and know that your heart's desires will present itself in its own time.

Cameron, you are smart, witty and have a big heart, but most of all, you are respectful, so carry those qualities throughout your life's journey and never forget that I am raising a King. You are both my Heartbeats and my love for you is unconditional. Love always – your Mum. XX

To all the survivors and anyone who is still enduring domestic abuse, I want you to remember that there is always hope and help available out there for you. Your journey to freedom may be a long and painful road but you will know when it is your time and along the way, you will meet and recapture your self-empowerment, inner strength, self-respect, self-esteem and self- love. Embrace and reconnect with all these valuable tools as they are the key to your personal growth! You will also meet women like me who will uplift you, encourage and support you to 'keep it moving forward'.

Tell your story for you never know who is waiting to hear it and be inspired by it. Any suffering that is inflicted upon you is not your shame to hold. Break the silence and be free. I did.

MAUREEN ELIZABETH WORRELL - THE DEFINITION OF I & I

My name is Maureen Elizabeth Worrell aka Jah siSTAR and I am a multiple award-winning published Author, Counsellor, Writing Therapist and Non-Generic Book Manuscript Editor. I have written, edited and had published the first in the trilogy of my 'Journey Books' which is called 'The Journey of I & I'. I am currently editing my second book which is titled 'The Definition of I & I'. I am also the Founder, CEO and Director of my own company – MW Counselling & Consultancy – which primarily offers combined and complimentary bespoke services related to non- generic editing of book manuscripts and counselling throughout the process of writing your personal stories and/or autobiographies. I also offer ghost-writing services to those clients who require that specific service of specialised expertise.

I was asked by Andrea to edit the Surviving Queens Anthology book and to include my own personal Surviving Queens chapter. I would like to thank Andrea as I was inspired by her passionate vision to unite a group of phenomenal women who have survived various life experiences inclusive of trauma, abuse, domestic violence, eating disorders and so forth.

My passions are for writing and helping others to have their previously silenced voices to be heard through their written words, so this was a perfect and much appreciated opportunity for me to be involved in this Anthology.

To say that I am inspired by all the other chapters is an understatement. I am so very proud of each of the ladies who are involved in this project. This is a unique and phenomenal book and readers will be inspired, motivated and will resonate with the courage it has taken for all of us to reveal our hidden pains that will ultimately help us towards seeking and obtaining inner peace.

I would like to take this opportunity to dedicate my Surviving Queens Anthology chapter to my beloved and precious Grandsons. You are the reasons that I literally fought against taking my last breath during the onset of a very recent and sudden serious and life-threatening illness. As the life and energy was seeping from my body, it was the visions of your beautiful, smiling and loving faces that pulled me back from certain oblivion and back towards the light, that was symbolic of the two of you. Grandma loves you unconditionally and with all her heart and soul. Thank you for loving me back and for the special bonds that we share between us three.

My dedication means nothing without acknowledging my beloved two adult children, Vanessa and Jamahl. You are my heartbeats and the blood that runs through my veins. You are both my Original Inspirations in and for Life. My love for you and your wonderful life partners is limitless and I thank you all for always being there for me with your love, support, encouragement and respects. I love you all.

I dedicate my chapter to my beloved Mum and Dad. Your demonstrations of inner strength and dignity through times of personal pain and grief are astounding and a wonder to behold. I draw strength from watching how you both are in those moments of crisis, and I gratefully learn how to stand taller and be stronger for it. Thank you for almost sixty years of unconditional love and support. My love and admiration for you both knows no bounds.

Last but not least, I give thanks and praises to The Higher Powers and The Universe in gratitude for all my blessings.

THANK YOU ACKNOWLEDGEMENTS TO THE SURVIVING QUEENS ANTHOLOGY CHAPTER WRITERS BY MAUREEN ELIZABETH WORRELL ~ EDITOR

Surviving Queens Anthology is a unique and superb collection of chapters written by ten phenomenal ladies.

A wonderful collection of beautifully written chapters of personal stories of traumatic and challenging lived experiences.

Surviving Queens was lovingly created and developed through the courageous sharing of inspirational memories and experiences by a group of phenomenal women whose stories of resilience and of overcoming immense adversities and devastating examples of varying types of mental, physical, emotional, financial, sexual and spiritual abuse inflicted upon them, illustrates clearly how surviving those episodes of mental, emotional and physical debilitation has empowered them into being the dynamic and shining beacons of light and HOPE that they are today.

Andrea Maynard-Brade Cornita Taylor

Jannette Barrett Maxine Palmer-Hunter Sara Maynard

Anchila Kamala Mae Teresa KimolaKay

Maureen Elizabeth Worrell

To begin anew you must first say goodbye to who you once were.

Changes can be heart-breaking and scary, but it is necessary if you are to grow and evolve to rise above all adversities as a stronger and more joyful YOU! You cannot force others to comprehend a message that they are not ready to receive but you must never under-estimate the power of planting that seed!

Ladies, I salute you all for illustrating so eloquently how your once fearfully silent voices can now be heard through your written words.

THANK YOU ACKNOWLEDGEMENTS TO THE SURVIVING QUEENS ANTHOLOGY CHAPTER WRITERS BY ANDREA MAYNARD-BRADE ~ SURVIVING QUEENS ANTHOLOGY LEADER & VISIONARY

I feel privileged and honoured to take this opportunity to thank all the Surviving Queens who took part in creating this beautiful Anthology.

It has been a long journey of so many emotions, but I am so proud of the courage, determination, support and love that each of you has shown not just to me but to each other. I feel humbled and motivated by the sisterhood that has developed and evolved between us as the weeks and months have gone by.

We all have a beautiful gift to share between us and the world at large which helps us in serving our purpose here on earth.

I give all thanks and praises to The Creator for gracing us, The Original Surviving Queens, with the blessings of becoming one, united as survivors and female warriors against so many varying obstacles and adversities we have all faced and overcome in life.

I have had the pleasure and the honour of reading all your chapters and to say that I am blown away is an understatement! I embrace and salute you all. Thank you does not cover the words I am looking forward to expressing my gratitude and appreciations for your courage, determination, resilience, support, love, compassion, understanding and hard work throughout this process and journey. Well done and I love and respect you all.

There is an inner beauty about a woman who believes in herself, who knows that she is more than capable of succeeding at anything she puts her mind to. There is an inner beauty in her strength and determination and her belief to follow her own path in life and not be distracted by negative energies along the way. There is an inner beauty about a woman whose self-confidence originates from her life experiences, who is aware that she may fail but refuses to do anything other than to pick herself up and move on. You, ladies, are one of those beautiful women!

POSITIVE AFFIRMATIONS
DEDICATED TO OUR READERS

- When you trust the WHOLE healing process and stand firm in your personal truth and lived experiences, your silent voices are heard loud and clear through your written and verbal words.
- Do not allow a lack of genuine support and encouragement to diminish your beliefs in yourself and your capabilities.
- You are more capable and deserving of more than you think. It is during those challenging circumstances that you will shine the brightest. Release any traces of negativity and focus all your energy on love, happiness and your dreams and visions for a wonderful future.
- Life does not always give you the people you want in your life. Sometimes life gives you the people you need – those who will love you, hate you, inspire you, make or break you, to encourage you onto the path of being the person you were meant to be.
- Trust that everything is working in divine order and that the changes in your life are aligned with your soul's purpose and mission.
- When feelings and emotions awaken your soul, remain

grounded and cleanse your thoughts, focusing on things that allow you to express your hidden emotions.

- Life challenges allow you to discover things about yourself that you never really knew. Embrace those adversities so that you may learn and grow from them.
- Where you are at this very moment is where you are meant to be so embrace every moment with gratitude.
- The secret of health for both body and mind is not to mourn for the past, worry about the future or anticipate troubles, but to live in the present moment wisely, earnestly and authentically.
- Vulnerability is the birthplace of courage and the ability to show up no matter what.
- Liberate yourself by letting go and fully embracing inner peace of mind.
- Speak your positive desires into reality and be bold in interrupting the patterns of destructive thoughts and behaviours.
- Remove the burden of drama, chaos and toxicity from your life by acknowledging the childhood that you didn't have. Give yourself permission to get your inner self in order so that you can live your life in peaceful order.
- Give yourself permission to shed tears of cleansing so you can heal from within and in so doing, be kind and loving to yourself.
- Never suffer alone or in silence. You cannot begin to heal that which is left unspoken.
- You cannot grow and heal from within without discomfort. Remember that when you feel unworthy you are forgetting to value yourself.
- Denial and avoidance create inner turmoil. Awareness is powerful and empowering. Acknowledge. Affirm. Appreciate.
- Healing is a way of being. What you do not transform from within and externally will be transferred to others and the next generations.
- The empowerment of forgiveness is letting others know how

the hurt made you feel and then letting go and moving forward with your life.

- When others show you who they are, believe them and love yourself enough to walk away.
- Know that you too can step out of the chains of shame and guilt associated with secrets and lies enforced upon you. Hidden secrets only keep you from being fully present in your life and in the lives of your loved ones.
- The misrepresentation of your personal truth is a betrayal to yourself.
- Create your own positive reality by trusting yourself that you will be OK.
- Validate yourself and worthiness in recognising that fear itself is what is holding you back in life. Sometimes the truth may be painful but remember that you are ENOUGH.
- Set peace of mind as your goal and aim to live with inner peace day by day.
- You owe yourself the love that you so freely give to other people.
- We rise by lifting others.
- Envision your dream goal. Understand the potential obstacles. Create a positive mental image. Clear your mind of any self-doubts and negative thoughts. Embrace the challenge. Stay focused and then show the world that you can do it!
- Invest in your dreams and take it one step at a time.
- Keep elevating yourselves as knowledge empowers you.
- Loving yourself begins with liking yourself, which commences with respecting yourself, which originates from thinking of yourself in positive ways.
- Honour your truth by not allowing fear to keep you silent.
- Live unapologetically and authentically and inspire others to shine.
- Allow nothing and no-one to dim the light that shines from within you.
- Be somebody who makes everybody feel like somebody.

- Remember that just one kind word can change a person's life forever.
- Do not allow the fears in your thoughts to define you. Let the dreams you hold in your heart guide you to awesomeness!

You Are

Surviving Queens

Loved

Hope

Courage

Wisdom

Awarenes

Purpose

Passion

Authentic

Unique

Creative

Valuable

Worthy

Deserving

Empowered

Amazing

Healing

My siSTAR

Limitless

Spiritual

Integrity

Respected

Heard

Perfect In Your Imperfections

Your Own Truth

An Inspiration

CONTACT INFORMATION
SURVIVING QUEENS
ANTHOLOGY CHAPTER
AUTHORS

Andrea Maynard-Brade

Email: positivebrade313@gmail.com

Cornita Taylor

Email: head2toemassage18@gmail.com

Jannette Barrett

Email: jancancare1@gmail.com

Maxine Palmer-Hunter

Email: palmermaxine50@hotmail.com

Sara Maynard

Email: sarzmaynard09@gmail.com

Anchila Kamala

Email: kamalaanch@gmail.com

Mae Teresa

Email: hannahtsanya@gmail.com

KimolaKay

Email: kimmysnibbles@hotmail.com

Maureen Elizabeth Worrell Email: mrnworrell@yahoo.co.uk

Surviving Queens

POSITIVE AFFIRMATION
QUOTES

Be grateful that your life is changing course towards a new and positive direction

Embrace your intuition to boldly step into your new life borne of courage

Our souls are here with a destiny and desire to fulfil certain conditions, goals and lessons learnt during our life journeys

Live authentically and treat Self and Others with kindness, understanding, compassion, empathy, love and respect

Trust yourself to know that you will be guided to the truths of your soul

And that whatever your heart desires are already on its way to you Be the voice of self-awareness so that you can learn how to analyse Discuss and communicate without destructive criticism or judgement Allow your consciousness to guide you towards the truth

Focus your thoughts and emotions on what you desire

From a place of love declare your positive intentions and live your life in and with purpose

Surviving Queens

Silence protects the perpetrator and imprisons the victim
Take back your life and break the silence

THERE IS SOLACE IN BREAKING OUR SILENCE

A STRENGTH OF SPIRIT WHEN SHARING OUR TRUTHS

It all commences with the choice to live on the other side of being a victim

Our ego says that once everything falls into place, we will find peace

Our spirit tells us that we when we find peace then everything else will fall into place

Your perception of me is just a reflection of you My reaction to you is an awareness of me

When you carry love in your heart you have the capacity to heal at any moment

Stand up for me and Protect me Educate others and Advocate for me

Know the signs, understand them and prevent them

Printed in Great Britain
by Amazon